Power and Greed

Power and Greed

Monopolies, Mergers, and Cartels on the American Stage

Spencer Weber Waller

BLOOMSBURY ACADEMIC
LONDON • NEW YORK • OXFORD • NEW DELHI • SYDNEY

METHUEN DRAMA
Bloomsbury Publishing Plc, 50 Bedford Square, London, WC1B 3DP, UK
Bloomsbury Publishing Inc, 1359 Broadway, New York, NY 10018, USA
Bloomsbury Publishing Ireland, 29 Earlsfort Terrace, Dublin 2, D02 AY28, Ireland

BLOOMSBURY, METHUEN DRAMA and the Methuen Drama logo are trademarks of Bloomsbury Publishing Plc

First published in Great Britain 2026

Cover design and illustration by Megan Wilson

A catalogue record for this book is available from the British Library.

A catalog record for this book is available from the Library of Congress.

ISBN: HB: 978-1-3505-7809-8
ePDF: 978-1-3505-7810-4
eBook: 978-1-3505-7811-1

Typeset by RefineCatch Limited, Bungay, Suffolk
Printed and bound in Great Britain

For product safety related questions contact productsafety@bloomsbury.com.

To find out more about our authors and books visit www.bloomsbury.com and sign up for our newsletters.

To Laura and Jordan

For Making Sure That I Did Not Throw Away My Shot

Contents

Cast of Characters ix

Act I THE CREATION OF A NATIONAL THEATER INDUSTRY 1

Introduction: Setting the Stage 3

Chapter 1 Live Entertainment Becomes a National Business 9

Act II THE CARTELS 23

Chapter 2 The Entertainment Barons of the Gilded Age 25

Chapter 3 The Rise of the Syndicate 35

Chapter 4 Trustbusting and its Loopholes 51

Chapter 5 The Price of Independence 59

Chapter 6 The Shubert Challenge 69

Chapter 7 War, Peace, and Dirty Tricks 85

Chapter 8 The First Vaudeville War and Dreams of Global Domination 97

Chapter 9 Labor and Monopoly 113

Act III THE MONOPOLIST 127

Chapter 10 Empire 129

Chapter 11 Survival 145

Chapter 12 The Quiet Life 161

Act IV THE BREAKUP 171

Chapter 13 Justice 173

Chapter 14 The End of the Road 189

Act V THE MERGERS 199

Chapter 15 The New Bottlenecks of Broadway 201

Chapter 16 Pearl Jam, Taylor Swift, and Live Nation 215

Epilogue 225

Appendix A The Syndicate Agreement 229

Appendix B United States v. Shubert, Supreme Court opinion (1955). 233

Notes 237

Bibliography 259

Acknowledgements 265

Index 269

Cast of Characters

The Barons of Vaudeville

Benjamin Franklin (B.F.) Keith

Founder of the Keith-Albee Circuit controlling big time vaudeville in the Eastern United States and the United Booking Office (UBO) controlling the national bookings of vaudeville acts.

Edward Franklin Albee

Partner of B.F. Keith and eventual successor as head of the Keith-Albee circuit. Grandfather of playwright Edward Albee.

Martin Beck

Head of the Orpheum Circuit controlling vaudeville in the Western half of the United States and part owner of the Palace Theater in New York City.

Joseph Kennedy

Father of President John F. Kennedy and financier who bought the remains of the vaudeville Combine to incorporate the vaudeville theaters into his growing movie studio.

The American Theatrical Syndicate and Associates

Abraham Lincoln (Abe) Erlanger

The feared, brutal, and vilified head of the 1896 American Theatrical Syndicate controlling the production, booking, and presentation of legitimate theater on Broadway and on tour until the rise of the Shubert brothers as competitors.

Marc Klaw

Erlanger's partner during the heyday of the Syndicate. A lawyer by training and softer spoken in style than Erlanger.

Charles Frohman

Courtly and best liked member of the Syndicate. Producer, booking agent, and theater owner with strong connections in England and Europe bringing hits to the United States such as *Peter Pan*.

Daniel Frohman

Brother of Charles Frohman and well-regarded producer in his own right. Never an official member of the Syndicate but benefited from his association with the cartel.

Al Hayman

Partner and general manager for Charles Frohman with strong network of presenting theaters on the West Coast.

Sam Nixon

Partner of Fred Zimmerman controlling key theaters in Pennsylvania and Ohio.

Fred Zimmerman

Partner of Sam Nixon controlling key theaters in Pennsylvania and Ohio.

The Independents

Harrison Grey Fiske

Publisher of the *New York Dramatic Mirror*, outspoken critic of the Syndicate, and husband of Minnie Maddern Fiske.

Minnie Maddern Fiske

Leading actress of the 1890s and 1900s, vocal opponent of the Syndicate, and wife of Harrison Grey Fiske.

David Belasco

Actor, producer, playwright who worked with the Syndicate and the Shuberts whenever it suited his interests.

Richard Mansfield
Vociferous Syndicate critic and leading actor who helped establish the credibility of the Shuberts by starring in their early New York City productions.

The Shubert Brothers and Allies

Sam Shubert
The beloved boy genius of the family who led the creation of the fledging Shubert network of theaters and productions in New York City and on tour before his untimely death at the age of thirty.

Lee Shubert
The oldest of the Shubert brothers, who led the growing network of theater operations in their heyday. Known for his polite but icy demeanor, hard bargaining, and litigiousness.

Jacob (J.J.) Shubert
The youngest and most volatile of the Shubert Brothers harboring resentments at Lee and outsiders for slights both real and imagined.

John Shubert
J.J.'s son and Harvard Law School graduate who briefly led The Shubert theatrical operations after the death of Lee and J.J.

Gerald Shoenfeld
Joined the Shuberts as a young lawyer, guided their defense against the government's antitrust case in the 1950s, and became the first non-family member to lead the Shubert Organization.

Marcus Loewe
Key friend and ally of Lee and J.J. who built vaudeville and movie empire often partnering but never competing with Lee and J.J.

Current Live Entertainment Firms

The Shubert Organization
The surviving operations of the Shubert empire after the court-ordered breakup. Still a significant Broadway theater owner and producer with limited theater operations outside New York City.

Nederlander Organization
Originally presenters in the Detroit area, now a producer and owner or operator of theaters on Broadway and around the country.

Ambassador Theatre Group
Owner/operator of theaters on Broadway, London, and in growing number of markets across the United States.

Broadway Across America
Leading owner or manager of venues presenting touring Broadway musicals and plays in more than forty cities in North America.

Independent Producer Network
Loose network of producers and venues presenting Broadway musicals and dramas outside of New York City.

Live Nation/Ticketmaster
Largest integrated live music firm owning leading talent management, booking, venues, ticketing, merchandising, as well as food and beverage operations for concerts. Now in litigation accused of monopolization in the United States and other countries. Acquired leading primary ticketing provider Ticketmaster in 2010.

Act I

The Creation of A National Theater Industry

Introduction

Setting the Stage

One day during the pandemic my wife was reading a best-selling book on the history of Broadway and asked me if I had heard of something called "The Syndicate." My mind raced back to my days as a federal organized crime prosecutor in Chicago, where the organized crime gang of Al Capone was also known as "the Syndicate." She assured me that she was not talking about *that* Syndicate, but something else entirely: the American Theatrical Syndicate from the 1890s.

Although I had spent a couple of years investigating and prosecuting the other Syndicate for the U.S. Department of Justice, this was music to my ears for a very different reason. Since leaving the Justice Department, I have spent much of my career practicing and teaching antitrust law—the law of competition—that in general prohibits things like cartels and monopolies. The Theatrical Syndicate was most definitely one or both. I eagerly read the short chapter on the Theatrical Syndicate in the book my wife shared.[1]

Much to my amazement, the story of the Theatrical Syndicate, and what followed, was almost the same story of the rise and fall of the large industrial combinations that formed in the first Gilded Age of the 19th century. These cartels, also known as "trusts," were the reason the federal antitrust laws were passed in 1890. Since then, countless antitrust cases have been prosecuted by the federal government and brought by private plaintiffs seeking damages from violations of the law.

Like more famous companies such as Standard Oil and U.S. Steel, the history of the theater and vaudeville industry is intertwined with that of the antitrust laws. As I learned more, I realized that this story had never been told in a comprehensive fashion.

For nearly a century, these industries were dominated by colorful characters who conspired, monopolized, but also fiercely competed to present great works of art, and more commercial fare, on the stage. These same competitors similarly connived backstage to dominate the theater industry and the related, but more populist, vaudeville circuits.

Producing dramas, comedies, musicals, and variety shows obviously is not the same as producing sugar, copper wire, oil, or whiskey. But in entertainment as well as manufacturing, human nature and greed seek to make the most amount of money with the least amount of competition possible. For decades, the Theatrical Syndicate, the later Shubert Organization, and the two dominant vaudeville circuits, that also worked together under the name of the Combine, fought, attempted to squeeze each other out of the market, and colluded with each other whenever it was advantageous to do so.

They also tangled with the antitrust laws designed to prevent this sort of behavior. These powerful combinations controlled—at different times—what people saw on the stage, where they saw it, how much they paid for it, and how those enormous profits were shared. Only they were not selling sugar, copper wire, or whiskey. They were selling William Shakespeare, W.C. Fields, Buster Keaton, Al Jolson, The Marx Brothers, Ethel Merman, and the glamour of show business itself.

This is also a tale of how industries deal with new technologies and new forms of competition. While live theater has existed since the earliest days of ancient Greece, if not before, we only have a few centuries of theater in a recognizably modern form. In the 20th century, newer forms of technology, such as silent films, radio, talking pictures, and then television challenged legitimate theater, vaudeville, and other forms of live entertainment, competing for both the attention and dollars of audiences.

While the titans of theater and vaudeville could prevent competition within their industry, they were far less successful in responding to competition from new technologies that enticed people to enjoy entertainment on the radio in their homes or at the movie palaces of their day. This is a trend that continues today with new forms of mass entertainment such as streaming services, online gaming, and virtual reality. The urge to control competition for live and recorded forms of entertainment is alive and well.

The story of the growth of a truly national entertainment industry begins with the end of the Civil War. It continues in the late 19th century with the rise of the Theatrical Syndicate and ends with the forced dismemberment of the Shubert theater empire under the antitrust laws in the late 1950s. Competitive concerns still exist today both for live theater and the concert business where the role of antitrust law is still being played out in the courts. The story of the creation of the national vaudeville circuits, the Theatrical Syndicate, the Shubert Organization, and what follows, is both good history and a wakeup call for how we should look at the entertainment giants of today.

***

Most critics and historians agree that the September 12, 1866, opening of *The Black Crook* was the first example of a true Broadway musical comedy that became a nationwide phenomenon. Even those who point to earlier shows as the first modern musical acknowledge that *The Black Crook* was the first musical to enjoy nationwide commercial success.

It was a five-and-a-half-hour extravaganza with a loose plot pulling together many styles, genres, and variety acts. The plot (using that term loosely) by Charles Barras is billed as an "original magical and spectacular drama in four acts." The play was set in the Hartz mountains of Germany in 1600 and featured nobles, servants, a poor artist, an alchemist/sorcerer named the Black Crook, young lovers, their relatives, peasants, travelers, immortals, amphibea, gnomes, infernals, and "skeletons, apparitions, demons, monsters, etc. etc.".[2]

The Black Crook himself is identified in the language of that time as having a hideous deformity, with a leaden complexion, humped-back, knotted limbs, crooked body, and lame. The story is vaguely based on Faust and his obsession with magic. The plot of The Black Crook was described as "both convoluted and flimsy." It mixed comedy with melodrama and was overacted to the extreme.

The play featured over 100 scantily clad ballet dancers assembled in Europe by the producers. The dancers had been brought to New York for a different extravaganza at the Academy of Music. Sadly, that theater burned down. The manager of the nearby Niblo's Garden bought the dance troupe, the costumes, and the scenery and then shrewdly saw the potential of *The Black Crook* as a vehicle to present these new assets to the public with state-of-the-art special effects and theater magic.

The show was praised as a gorgeous and magnificent spectacle. The dancers were as much an attraction for the critics as the audience and were often praised in the reviews of the show. The New York Times noted positively that the women "wear no clothes to speak of". Even the clergy and critics who condemned the immorality of the ballet only heightened the interest of parishioners and readers to see the show for themselves.

Whatever its artistic failings, *The Black Crook* was a huge commercial success. It played for 475 performances over the 16 months of its initial New York run at the Niblo's Garden Theater. It grossed more than a $1 million, had net profits of well over $660,000 (on a budget of $55,000) and was revived on Broadway and the road several times over the coming decades as late as 1936.

All but one of these productions were highly profitable for the Kiralfy brothers who controlled the rights to the production. The 1879 Broadway revival was on its way to being equally successful until the theater lessee absconded with the proceeds of the run and left the cast and crew without ten days of pay amounting to some $2400.

The Black Crook had an even greater life on the road. It toured the United States and Canada for more than forty years, beginning in the administration of President Andrew Johnson and ending in that of William Howard Taft. In April 1894, Willa Cather, while still a student at the University of Nebraska, reviewed one of the more thread-bare versions of the tour in Lincoln. She wrote:

> "Of course the "Black Crook" drew. It always does, and the Lansing was pretty well filled from "bald-headed row" to gallery. Of course a spectacular play, when playing to one night stands, loses one of its chief attractions, the confusing number of dancers. No matter how far the imagination may stretch, eight will not take the place of eighty, and an army of a dozen amazons will not be imposing."[3]

The Black Crook helped create Broadway as we know it and the touring system that brings "direct from Broadway" productions to hundreds of cities across the United States and Canada. Its many productions spanned the era of local theatrical fiefdoms, the growth of small regional circuits for tours under the control of individual entrepreneurs, the growth of cartels and monopolies dominating live entertainment, periods of intense competition, and the onslaught of new technologies.

***

The lifespan of *The Black Crook* also included the rise of the modern business of Broadway and its biggest players: the American Theatrical Syndicate, the Shubert Organization, and a Combine of the two dominant vaudeville circuits. At different times, these organizations competed and colluded in dealing with the business and economic challenges of their time.

These were the robber barons and the monopolists of the theater industry. While much has been written about the history of the Gilded Age and the titans who controlled the industrial corporations of the United States, relatively little has been written about how the forces of competition and collusion defined the live entertainment industry both on Broadway and across North America.

Antitrust law plays an important part of this story both then and now. Senator John Sherman of Ohio spoke passionately on the floor of the United States Senate in support of the Sherman Act, the federal antitrust law that bears his name. He declared that monopolies are:

> "inconsistent with our form of government. . . . If we will not endure a king as a political power, we should not endure a king over the production, transportation, and sale of any of the necessaries of life. If we would not submit to an emperor, we should not submit to an autocrat of trade . . . ."[4]

The final vote on the Sherman antitrust act was 51-1 in the Senate and 242-0 in the House. It banned agreements in restraint of trade, monopolization, and attempted monopolization. The Sherman Act also created criminal penalties for convicted defendants, the right to seek injunctions to stop illegal conduct, and provided triple damages for any persons injured in their business or property by a violation of the law.

No one was thinking specifically about the theater or vaudeville industries at the time. The members of the House and Senate and the White House of one term president Benjamin Harrison were mostly concerned about the Standard Oil trust (hence the term antitrust), and similar cartels in manufacturing industries such as railroads, whiskey, barrels, lumber, and salt.

It would be years before these laws were applied to the cartels and monopolies that dominated the theater and vaudeville industries. Often those laws were applied weakly and inconsistently and became merely a cost of doing business for industry leaders. More often market forces, changing audience tastes, and the development of new technologies like radio and movies had far more impact on live entertainment.

Eventually the law would catch up, even if much of the damage had been done. Sometimes competitors were destroyed before the government, or the courts, could act. Sometimes competitors became coconspirators with dreams of global domination. Along the way, profits were extorted, performers and workers were abused, and consumers were taken advantage of. The art often suffered and took a backseat to the needs of monopoly profits.

These concerns still resonate today, Although the literal cartels and monopolies of the past are long gone, modern theater is still controlled by key players who dictate the art that we see on the stage. If anything, the concert business is of even greater modern concern (ask any Taylor Swift fan) and the government is once again embroiled in a monumental antitrust case against Live Nation, the dominant firm that determines what bands we see, where they play, and the price we pay. It took the government nearly seventy years to use the antitrust laws to break up the Shubert Organization, the last remaining theatrical monopoly of its time. We cannot afford to wait that long to take action against the monopolies and cartels of today in the entertainment field and beyond.

This is a story that spans from the end of the Civil War in 1865 and continues to the present day. We raise the curtain nearly two hundred years before *The Black Crook* made its debut.

1

Live Entertainment Becomes a National Business

Live entertainment has been part of human culture for thousands of years. But the **business** of live entertainment in the United States is less than two hundred years old. Starting in the mid-19th Century legitimate theater (full-length dramas, comedies, and musicals with a plot driven story) and vaudeville (variety show of different unconnected types of performers) became the dominant forms of commercial popular live entertainment in the United States. While there were many other types of live entertainment in the late 19th century vying for the audience's time and money, these other forms of entertainment eventually faded away or were coopted into either the legitimate theater or vaudeville.

The first known theatrical production in colonial America was in Accomac, Virginia in 1665. The performers of *Ye Bare and Ye Cubb* were later hauled into court on indecency charges but were acquitted on all counts. The first known musical work for the theater by an American writer was the 1767 production ironically titled *The Disappointment*. *The Disappointment* was advertised and scheduled to premiere in the Philadelphia area by the American Theater, an early East Coast traveling theater company. *The Disappointment* never made it to the stage, being withdrawn before its first performance as "unfit for the stage."

A mere four days after the failed premiere, the American Theater Company mounted Thomas Godfrey's *The Prince of Partha*, marking the first known professional performance of a play written by an American. It would not be until fourteen years later and after the Revolution that the next such play by an American playwright would be staged.

It was often hard to distinguish between musicals and dramas in the theater of the late 18th century and early 19th century. Productions were described as ballad operas, comic operas, comic burletta, melodramas, or simply operas. Even dramas normally contained musical numbers, or at least musical interludes, including well-known Shakespearean classics. The theaters also normally had full orchestras and singers to entertain the audience before the show and between acts.

The first half of the 19th century also featured the beginning of burlesque, variety shows, and minstrel shows. Over time, elements of these early forms of popular entertainment were incorporated into mainstream Broadway theater and vaudeville productions.

As the United States expanded westward across the Appalachian Mountains, theaters, actors, and productions followed, with permanent theaters established in many cities and numerous itinerant touring companies roaming the rapidly expanding country. Following the gold rush in the West, the earliest theaters and performances in that part of the country were often little more than sideshows at saloons, casinos, and bordellos. As a result, early theater had a terrible reputation in the states and territories and was often prohibited by law with such bans persisting in some states until the mid-19th century.

As the labor economist Alfred Bernheim described these early days:

> The first [stage of American theater] we may call the nomadic, when acting companies were still strolling players and were without a permanent theatre for a home. Then came the pastoral stage, when established companies settled down to cultivate their own territories and became attached to specific theatres. This happened first in the larger cities and later in the newer and smaller communities. The two stages, of course, overlapped somewhat. The nomads might settle in a community for weeks, sometimes for an entire season, before folding their tents and moving onward. The

> established companies might travel for a part of the season. But there was a clear distinction between that were identified season in, season out, with a specific theatre and those that were not; and it is a fact that drama in the newer settlements was first supplied by traveling companies and later largely by residential companies.[1]

The hazards of touring in the early days were substantial. Travel was an arduous mixture of wagons, coaches, barges, boats, and limited railroad lines with unpredictable operations and schedules. Early nomadic companies had to move on quickly as the audience and box office potential for any individual show was rapidly exhausted. In the worst case scenarios, shows would fail and the company and its manager had no money to pay for anyone to return home.

The perils of touring the West, even in the post-Civil War era, are nicely illustrated in a memoir by producer Daniel Frohman, the brother of Charles Frohman, one of the founding members of the Theatrical Syndicate. While prone to exaggeration in places, Daniel recounts how Charles Frohman reacted when a group of cowboys started shooting up the stalled train while Charles and his theatrical company were near Miles City, Montana. Frohman explained to the cowboys that they were a theatrical company and instructed one member to perform. According to Daniel's memoir, the cowboys were amused and allowed the group to go on their way.[2]

For the local resident stock companies, there were similar hazards of shows quickly outliving the demand in any given town and having to mount new productions to replenish the audience and the coffers of the company. Small tours of surrounding towns or territories were an additional potential source of income and reputation, but subject to hazards of weather, harvest cycles, transportation glitches, audience demand, and the always present danger of fire or other natural disasters destroying the flimsy wooden theaters.

By the 1820s, a star system had evolved where the leading actors and actresses from the United States and England performed first in New York and then toured the United States and Canada. These stage legends included British stars Edmund and Charles Kean, Junius Brutus Booth (father of John Wilkes Booth and his less infamous and better-known fellow actor Edwin Booth) as well as the early American stars Edwin Forrest, Joseph Jefferson, and James Hackett.

These actors, and other less prominent thespians, crisscrossed the United States, performing the lead roles they had memorized with the resident stock companies in the larger cities where they played familiar roles in the handful of plays in their repertoire. Once such stars were booked, the resident stock companies had time to rehearse the shows and presumably sell more tickets at a higher price than in the earlier era when the "star" was merely the member of the stock company selected to play the lead role of any particular production. Such star-stock company joint ventures were the norm from roughly 1820 to 1860. The nomadic combination system eventually disappeared as the industry matured and the newer star system first coopted, and then destroyed, the resident stock companies.

A "combination" system developed later where the star actor/manager would create a complete company to perform a particular show for New York and/or a tour of as many cities as possible. The star actor/manager would hire an ongoing company of supporting actors, crew, and musicians, and arrange for the scenery and costumes needed for a particular production. This provided for more artistic control, as well as the prospect of greater profits if the performance was a long running success.

This was also a much more expensive, risky venture, but this type of more integrated and artistically coherent organization became the norm by 1890. Resident stock theater companies gradually faded away, except as amateur or quaint summer productions outside urban locations. The local theater managers, without a fulltime stock company to run, ceased to be producers in any normal sense of the word. They became what we would call today presenters, operating a venue that was leased to traveling productions controlled by others for either a fixed rental, a share of the revenues, or some combination thereof. Many in the industry bemoaned the transformation of independent businessmen into what one critic called "glorified janitors."

***

Modern industry on a national scale, whether theatrical or manufacturing, simply was not possible until the end of the Civil War. It is not a coincidence that *The Black Crook* premiered in 1866, only one year after the end of the war and Lincoln's assassination at Ford's Theatre during a performance of *My American Cousin* while it toured on the East Coast.

Truly national industry required the political and economic reunification of the nation. It also required national transportation. After the war, it took time to restore the damage to the fledging railroad industry and reintegrate rail lines in the North and the South. A national transportation system also required massive new rail lines that connected the East and West Coast, which did not occur until 1869. It was only then the railroads could efficiently transport people and freight in bulk throughout the United States. National communications did not exist until the telegraph and telephone industries built out their national networks.

In the rapidly developing commercial theater industry, barnstorming and short local tours after the end of the stock company's local season were replaced by lengthier tours of combination productions. This in turn led to the development of "circuits" where lengthy, and potentially profitable, routes could be planned and performed in an efficient manner that did not exhaust the cast and crew, cost less to produce, and attracted a larger audience of national ticket buyers. Theater was becoming a national industry like so many manufactured goods that had once been local in nature.

The next step was the growth of booking offices to expertly design the routes for the productions and negotiate the contracts with the theaters where the productions would perform across a region or nationwide. As Bernheim notes: "Through booking offices a large number of theatres over a wide territory were linked in a sort of amorphous super-circuit, held together not by direct contact between the theatres themselves, but by the centripetal force of booking offices."[3]

The booking offices not only served as agents connecting the theaters and the producers of tours. The growth of the booking office marked the effective beginning of a national theater industry linking production, distribution, and consumption of theater in a vertically integrated supply chain, not unlike the burgeoning industrial economy.

The risks in the theater industry were similar to those the many industrial industries with high fixed costs and fluctuating revenues. The booms and busts of the economy in the second half of the 19th century led to a high rate of business failures and bankruptcies. Rapid new entry normally was followed by overproduction and fierce price competition, followed by recession and depressions where demand plummeted. Market prices often failed to cover costs of production, let alone pay down debt or provide profits for the owners or investors.

It was the same in the legitimate theater industry. Each new production required raising substantial funds to pay for a script, music, actors, directors, musicians, crew, scenery, and costumes, renting theaters, advertising the show, as well as transporting, housing, and feeding the company for the run of the show.

While costs were high, revenues were quite uncertain. A production could end up a flop for any number of reasons. The show might not be any good, fail to appeal to audience tastes, appear too similar to previous shows in that city, lack a star of sufficient fame to sell tickets, or simply have the bad luck to play during bad weather, financial downturns, or other natural disaster.

Every industry struggled to find ways to limit their risks, keep revenues high, and reduce costs. There were attempts by manufacturers to reach informal agreements to keep prices high and prevent price wars from breaking out. Gentlemen's agreements and other informal arrangements had two basic problems. First there were numerous temptations to cheat on any agreed upon price, production level, or territories, and second, these informal agreements were rarely enforceable, either legally or practically.

Eventually, cartels became more formalized, firms acquired other firms, and the trust was created as a legally enforceable agreement consolidating control of an entire industry. The resulting excesses of the cartels, trusts, monopolies, mergers, and robber barons of the first Gilded Age brought with it the passage of the largely ineffective state antitrust laws in the 1880s and eventually the federal Sherman Act in 1890. Eventually cartels and monopolies would dominate vaudeville and the legitimate theater while other forms of live entertainment failed to maintain a true national audience.

***

After the Civil War, many forms of live entertainment vied for a national or regional audience. These included wild west shows, circuses, magic acts, minstrel shows, opera, vaudeville, and legitimate theater. By the end of the 19th century only vaudeville and the theatrical theater remained as truly national industries with burlesque a distant third.

Irving Berlin wrote in the 1946 hit musical *Annie Get Your Gun* about a travelling Wild West show that included the anthem *There's No Business Like Show Business.* This enormous hit declares:

> There's no business like show business, like no business I know
>
> Everything about it is appealing, everything that traffic will allow
>
> Nowhere could you get that happy feeling when you are stealing that extra bow
>
> There's no people like show people, they smile when they are low
>
> Even with a turkey that you know will fold, you may be stranded out in the cold
>
> Still you wouldn't change it for a sack of gold, let's go on with the show . . .[4]

Annie Get Your Gun was a Broadway musical comedy (and later 1950 film) about a Wild West Show that no one would confuse with modern musical theater. As a genre, the Wild West shows mythologized the American West and the cowboy and trafficked in derogatory stereotypes of Native Americans. Some versions were performed indoors in actual theaters, but the majority, like the most famous *Buffalo Bill's Wild West Show,* were performed outdoors. Most versions of this type of show were three to four hours long and featured heavily fictionalized vignettes reenacting history, combined with animal acts, shooting exhibitions, and rodeo events.

The circus was also an important form of popular entertainment in America beginning in the 1790s. The traditional big top circus which presented one or more "rings" of animal or acrobatic acts lasted until very recently when changing audience tastes, concerns over the treatment of animals, and the COVID pandemic forced Ringling Brothers, the last nationally touring circus, to close. Animal acts and acrobatics became part of the vaudeville circuits and continue to exist today in Las Vegas and elsewhere. While the human acrobatic aspects of circus continue to survive in the Cirque du Soleil type shows, and a revived animal-free Ringling Brother circus tour, the traditional big top multiple ring circus is defunct. The circus was exciting, but largely a form of family entertainment. Few would view it as a serious alternative for an evening of legitimate theater.

Professional operas have been performed in the United States since 1735. These early productions often were performed in the same theaters as legitimate dramas, comedies, and musicals. Over the course of the 20th century, opera matured into primarily specialized companies, dedicated theaters, and a subscription-based audience with the need for heavy philanthropic support. It was no longer the stuff of popular culture.

In late 19th century Gilded Age New York City, older audiences still attended opera and symphony at the Academy of Music located at 14th and Irving Place, near Union Square. The newer and younger money crowd could never acquire the limited number of coveted boxes at the Academy which led the drive to establish the new Metropolitan Opera House further uptown at 39th and Broadway. Ironically, the Academy later tried to compete by turning itself into a vaudeville house but eventually went out of business.[5]

The business of producing opera became its own niche, with different entrepreneurs with their own skill sets and know-how. In the modern era, an audience member may well attend a musical comedy one night and an opera the following evening, but it is a rare, and probably foolhardy, Broadway producer or investor who funds traditional opera in the hope of finding the next hit on the scale of *Rent*, *Wicked*, or *Hamilton*. It is more common for today's opera houses to present their own versions of Broadway musicals to attract new subscribers and younger audiences.

Operettas, light operas, and so-called comic operas enjoyed more enduring success. These largely interchangeable terms are an important bridge between the traditional Europe opera and the musicals of the Broadway stage. No matter what you call them, these productions tell their story primarily through song. These productions were shorter and lighter in tone than traditional opera. Over time operettas were increasingly written and performed in English, and became popular enough for long and profitable runs in New York City and around the country.

The operettas of Gilbert and Sullivan were an original and quite popular alternative to more old-fashioned operettas from the continent. They were hits first in London and then in the United States, where both authorized and pirated versions were presented around the U.S. in the later 19th century and early 20th century. One of the most famous is *The Pirates of Penzance* which remains in production after nearly 150 years with a modern adaptation playing on Broadway in 2025.

After the heyday of the Gilbert and Sullivan operettas, U.S. producers sought to import operettas from England and Europe or create their own. As we shall see, the operetta was a key component of how the Syndicate, the Shubert Organization, and in condensed form the vaudeville circuits, kept their theaters full and their audiences happy.

***

Magic was another form of live entertainment that gradually became part of vaudeville and legitimate theater except for the handful of top magicians who could draw a national audience on their own. Magicians presenting grand illusions have been big business in Europe since the mid-19th century and became popular in the United States shortly thereafter. The top magicians performed solo shows, either booked by themselves or by agents. They performed in salons, clubs, theaters, and other venues both large and small depending on the performer's popularity. Magicians also appeared on the Chautauqua and Lyceum circuits, better known for their lectures and monologues. Lesser-known magical talents performed in private homes, saloons, fairs, smaller commercial venues, and on the streets.

As variety and vaudeville shows evolved, magicians began to perform segments on bills featuring numerous other talents including singers, comedians, dancers, acrobatics, animal acts, short plays or operetta, strong man acts, minstrel performers, and lecturers. Later, magicians also performed on Broadway in reviews or musicals specially tailored to showcase their famous acts.

The most famous performed in their own one-person shows. For example, Harry Houdini began in circuses and dime museums before making his reputation as a conventional stage magician in vaudeville. It was not until he was persuaded to drop the standard stage magic sleight of hand and more complex illusions using equipment, in favor of astonishing escape acts, that he became a worldwide sensation headlining his own shows until his death in 1926.

Houdini's brother, who performed under the name Hardeen, was also a headlining magician with strong vaudeville roots. Although they initially performed together, once the brothers were established stars, they typically performed with different vaudeville circuits, marketing themselves as fierce competitors, despite their close relations until Houdini's death.

While minstrel shows as a separate circuit were largely gone by the late 1890s, some of the more famous performers, both white and Black, continued to perform in vaudeville, on the legitimate stage, and in the movies. The Syndicate regularly featured Bert Williams, an African American man who performed in black face, in its massively profitable *Ziegfeld Follies*. The up-and-coming Shuberts cast Al Jolson (one of the most famous white actors performing in black face) in its competing *Passing Show* musical reviews, before Jolson left to star in the movies.

***

Burlesque and vaudeville are two forms of theatrical entertainment that emerged in the United States in the late 19th century and flourished through the early 20th century. While they share some similarities, such as their origins in popular culture and their use of variety acts, they are distinct genres with different histories, styles, and audiences.

Burlesque originated in the 1860s as a form of parody and satire, often featuring risqué humor, songs, and dance. It was a type of entertainment that poked fun at the established order and social conventions, often using sexual innuendo and bawdy humor. Burlesque shows usually consisted of a series of acts that ranged from comedic skits to striptease performances.

Vaudeville, on the other hand, began as the variety shows that were presented in saloons, casinos, and bordellos in the second half of the 19th century. It also drew on the minstrel shows which presented at most loosely connected sketches and acts over the course of an evening's performance. Over time the variety shows outgrew these settings and eventually found permanent homes attracting mixed audiences of men and women seeking more professional and less vulgar entertainment. It is not clear exactly when and where the term vaudeville was first used in the United States, but a touring company was using the term in the 1880s and a theater in San Antonio used the name Vaudeville Theatre as early as 1882.

Vaudeville eventually emerged in the 1880s as a relatively family-friendly form of entertainment (at least in its East Coast incarnation through the work of B.F. Keith) designed to appeal to a broad audience of both men and women. Tony Pastor (known as the King of Vaudeville despite never liking the term vaudeville) became one of the famed early vaudeville producer/managers first touring and later establishing one of the first clean vaudeville shows in America in a posh theater in 1881 on 14th street near Union Square in New York City. Pastor featured a variety of acts, including singers, dancers, comedians, magicians, and acrobats, and aimed to provide reasonably priced all-ages entertainment.

Vaudeville eventually divided into two types of circuits (so-called big time and small time) and some independent theaters that booked whatever acts they could get. The big time vaudeville circuits produced high quality two-a-day shows that toured the country for months or years at a time with a rotating cast of well-known headliners and more journeyman performers.

Big time vaudeville quickly became dominated by two circuits—the Keith-Albee Circuit in the East and the Orpheum Circuit in the West, which cooperated with each other more than they competed. These two friendly mega circuits had some competition from smaller more local circuits (particularly on the West Coast) in the so-called small time vaudeville circuit which featured less attractive theaters, three, four, or even continuous shows each day, and less famous and lower paid casts of performers.

Burlesque and vaudeville differed in their style and content. Burlesque was known for its outrageous and often titillating performances, which featured scantily clad women and suggestive humor. It reveled in its own excess, using over-the-top costumes, elaborate sets, and larger-than-life characters to create a sense of spectacle.

Vaudeville, by contrast, was more focused on skill and professionalism. Performers were expected to be polished and entertaining, but also respectful and appropriate for all audiences and age groups. While there were some risqué elements in vaudeville, they were generally more subtle rather than explicit.

These differences were more of a spectrum rather than a bright line divide. Big time vaudeville aimed for a cleaner and more family-friendly show, small time vaudeville was often more risqué, and burlesque more regularly featured vulgar and racy content. A performer could appear anywhere, but the higher paying, less taxing schedule, and the better conditions of big time vaudeville gave most performers a real incentive to work clean for more money and fewer shows a night.

Burlesque and vaudeville also had different audiences. Burlesque was primarily aimed at working-class men, who were drawn to its ribald humor and more racy content. It was a form of entertainment that was seen as vulgar and lowbrow by the middle and upper classes, who considered it inappropriate for women and children.

Vaudeville, over time, increasingly was designed to appeal to a broader demographic, including families and middle-class audiences. It was a form of entertainment that was eventually considered respectable and mainstream and was seen as a way for people of all ages and backgrounds to have a fun afternoon or night out.

The best example of the differences between vaudeville, Broadway, and burlesque is the very plot of the beloved 1959 Broadway musical *Gypsy*, regarded by many as the perfect Broadway musical. *Gypsy* tells the story of Mama Rose, the ultimate stage mother, living out her show business ambitions through the lives of her daughters June and Louise. Rose takes her children on the road in a family-friendly, but second rate, vaudeville act featuring "Baby" June as the star and Louise as part of the supporting ensemble. Rose controls all aspects of their business and lives as they achieve eventually some success in big time vaudeville.

As the kids age, and the act becomes increasingly cringey and threadbare, bookings become harder to come by. Soon the family act is reduced to playing increasingly small-time vaudeville theaters under worse and worse conditions and receiving ever smaller fees.

The now grown June leaves with her fiancé (one of the dancers from their vaudeville act) to audition for the Broadway stage. Mama Rose then pressures the more introverted Louise to take over the vaudeville act and become the family star.

Louise flounders as the lead, and the money begins to run out. They accept a desperation booking as the only "legitimate" act in a raunchy burlesque theater featuring mostly strippers, as a front for the theater owner trying to stave off being closed by the local police for indecency. Just before curtain, the burlesque house loses its top stripper, and Mama Rose literally pushes Louise on stage in one last final attempt to make her the star of the family.

Louise stumbles through a modest and inept strip tease routine, woefully singing "Let Me Entertain You" from their now dead vaudeville act. She somehow perseveres in this new role, gains confidence and strength, and becomes a burlesque star as a stripper, far beyond anything Mama Rose could have dreamed of.

Gypsy is a loose adaptation of the real-life story of Gypsy Rose Lee, the greatest stripper of the waning era of Burlesque, and the stage name of Rosalie Hovick, the younger daughter of the domineering Momma Rose Hovick. Baby June eventually became the acclaimed Broadway, film, and television actress and director June Havoc, but never achieved the cultural renown of her sister Gypsy Rose Lee, or the dreams of her mother.

The 1959 Broadway musical version featured a creative team of Broadway royalty with Jerome Robbins as director, music by Jule Styne, lyrics by Stephen Sondheim, and book by Arthur Laurents. It was an artistic and commercial success, playing for more than 700 performances and receiving eight Tony Award nominations and a Grammy award for best cast album.

The initial production starred Ethel Merman as the unstoppable Momma Rose and the role has been successfully revived many times featuring such stars as Angela Lansbury, Bernadette Peters, Patti LuPone, Imelda Staunton, and most recently Audra McDonald in a 2024 production.

Gypsy has been produced and revived in London and has toured North America multiple times. It also was made into a 1962 movie musical starring Rosalind Russell (not much of a singer) and a 1993 television version starring the incomparable Bette Midler.

Both burlesque and vaudeville declined in popularity by the end of the 1920s, as radio, television, and other forms of popular entertainment became more prevalent. Today, burlesque has experienced a niche revival in many parts of the world, and particularly in the LGBT+ community, as performers and audiences have rediscovered its playful, irreverent spirit. Modern burlesque shows often incorporate elements of comedy, theater, and music, and celebrate body positivity and diversity.

Vaudeville, meanwhile, has largely been forgotten by modern audiences, although its influence can still be felt in many areas of popular culture. The variety show format that vaudeville pioneered became a staple of the early days of television and inspired the format of many beloved TV shows ranging from *The Ed Sullivan Show, The Muppet Show, Saturday Night Live*, reality competitions like *America's Got Talent*, and more niche live events. Many of the stars of vaudeville and burlesque, such as W.C. Fields, Mae West, Buster Keaton, the Marx Brothers, Bob Hope, and Charlie Chaplin are still revered as icons of American entertainment. Vaudeville continues to exist today but is no longer a national commercial industry.[6]

One prominent historian ascribes even greater importance to the legacy of vaudeville. Robert Synder wrote that vaudeville's most important contribution to American pop culture "was to erode the local orientation of nineteenth century audiences, and knit them, despite their diversity, into a modern audience of national proportions."[7] Another historian wrote more bluntly: "The men who founded vaudeville in America sought to make money by satisfying the needs of the working class for inexpensive and popular entertainment."[8] Both vaudeville and the legitimate theater entered the Gilded Age of the late 19th century with a growing national audience and a business model that would produce untold wealth for the men who would vie for control of the business of live entertainment. What began as a localized form of entertainment for working men quickly became a highly regimented form of mass entertainment for the whole family, but under the control of the first entertainment monopoly in the history of the United States.

Act II

The Cartels

2

The Entertainment Barons of the Gilded Age

By the 1870s and 1880s there were mini-circuits where vaudeville programs could tour to a small handful of affiliated theaters extending the contracts of performers and the profits of the producers and managers. But the business of vaudeville would soon be dominated by two circuits on opposite ends of the United States.

One of the main roots of East Coast vaudeville came from the so-called dime museum shows, named for the price of admission. The great P.T. Barnum of circus fame opened his American Museum in New York in 1841. It was a museum of oddities that included a theater featuring a variety of live acts. The museum's theater ran continuously with a schedule of rotating acts to keep customers returning on a regular basis.

The performances included everything from temperance lectures to scenes from Shakespeare to more exotic acts such as trained animals, acrobats, magicians, and opera singers. Attending the theaters made the museums an acceptable public space for middle-class women and families and became a rare melting pot of people from different social strata.

The shows ran all day from the opening of the museum around 9 AM until closing in the evening at 10 or 11 PM. This meant between five and thirteen shows a day for the mostly exhausted and poorly paid performers. In contrast, the more famous headliners were paid significantly more and only had to perform twice a day at a matinee and then a prime-time evening performance. It was only later when big time vaudeville separated itself from the museum business that two-a-day shows became the industry standard, and three to five shows a day became the norm for the small time and even more down-market vaudeville houses.

Barnum's success with variety shows led to many imitators. The most successful was Benjamin Franklin (B.F.) Keith in Boston who was instrumental in the creation of modern big time vaudeville. Keith was born in 1846 in New Hampshire and grew up on a farm. He began his show business career working in the circus for P.T. Barnum and others. While in the circus trade, Keith worked mostly as a "grafter" selling such dubious merchandise such as "blood testers" on the circus grounds.

In 1883, then in his thirties, Keith opened his own dime museum in Boston and tried ways to keep existing customers coming back on a regular basis. He also sought to make the museum a more reputable enterprise to broaden its appeal as more family entertainment. He hired bouncers to control the rowdier customers in the gallery, required hats and caps to be removed, banned smoking, spitting, whistling, stomping, and even prohibited tossing crunchy peanut shells on the floor.[1]

He began to present live shows on a continuous basis in a 300-seat theater that was part of the museum. The shows changed frequently so customers would return more than once. People could stay in the theater as long as they wanted. However, the program was the same all day long, and most people moved on once they realized they had seen everything before.

Keith soon partnered with Edward Franklin (E.F.) Albee, the grandfather of the acclaimed playwright. Albee was born in 1857 in a bleak Maine village and soon left school also to work in the circus (including for P.T. Barnum) selling overpriced admission tickets to gullible customers with the promise of skipping the regular ticket lines. Albee eventually found his way to Boston and hustled his way into working for Keith's dime museum by acting as a shill for the museum to drum up interest and admissions for crowds in the street.

The variety acts became more popular than the museum and Keith and Albee eventually separated the theaters and closed the museums. They opened their first vaudeville palace in 1894 and soon expanded throughout the eastern United States. So began what became modern vaudeville.

As their vaudeville theater empire expanded, Keith and Albee continued to crack down on the rambunctious men and boys who threatened the more lucrative and growing family audience. They were equally strict with the performers. Backstage signs went so far as to ban words like "slob" and "son of a gun" as not fit for family consumption. Dime museums and less family friendly forms of vaudeville and burlesque survived for several decades, but became a lower-price, lower-class, form of entertainment for performers on their way up to, or down from, big time vaudeville.

In 1898, Keith wrote about his career and business strategy in *National Magazine*. When asked how he came up with the idea of the continuous performance that formed the spine of early vaudeville he replied "Because I had to do something" to keep folks coming back to the theater. [2]

The Keith-Albee Circuit concentrated on the East Coast and insisted on family entertainment without a hint of vulgarity or lewdness to encourage families to attend and avoid any association with the more adult-style entertainment in burlesque or the variety acts in saloons. For a time, Keith also maintained a stock company to present short plays and farces, but the program quickly began to include comedians, singers, dancers, magicians, trained animal acts, ventriloquists, monologists, gymnasts, strong man acts, and eventually short films.

Keith built his vaudeville empire through controlling the booking of the performers, first at his own theaters and then nationwide. Most of the profits came through the fees earned as the middleman connecting performers and theater managers.

The key to this vast network was the United Booking Office (UBO)[3] which Keith formed in 1906, based on the success of the American Theatrical Syndicate agreement in controlling the booking of legitimate theater. The UBO eventually was located on the sixth floor of the Palace Theater in New York City, the most prestigious big time vaudeville venue. The UBO resembled more of a stock exchange style trading floor than an office. There was an open space where booking agents representing performers and theaters sought to put together programs and secure lineups for their clients for weeks, or even entire seasons, at a time.

Each vaudeville bill typically included eight to twelve acts arranged in an order to accommodate audience tastes and to build interest as the audience got settled until a big-name performer appeared shortly before intermission. Another four or more different acts would follow the intermission with the star of the show, usually second to last. Each act was rated by the local managers with reports sent back to the national booking agents. Salaries increased and decreased depending on the ratings, and performers were often dropped from the rosters if these secret ratings remained low.

The UBO's fee normally was 5% of the act's weekly salary. They also charged another 2.5% of the act's salary representing half of the fee for the agent representing the performer. Performers made vastly different amounts of money, but with up to nearly 8,000 acts booked a year, the UBO profits were immense.

Vaudeville theaters around the country received a steady supply of proven talent who were contractually obligated to appear, on pain of losing the rest of the bookings on their tour. Agents were guaranteed to receive at least half their fee remitted directly from the UBO rather than going through the client. The theaters also benefited from the reputation of the Keith-Albee name and the publicity this provided for acts on the road. The performers received a route that was conducive to a long and profitable tour without too many dark nights or lengthy railroad trips between markets.

Both the performers and the theaters were obliged to use the UBO for everything, or not at all. Moreover, the contracts also allowed cancellation of any act for vulgarity, lack of professionalism, failure to appear, or virtually any other reason that the Keith-Albee organization could assert.

***

Vaudeville had a very different and bawdier origin story on the West Coast. In San Francisco, Gustav Walter operated the Fountain, and then the Vienna Gardens, both based on German beers halls. These venues catered to a more adult audience, served alcohol and featured a more vulgar and less family-friendly atmosphere and style of entertainment. The Vienna Gardens and most saloons of this era offered some entertainment mostly to keep patrons staying longer and drinking more.

Walter later opened several theaters, including the Orpheum Opera House in 1887. He presented variety acts that he booked from across the United States and Europe including singers, dancers, and magicians and made no serious attempt to censor their material or cater to women and children. The Orpheum was open well into the early hours of the morning and often welcomed audiences coming from the legitimate theater and other live events in town.

Walter's reputation was destroyed by shady finances and growing debts. Ownership of the Orpheum eventually passed into the hands of Morris Meyerfeld, an entrepreneur in the tobacco and liquor industry, who sought to expand the entertainment options of the Orpheum. He wanted to hire top talent from Europe and the East Coast but quickly found it was costly and unappealing for the stars to travel to San Francisco on a lengthy and uncomfortable train trip for a short run. His solution was to create a circuit of Orpheum properties throughout the Western half of the United States and in portions of the South to attract and profit from such top performers by offering them longer engagements and less arduous travel schedules.

Meyerfeld hired Martin Beck, a former vaudeville performer and waiter in a Chicago beer hall, to run the Chicago office that eventually became the hub of the Orpheum circuit dominating the Western half of the United States. Beck became the leader of the Orpheum Circuit which rivaled (but rarely competed with) the Keith-Albee circuit in the Eastern half of the country. Over time, the Orpheum's programs became more family-friendly like the Keith-Albee shows making it possible for the two circuits to offer a combined true national tour. The combined Keith-Albee and Orpheum circuits could provide a year or more tour for any vaudeville act or program playing weekly engagements in a series of well-planned short jumps via railroad between major markets with intermediate stops in smaller markets similar to the national tours of legitimate theater productions.

Each of the vaudeville circuits faced local or regional challengers that they usually coopted, colluded with, acquired, marginalized, or destroyed. The Keith-Albee circuit divided up the lucrative New York City market among smaller vaudeville presenters, such as Oscar Hammerstein, the operator of his own high-end theaters in the city (and the grandfather of the famed composer). Beck himself tried to present vaudeville in New York City, but settled for the booking rights and a small ownership stake in the Palace Theatre, the crown jewel of the vaudeville empire.[4] The Orpheum circuit had its own local and regional competitors, including the Pantages and Loews chains, none of which grew to the scale of a serious challenger.

Numerous Broadway stars got their start in vaudeville, beginning with George M. Cohan as a ten-year old trick violinist performing with his siblings. Buster Keaton began his career as a seven-year-old performing as part of a family act where he was thrown about (and off) the stage like a rag doll. Houdini and the Marx Brothers got their starts in vaudeville before moving onto bigger fame and fortune. W.C. Fields began as a trick juggler long before he switched to comedy.[5] But for decades, vaudeville (particularly the small time variety) remained associated with low class entertainment, while the so-called "legitimate" theater enjoyed a more upscale reputation and audience.

***

The legitimate theater soon after began its own process of centralization and concentration in the hands of a small group of powerful men. New York City quickly became the capital for legitimate theater. It was the largest and wealthiest city and already functioned as the arbiter of taste for the rest of the country. New York City also had the densest number of theaters, and more importantly, the most actors, producers, financiers, writers, and trained crew in the country. It quickly became "the only city where all the plays could be cast and mounted that were needed to supply the theatres throughout the country."[6]

The maximum financial reward went to the producers who had the longest runs in New York City (increasingly in the neighborhood now known as Times Square as the theater district moved ever northward) followed by the lengthiest national tour possible. A well-organized tour would play the biggest cities first for weeks at a time, connected by one-to-three-night engagements in the smaller cities until the audience's appetite for any particular production was exhausted and the producers and their investors were flush with profits.

On occasion, a show might originate in a city other than New York for a pre-Broadway try out, or tour, to make sure the show was appealing to audiences and to give the producers time to fix any problems before it opened on Broadway. On occasion, the out-of-town tryout closed, and never made it to Broadway, if it was an irredeemable flop.

The touring of live theater was a chaotic affair in the 1870s, 1880s, and 1890s. A producer had to negotiate with numerous theater owners or managers to book his show in New York City and enough markets around the country to be profitable. The tour also had to be organized in an efficient enough manner so the actors, crew, musicians, scenery, and costumes could move as quickly and cheaply as possible via railroad between towns that were not too far apart.

It made no sense for a tour to play a theater in Michigan, followed by one in Maryland, and then one in South Carolina. Ideally, you wanted to play adjacent markets in one part of the country before moving on to the next part of the tour to save on rail transportation.

At the same time, a theater owner or manager in Chicago, St. Louis, or Salt Lake City had to fill their theater, ideally for the entire year. This required booking and presenting multiple shows of differing styles, stars, and plots each for all or most of the year. This was an expensive and cumbersome process with the local presenter working long distance to work out contracts with producers or booking agents usually in New York.

The theater owners and managers on the road were faced with the challenge of putting together a Rubik's Cube of shows, schedules, and contracts that would allow the touring show to be able to load in, play the agreed upon number of performances, and then load out to travel to the subsequent destination of the tour. Similarly, actors, both stars and company members, wanted the longest runs possible, so their livelihood could be guaranteed as much as possible for the longest period of time.

Worst case scenario, a touring production would have long gaps in their schedule, find a stop on their tour already booked with another attraction, a shuttered theater, or a bankrupt presenter with no funds to pay them. Actors, crews, managers, and advance agents often were stranded without pay on the road in a distant city if the tour ended before its scheduled runs. Theater operators would stay dark for long stretches if no substitute attractions were available on short notice.

A new type of intermediary, the booking agent, arose to fill this need. The first theatrical booking agents in New York City appeared in 1859. By the 1870s there were numerous honest and shady booking agents each seeking the same clients. The theater owners and managers often traveled to New York City multiple times a year to work out the arrangements for the coming year. Meetings were held in hotel lobbies, saloons, park benches, and on the sidewalks of Union Square in Manhattan.[7] This mostly outdoor market of managers and bookers trying to make verbal deals looked like a combination of the modern farmer markets that crowd the west edge of the park today and the early days of the downtown curb markets for securities that preceded the growth of Wall Street.

The old-style oral contracts that ensued were risky for both parties. Mistakes were made and both sides often reneged at the last minute when a better deal was available. By 1880, there were 250 touring companies seeking bookings in more than 5,000 theaters in 3,500 cities, posing an immense logistical challenge separate from the problems caused by opportunistic behavior by the parties in this three-tiered system.

This led to the growth of a variety of circuits by the 1870s where the theater owners and producers could be assured of at least a regionally coherent schedule that maximized the chance of both the producers and the theater owners making a profit. The simplest definition of a circuit for theatrical purposes is "a group of theatres so related to each other geographically that they form a logical route for a touring theatrical company."[8]

Sometimes the circuits were as small as three or four theaters contracting for attractions together or operating together under common ownership or management. More typically, the circuit included twelve or more theaters covering all the smaller and midsized cities in such locations as Southern Illinois, Eastern Pennsylvania, Northern Michigan, or the Pacific Northwest. Over time, such circuits grew in both number of theaters and the geographic area they covered.

The circuits that had the most bargaining power depended on their size and location. The more weeks a circuit could supply in a geographically coherent pattern in an important section of the country, or connecting two more major markets, the greater the bargaining power and the better the terms for presenting the touring production. The presenters cared about price but cared equally about getting the most attractive shows and the most favorable times of year for local conditions and tastes. From the producer and booking agent side, this was still an attractive deal given the ability to one-stop shop for an important slice of a multiweek or year-long tour.

The circuits eventually developed an all or nothing policy to further increase their bargaining leverage. Producers had to agree to perform in all the theaters in a particular circuit, rather than cherry pick only the larger and most desirable theaters. Who won the better terms for any particular tour, or circuit, depended on the powers of the parties and the skills of the negotiators.

As the theater industry continued to grow, producers, theater owners, and managers began to serve as booking agents. Booking offices grew bigger, more formal, and covered larger segments of North America. From the producers' perspective this was a mixed blessing, but a tolerable arrangement as long as there was some competition among booking offices for the best deals. But that was about to change.

3

The Rise of the Syndicate

On August 31, 1896, six barons of the theater industry met for lunch in the Holland House Hotel in New York City to form the American Theatrical Syndicate. Its founders—Abraham Lincoln Erlanger, Marc Klaw, Charles Frohman, Sam Nixon, Fred Zimmerman, and Al Hyman combined different aspects of producing, booking, and presenting theatrical productions in New York and the major touring markets on the road.

The Syndicate agreement was a written contract forming a partnership of the existing three businesses operated by the founders. Article two of the agreement listed the theaters controlled by the partners and those where the partners already did the booking. The Syndicate partners paid no booking fees for their own productions and agreed to "pool net profits and other income" and divide the profits equally among the three partner firms: Klaw & Erlanger, Hayman & Frohman, and Nixon & Zimmerman. The agreement was renewed for another five years in 1900.

The Syndicate Agreement created a new arrangement among the three partnerships. It began with a five-part preamble which asserted that the theatrical business has resulted in "great losses from indiscriminate bookings" where "similar first class attractions often directly compete and injure the other"; that arranging tours often resulted in unnecessary expenses particularly from railroad fares and freight charges; and that a new arrangement was necessary to guard against such losses from "indiscriminate bookings."[1]

The core of the Syndicate agreement was that the three partnerships agreed to centralize all bookings for the full range of theaters they owned, managed, leased, or booked in New York City, as well as in a wide array of other cities across the United States. The partners could not book or present competing attractions in other theaters in those cities without the consent of the three partnerships comprising the Syndicate.

Under the agreement, net profits would be pooled and divided among the partners. Each partnership had to keep accurate records and share with the rest of the Syndicate upon request to verify profits (or losses). This relatively short agreement (which largely reflected the current practices of the partnerships) was solemnly witnessed by one Alfred Rhemshom (otherwise lost to history), and executed in triplicate.

Al Hayman had the chutzpah to state to the press after returning home from the New York lunch: "There is no syndicate or trust," despite just having signed in triplicate an agreement with the word "Syndicate" in the title. The modern perpetrators of a cartel like the Syndicate would operate in great secrecy. Instead, these former competitors met in the proverbial smoke-filled room, enjoyed a nice lunch, and signed a written contract that lasted formally, or informally, for nearly three decades.

Two of the Syndicate members had previously already tried to create regional versions of the Syndicate in the South and on the West Coast. The Syndicate members also had done business with each other for years. The idea of finally centralizing the national booking and presenting of Broadway across the United States must have seemed to all six men as the natural outcome of the growth of the various circuits in the industry and the best ways to assure steady profits in a boom-and-bust business cycle. However, it was an act of sheer deceit, or selective memory, when Marc Klaw wrote in the Saturday Evening Post thirteen years later that the men met "by chance" that day in 1896.

Today, we call this kind of meeting a cartel and expect it to be held in secret. Forming such an agreement would now be a felony, and the conspirators (if convicted) would be spending several years in a federal prison. Back then, however, it was held in the open with everyone signing a written contract in triplicate in front of witnesses.

There had been past attempts to form cartels and monopolize the legitimate theater, but all had failed. Sometimes the attempts to corner the theater market failed because they were just too small to succeed, because the managers involved were not competent enough to pull off the scheme, or because the cartels couldn't keep new competition from ruining their plans for national or regional supremacy.[2]

***

This time the Syndicate would succeed because it brought together the key players in the burgeoning national theater industry and because controlling the booking of the New York City and road theaters allowed them to control the producers, actors, and the theatrical managers who depended on the bookers to make their living.

The key players were Abraham Lincoln Erlanger and Marc Klaw who were already powerful bookers based in New York City. Together they owned or leased several theaters and controlled the booking rights to many theaters in smaller cities on the East Coast and in the South. They rose to prominence starting in 1888 by acquiring the Taylor Agency, the most prominent booking office of its time representing producers, theaters, and actors in North America, as well as England.[3]

Erlanger was born in 1860 in Buffalo, New York and, like most of the early pioneers of commercial theater, he had little formal education. His first introduction to the business of the theater was as a cloakroom attendant and opera glass vendor at the Academy of Music in Cleveland where his family had moved. He was transferred to the box office and eventually became treasurer of the Academy.

Erlanger was short, heavy, thick-necked, bald, and nattily dressed. He resembled a smaller version of the Kingpin, a villain in the Marvel *Daredevil* comic books. Erlanger received the most press of all the members of the Syndicate and was viewed by the public and the industry as the kingpin of the Syndicate.

Most of the press about him (except in the newspaper owned or controlled by the Syndicate) was negative, and Erlanger became the symbol of the monopolistic greed of the Syndicate. It was reported that he considered himself "little less than a reincarnation of Napoleon, living in a house full of busts and mementos of the Little Corporal, and of books about him."[4] Erlanger also received an enormous share of anti-Semitic slurs as his wealth and standing in the industry increased.

Marc Klaw was taller, thinner, and a lawyer by training. While Erlanger routinely was described as "crude" or "arrogant," Klaw was more often described as "softspoken, suave, and reticent."[5] While still working in the newspaper industry, he had done legal work fighting play piracy for Charles Frohman, the main producing partner in the Syndicate.

The firm of Klaw and Erlanger was organized in 1887. Early on, they managed a tour of *Alladin* and produced two shows of their own. Erlanger also managed the Southern tour of the great 19th century acting legend Joseph Jefferson and acted as the advance agent for the star.

Klaw and Erlanger soon operated a booking office for several smaller circuits, mostly south and west of Chicago. Even then, they insisted on exclusive booking rights for the circuits they represented. For a time, they operated a partnership with Charles Jefferson, the son of the storied actor Erlanger had previously represented, but that partnership dissolved by 1895 prior to the formation of the Syndicate.

Charles Frohman enjoyed the best reputation of the six partners in the Syndicate. He was a shrewd businessman but also more gentle, erudite, often kind, and committed to producing great art -- if it could be done profitably.

Frohman began as both a local presenter and booker in the mid-1880s in upstate New York State for a local circuit. By 1884, he was already dreaming of a far grander coast-to-coast circuit that would prove to be a model for the Syndicate.

He and his older brother Gustave (Gus) took over the booking operations of the International Amusement Exchange (IAE) and obtained IAE's financial backing for future productions and tours.[6] The Frohman brothers quickly set up their own offices on Broadway in the building that housed Augustin Daily's renowned theater company. Over time, Charles worked with most of the theaters, railroads, and hotels that formed the backbone of a successful tour.

By the mid-1890s, Frohman mostly produced plays and musicals but also owned or managed theaters in Boston, New York, and other markets on the road. He also managed one of the few surviving stock companies based in New York.

Charles Frohman was the son of German Jewish immigrants. His father began his work in the United States as a peddler. Frohman's father enjoyed increasing prosperity as his business expanded to include a cigar factory and a bar-restaurant in Sandusky, Ohio.

While in Sandusky Ohio, Charles's father was a member of the Little German Theatrical Company, an amateur theatrical troupe. At the mother's insistence, they eventually relocated back to New York City in the early 1860s where the father opened a soap factory on East Broadway which failed. This venture was followed in rapid succession by a distillery in Hoboken, New Jersey which burned down, and then a retail cigar shop on Broadway near Greenwich Village in what was then the heart of the theater district.[7]

According to a family memoir, Charles's first theatrical experience was in the late 1860s as an eight-year-old. He snuck away from home to join his older brother Daniel to watch a performance of (you guessed it) *The Black Crook* at Niblo's Garden from the cheap seats in the gallery. Family lore has it that he stayed to the end, transfixed until the final curtain. Supposedly all Charles could say when he returned home to an uproar was "I have seen a play. It's wonderful!"[8]

Frohman's first business experience in the theater was watching his older brother Gus hawk programs at the old opera house on Union Square and finding a $5 bill on the floor of the streetcar they took home.[9] He made his one and only appearance on the stage for one night at the age of nine as a non-speaking flag carrier in a production of *The Field of Gold.*

Frohman began his professional career in the theater business working as the summer box office manager for the famous Callender Minstrel troupe during their summer 1874 Brooklyn engagement, working for his older brother Gustave, who then managed the troupe. Gustave later invited Charles to go out on the road as an advance agent for a comedy acting company headed by John Dillon, a famous Western comedian of the era. As an advance man, Charles went from town to town printing advertising bills and then plastering them around town to drum up ticket sales before the performers they arrived in town.

Charles normally would get his transportation, lodging, and printing on credit advanced against payment from upcoming box office receipts. If the show was a flop, the creditor would simply seize the baggage of the company, leaving them stranded. During this period, theatrical productions were disfavored by creditors, who preferred dealing with the more reliably lucrative variety shows, minstrel shows, and circuses. As part of his advance duties, Charles would arrange for "benefits" on behalf of firemen, widows, orphans, or any cause that was likely to sell enough tickets to fill the theater.[10]

Charles continued to follow his older brothers in their theatrical endeavors. He became the treasurer for the Haverly Mastodons Minstrel show which featured a company of forty performers and used the effective, if rather literal, slogan "Forty – Count 'em – Forty." Gustave Frohman was the advance agent for the troupe and later managed touring companies for Charles for most of his career.

The Haverly Mastodons successfully toured the country, including playing Washington D.C. and marching in the processions for both the inauguration of President James Garfield and the funeral following his assassination. They continued to tour London and across England, including a performance for the future King Edward VII.

Charles gradually assumed most of the duties, and eventually the title, of manager of the company. He met Erlanger at the box office of the Cleveland Opera House, and later in Philadelphia met Al Hayman (who became his general manager for all his productions and partner in the Syndicate). While in San Francisco, Frohman first encountered David Belasco who was just beginning his turn from actor to author, manager, and producer.[11]

Frohman's days on the road were numbered. By 1881, he was back in New York working with his brothers, Gustave and Daniel, at the Madison Square Theater at 24th & Broadway. Frohman introduced a series of innovations that quickly became the industry standard. He was the first to use photos in the posters that were the principal form of advertising for the shows. Frohman is also credited with creating a version of the modern press release. He further began regularly granting playwrights a percentage royalty based on the profits for the production, standard practice today.

Charles Frohman was gracious and genuinely polite, assisting his younger brother Daniel in his own career as a producer, employing his older brother Gus as an advance man on the road, and dealing with the endless stream of would-be playwrights and actors who sought his time and patronage. He handled an enormous stream of correspondence on all aspects of his theatrical operations, even taking the time to personally write to Mark Twain, American's most famous author, that there were no tickets available for a particular matinee performance requested by Twain.

Frohman pioneered the use of multiple companies for a hit production with slightly tailored versions of the same show designed to appeal to different slices of the public. For example, the hit show *Hazel Kirke* had three different productions running at the same time in different theaters in New York, as well as many as fourteen different touring companies across the company. Later this would be commonplace in the early 20th century with more than one company in New York for the same show and with a dozen or more tours playing simultaneously for the most successful shows. In comparison, modern blockbusters like *Rent* and *Hamilton: The Musical* had only one company in New York and three or four North American tours at the height of their popularity.

Taking advantage of the play's popularity was not the only reason for having multiple tours of *Hazel Kirke*. This strategy was necessary at a time of limited copyright protection for play scripts. Creating multiple touring companies was designed to saturate the market before the plagiarizers could copy the script and present their own unauthorized versions of the production.

The perils of play piracy also led Frohman to Marc Klaw. Frohman needed Klaw's help in his capacity as a lawyer to stop additional unauthorized competing productions of *Hazel Kirke*. This type of play piracy was rampant in this era and the bane of any successful show. In the words of the memoir by Frohman's younger brother Daniel:

> Throughout the country local managers began to steal the Madison Square plays and put them on with "fly-by-night" companies. Since they were unable to get manuscripts of the play, the pirates sent stenographers to the theater to copy the scripts as performed. These stenographers had to sit in the dark and write surreptitiously. In many instances, in order to keep the lines of their notes straight, they stretched strings across their note-books.[12]

After successfully getting court injunctions against as many of the play pirates as possible,[13] Klaw went to New York and began working as manager of the "Number Two" *Hazel Kirke* company.

Around this time, Al Hayman joined Frohman's firm as a partner, bringing with him a virtual monopoly on theatrical bookings across some three hundred theaters on the West Coast. In addition, Hayman also booked and managed magic acts and tours throughout the West Coast, South America, and Australia. Hayman had begun his career as the manager of one of the many touring companies presenting *The Black Crook.* Hayman was an important part of the Syndicate but mostly handled tactics, and not strategy.

By 1890, Frohman began what became his annual trip to London to secure U.S. rights to leading English productions. On his first trip, he took with him legendary producer, David Belasco, and returned with the rights to *Jane*, which became one of his first true financial successes on Broadway. Frohman eventually established an office in the Covent Garden section of London. Frohman used his London office and growing transatlantic connections to bring to the United States a steady stream of playwrights, actors, and productions including J.M. Barrie's *Peter Pan.*

He began to bring U.S. attractions to the London stage as well. Ultimately, Frohman leased his own theater in London, the Duke of York, and produced nearly one hundred and twenty-five shows in London and a number of additional productions in Paris.

Daniel Frohman, Charles's older brother, was also a distinguished producer in his own right, though never an outright member of the Syndicate. Daniel left a career in the newspaper industry to begin his theater career as an advance agent for the Georgia Minstrels in the mid-1870s. He would occasionally run into Charles on the road. Their experience as advance men on the road made them formidable booking agents, because together they knew something about every opera house, theater, and rental hall throughout the country.[14]

All three Frohman brothers eventually left the road and worked together at the tiny Madison Square Theatre, then in an unfashionable neighborhood north of 14th Street and Union Square, where most of the legitimate theaters and variety halls were located. By the late 1880s, Daniel was managing and producing musicals and plays on his own and assembling his own stock company to mount productions. He and Charles were friendly competitors at times, but also informally divided up their London and New York productions so they never directly competed against each other in acquiring or presenting shows in either market.

Daniel never even mentions the theatrical trust or its members in his memoirs. Nonetheless, his Broadway and road productions benefitted from the association, long after Charles passed away in 1915.

Erlanger, Klaw, and Charles Frohman were the big three of the Syndicate. However, a Syndicate of national proportions still needed their other three members, including Al Hayman, the close associate of Frohman, who controlled booking for hundreds of theaters in the West. Hayman and Frohman helped each other immeasurably in the early days of their careers with Frohman representing Hayman in the East and Frohman providing Hayman with productions to present in theaters throughout the West. As a producer, Frohman could count on the best theaters and best routes for his tours from his partners in the Syndicate in a way that no other producer of his time received.

Sam Nixon and Fred Zimmerman were based in Philadelphia and controlled key theaters in both Pennsylvania and Ohio.[15] Nixon (nee Nidlinger) was born in in 1848 and grew up in Fort Wayne, Indiana. His first job in show business was sticking up posters and distributing flyers for a circus. He eventually worked as an advance agent for several road tours and settled in Philadelphia and formed a partnership with Fred Zimmerman. Francis Wilson, an actor and no friend of the Syndicate, once described Nixon as "he could squeeze more juice out of a business orange than any man I have ever met . . ."[16]

J. Frederick Zimmerman was from Philadelphia and had once been a baker. He began in the theater as the treasurer of the National Theater in Washington, D.C. and later was heralded as one of the best advance agents on the road.

**

The Syndicate was partly a reaction to the fear of ruinous competition as well as the economic havoc caused by the Depression of 1893. The Syndicate also was based on a similar plan that had been in existence in England.[17] In fact, the Syndicate had been operating informally for several months before they met for lunch and signed the written Syndicate agreement, making later statements that the lunch was an unplanned happy accident highly suspect.

Although the Syndicate included producers and theater owners, it was primarily a huge booking agency.[18] When it was created, the Syndicate faced competition from thirty to forty other booking agencies.[19] But soon it reigned supreme.

The press denounced the Syndicate as soon as it got wind of what had occurred at the Holland House. *The Buffalo Evening News* published a list of more than 50 newspapers across the country that condemned the Syndicate and confidently predicted: "Nothing could survive an onslaught like that made by the newspapers of the country against the evil combination that has seized upon the American theater." They were, of course, quite mistaken.

The full text of the original Syndicate agreement was published two years later in the *New York Dramatic Mirror*, a weekly newspaper published by Harrison Grey Fiske. Fiske was a fierce opponent of the Syndicate and the husband of Minnie Harrison Fiske, one of the leading actresses who refused to perform in Syndicate theaters.

The members of the Syndicate brought a libel action against Fiske and *The Dramatic Mirror* for its unrelenting attacks on the group. Fiske responded by publishing the court pleadings and highlights of the testimony from the case, and in March 1898 he published the full text of the Syndicate Agreement itself.[20]

By 1904, Broadway producer David Belasco estimated that the Syndicate controlled over 500 theaters through ownership, lease, or booking contracts.[21] If anything, this was an understatement. At its peak, the Syndicate could supply entire seasons of legitimate theater in New York City and in over a thousand theaters across the United States and Canada. It could profitably create tour routes that included all the major cities, and most importantly connect the top markets with all the smaller cities and towns along the way to maximize revenues and minimize railroad fares, by far the largest expense for any theatrical tour.

Such power naturally created many enemies along the way including critics, actors, producers, playwrights, and members of the press and public. But few theater owners complained. These owners and managers may have surrendered their independence, but they received a reliable source of supply for an entire season of shows. One actor, and a former opponent of the Syndicate, stated around 1911:

> The theatrical Syndicate has in fifteen years made more actors and managers rich, improved the drama to a greater extent, built more theaters and increased patronage more consistently than has been accomplished by any other factor during the last century.[22]

The Syndicate produced and/or booked new and classic dramas (many from England through Frohman), but mainly more profitable lighter comic operas, musical comedies, and musical revues. The Syndicate mostly provided what it thought would sell the most tickets and make a profit when it could on Broadway and then cleaned up on the burgeoning national road tours that eventually grew to over one thousand theaters.

These six men initially controlled only thirty-three theaters and a minute fraction of the productions on the road. The Syndicate grew by promising better pay and higher profits to actors, playwrights, and theater managers. As its power grew, the Syndicate used many of the same tactics as the industrial trusts and monopolies. It boycotted actors and producers who refused to sign on and bought, built, and leased competing theaters when the local venues or managers refused to book Syndicate attractions. Suddenly, independent venues faced cut-rate ticket prices for competing attractions at critically important points in the calendar. Many of the past evils the supporters of the Syndicate once decried were now the weapons it used to grow its hold over the market.

The Syndicate earned substantial fees in return. The booking fee was between five to ten percent of the net profits (minus certain agreed-upon expenses) for each engagement. There were additional profits and fees depending on whether the Syndicate also produced or presented any of the attractions in New York or on the road. It was not unheard of for the Syndicate to also request between twenty-five and fifty percent of the gross profits.

The Syndicate sometimes also demanded booking fees from the producers in addition to the fees collected from the theaters that presented the show. This included on occasion a percentage ownership of the production in return for booking a particular show on its national tour. At times, these investments were in the name of friendly third parties to disguise the sketchy nature of these transactions. Only nominal fees charged when a show was booked in a venue owned or controlled by a Syndicate member.

The Syndicate always demanded exclusivity. A theater that booked anything from the Syndicate could not present non-Syndicate productions. A producer working with the Syndicate could not present his work in a non-Syndicate theater. An actor for a Syndicate show (at least at the star level) could not perform in a non-Syndicate production or theater. Over time, theater goers often paid higher ticket prices, while actors often received lower salaries and suboptimal working conditions. This was true on Broadway, but especially on the road with its rigorous travel schedules.

Theater owners and managers were threatened and blacklisted if they booked any of the independent productions or performers. Producers who didn't comply were also blacklisted or given routes that virtually guaranteed financial ruin. At the same time, Syndicate productions and engagements could be extended or shortened as needed regardless of the effect on competing productions. Al Hayman, in testifying in the criminal libel case against Harrison Fiske, one of the leading critics of the Syndicate, blandly defended himself saying: "Where I control a theater I reserve the right of the tailor, to sell my clothing to whom I please."

Outside producers were probably the hardest hit by the Syndicate's growing booking monopoly. A good route without too many long travel legs or dead weeks was a matter of life or death artistically, financially, and occasionally personally. As Walter Prichard Eaton noted in *The American Magazine* in 1910:

> Frank Perley, once a manager, but forced out of the business, found one of his plays booked to jump from Philadelphia to East Liverpool, Ohio; from there to Dowagiac, Michigan; and then via a circuitous route with many relays to Charlotte, North Carolina, ... [and eventually back to Saginaw, Michigan].[23] Another manager of much experience, taste and skill has made but one or two productions a season for several years because he refused to meet certain implied demands of the Syndicate booking agents, and so was kept out of New York City. . . . Another small manager committed suicide, it is said, because he lost all his fortune paying railroad fares on a tour so arranged that profit was impossible.[24]

The Syndicate favored its own productions, or those of friends and associates, through better routes, better theaters, and better terms. Through

Charles Frohman, they further enjoyed a stranglehold on the best productions and actors coming over from England.

The Syndicate could coerce independent theater operators to join the Syndicate through a variety of means. It routinely threatened to buy or build "fighting" theaters near the independents to force them to go out of business unless they booked all shows through the Syndicate on an exclusive basis. It was not a coincidence that Marc Klaw embarked on a well-publicized tour of the West Coast promoting the new theaters the Syndicate was building, buying, or leasing, immediately after a longtime Syndicate presenter declared independence and announced that he would be booking attractions from the growing Shubert organization.

The Syndicate could also deny producers access to theaters outside of New York for pre-Broadway tryouts, raising their costs, increasing their risks, and losing the chance to generate favorable pre-Broadway buzz. The independents would be forced to open cold on Broadway with its more crowded field and higher costs.

The Syndicate charged higher or lower fees when it suited their purposes. It charged the highest fees where there was no competition or the producers competed with the Syndicate or its partners. It charged only nominal fees where the Syndicate needed product, where Frohman was the producer, where the theater owners or managers were on friendly terms with the Syndicate, or where the Syndicate needed to make an example of a troublesome independent competitor.

There was always a built-in conflict of interest for the Syndicate in being both a producer of its own shows and a booker of shows from other producers. Such arrangements gave the Syndicate both fees and access to sensitive information about routes and local conditions that gave it an inherent advantage with booking the shows of any competing producer.

Frenemies of the organization such as David Belasco often accused the Syndicate of misusing such information to favor its own productions. Belasco, who feuded with the Syndicate off and on throughout most of his career, accused the Syndicate of undermining his tour of a successful play on Broadway that was set in Japan. The Syndicate refused to book Belasco's production in the premier theater that it controlled in St. Louis during the

1904 World's Fair. This forced Belasco to book a less desirable independent theater during the height of the World's Fair and limited its access to the influx of tourists from around the country and the world.

To make matters worse, the Syndicate cancelled all the bookings of the tour in other cities, forcing Belasco into less profitable options. The Syndicate even went so far as to create its own less successful Japanese-themed play and booked it in many of the same cities shortly before Belasco's production played those same cities to sow confusion and sap ticket sales for its competitor.

Belasco called out the Syndicate in a public article for these shady tactics as well as confusing audiences on the road and diluting the demand for plays with similar themes and settings.[25] The fact that Belasco and Harrison Fiske controlled their own theaters limited the opportunities for such shenanigans for New York engagements but could easily make the difference between success or failure on the road.

On one occasion, Erlanger stopped rehearsals of a play by a playwright who had somehow offended him and for years blocked production of any of his plays. At one point, Erlanger even mounted a competing adaptation of the same work to play in the same cities before the blacklisted playwright's independently produced version could play in those cities. It took a court injunction to stop this tactic, but this incident only reinforced the power of the Syndicate and its very public and spiteful leader.[26] On one occasion, Henrietta Crossman's independent production of *Sweet Nell* was booked to follow week after week a Syndicate production called *Sweet Nell of Old Drury*.[27]

***

The Syndicate effectively controlled the length of any tour. At its height, it owned, leased, or booked nearly 2000 theaters in North America. This included hundreds of theaters in the larger cities and up to 1500 theaters in smaller cities where shows would play "split-week" or "one-nighters." Even if a producer could book on his own enough theaters for a tour of a year or more playing weekly engagements in the larger cities, the producer still needed the Syndicate for the split-weeks and one-nighters in order to have a coherent and profitable tour. Since the Syndicate operated on an all-or-nothing basis, the vast majority of producers booked everything through the Syndicate from pre-Broadway to Broadway and the entire tour for as many years as the audiences wanted to pay to see the attraction. In the words of John Shubert, the son of J.J. Shubert, they were "like the railroad barons."[28]

The Syndicate controlled the market for theaters through a combination of ownership, management, leasing, or booking. This included building—or threatening to build—theaters to compete with an independent venue on the road in a city or town capable of sustaining only one legitimate theater. It also included buying so-called popular-priced theaters to keep independents out of a particular market. Most of these theaters were subsequently resold with restrictive covenants keeping out the independents.

As it expanded, the Syndicate needed more blockbusters that could run for years in New York City and on the road. One of its perennial hits was the *Ziegfeld Follies*, loosely based on the *Follies Bergere* from Paris, which the Syndicate booked annually in New York from 1907 through 1924, and on the road in multiple tours for months at a time on an annual basis. The *Ziegfeld Follies* were a spectacle on the scale of *The Black Crook*, but with bigger budgets, and famous stars over the years such as W.C. Fields, Eddie Cantor, Josephine Baker, Fanny Brice, Bert Williams, Bob Hope, and Will Rogers. The *Ziegfeld Follies* consisted of numerous sketches akin to vaudeville, and in the words of producer Flo Ziegfeld: "Girls, girls, girls."[29]

On the drama side, some of the long running hits were *Charley's Aunt*, and *Peter Pan*, with its high-flying aerial acrobatics and Peter's impassioned plea to the audience to save Tinkerbell. Another perennial was the stage version of *Ben Hur*, which wowed audiences with its recreation of the epic chariot race, later made famous in a successful 1926 silent movie, and eventually the Oscar-winning film starring Charlton Heston in 1959.

These perennials were joined by dozens of lesser-known shows, that even if not profitable on Broadway, London, or Paris, became quite lucrative on the road where these "Direct from Broadway" attractions ran for months, if not years, after the show closed in New York City. At its best, the original cast, or at least the stars, toured after leaving Broadway. These kind of "Direct from Broadway" shows were more sumptuous productions with elaborate costumes, sets, and orchestras. For other road productions, "Direct from Broadway" was more of an empty slogan for a cut-rate company with little connection or resemblance to the original Broadway show.

**

The Syndicate was a loose pool, an informal agreement. Originally, the six members "pooled" the sixteen theaters they owned or leased and the seventeen theaters, all in major markets, where they held exclusive booking rights. These theaters would be booked as a chain on an exclusive basis so that a producer who wanted to book a Syndicate theater in one city would have to book a Syndicate in any other market where there was one.

Though often described as a trust, monopoly, or a cartel, it was a partnership of partnerships. The Syndicate was never incorporated, although holding companies had been legal since 1890. In many ways, it was a throwback to earlier gentleman's agreements and informal pools in salt, whiskey, metals, cotton seed oil, gun powder, meat packing, railroads, coal, lumber, and brewing that had been in vogue for decades throughout the rest of the economy. What this meant as a practical matter was that the written Syndicate agreement probably was not legally enforceable among the members in the event of a dispute, of which there were plenty over the years.

The Syndicate functioned more like an umbrella of the three existing partnerships, rather than an integrated business enterprise like Standard Oil and U.S Steel, which were public enemy number one and two in the era of the gilded age robber barons. However, the Syndicate (and well as the industrial giants) also had to contend with the new federal antitrust laws. But the antitrust laws also had a gaping loophole that the Syndicate would exploit for the rest of its existence.

4

Trustbusting and its Loopholes

One prominent lawyer described the antitrust laws as prohibiting "bullying" and "ganging up."[1] The Syndicate certainly did both. The Syndicate's go-to moves were to demand exclusivity, divide markets with its occasional competitors, and boycott anyone who refused to enter their orbit. These practices almost certainly violated every one of the antitrust laws as they are understood today.

But there was a loophole. The federal antitrust laws only applied to "trade and commerce" that was "interstate," as opposed to local in nature. The Syndicate (and other businesses in the live entertainment field) relied on the difference between interstate and local commerce to act as if the antitrust laws did not apply them.

These limitations were plausible at the turn of the century when the Supreme Court had held that manufacturing was local, and not interstate, in nature, and so beyond the reach of the antitrust laws. However, claiming that any national business, let alone live entertainment that toured the country nonstop, was purely local was increasingly less credible as the decades rolled on. The Court did not definitively eliminate this loophole for the theater industry until the 1950s, long after the Syndicate had left the scene.

***

The antitrust laws regulate competition. They were originally intended to protect consumers, workers, farmers, small businesses, and suppliers from the powerful trusts, cartels, and monopolies that dominated the American economy in the late 19th century.

The federal antitrust laws are short and very general. They prohibit unfair and abusive business practices like price fixing, dividing markets, boycotting, monopolizing, and harmful mergers. The main antitrust law is the Sherman Act of 1890 named for Senator John Sherman of Ohio, a former Secretary of both the State and Treasury Departments, and the brother of the famous Union Civil War General William Tecumseh Sherman.

The Sherman Act uses vague and antiquated phrases that are still being debated in Congress and the courts today. For example, Section One of the Sherman Act prohibits agreements "in restraint of trade." Section Two prohibits monopolization, attempted monopolization, and conspiracies to monopolize. Under later laws, mergers and acquisitions can be prohibited if they tend to "substantially lessen competition." The Department of Justice can bring both criminal and civil charges against any person or business that violates the law.[2]

In addition, private parties injured by antitrust violations can sue for **triple** damages, plus attorney fees and costs.[3] Plaintiffs in these cases are typically either customers who were overcharged by price fixing or competitors who were harmed by abusive or exclusionary conduct.

These private antitrust cases are almost always about money, and lots of it. This type of litigation can be costly and often involve settlements where the defendants pay hefty amounts of money, but never actually admit they broke the law. Such cases almost never involve breaking up the defendant's business, unless the government itself sues the defendant as an unlawful monopoly.

***

The earliest big antitrust cases brought by the federal government involved the railroads and other national businesses where the requirement of interstate commerce was not in serious doubt. The Justice Department prevailed in the Supreme Court's 1911 *Standard Oil* and *American Tobacco* decisions, breaking up the existing oil and tobacco monopolies.[4] These cases pleased almost no one, given the lengthy and vague reasoning of the decisions. Both trustbusters and corporate defenders thought the decisions left too much discretion to the courts to determine whether businesses had behaved "unreasonably" and therefore broke the law.

It is almost hard to believe today, but the presidential election of 1912 was fought in large part about what chould be done to improve the antitrust laws. The incumbent Republican William Howard Taft, the Democratic challenger Woodrow Wilson, the former President Theodore Roosevelt, and the socialist Eugene Debs all had their own antitrust proposals that were heavily debated.[5]

Following Wilson's victory, Congress passed two additional antitrust laws. The 1914 Clayton Act prohibited mergers and acquisitions that tend to harm competition. The Clayton Act further barred companies from using unfair tactics like price discrimination, tying, exclusive dealing, and other practices that tend to harm competition.[6] The same year Congress also passed the Federal Trade Commission Act creating a second federal antitrust enforcer with the even broader power to prohibit "unfair methods of competition."[7]

***

While most of what the Syndicate qualified as a "restraint of trade," an unfair method of competition, and unlawful monopolization within the meaning of the antitrust laws, there was a reasonable argument that the Syndicate was lawful at the time of its founding in 1896. The Sherman Act, like any federal legislation, must fall within one of Congress's powers under the Constitution to be lawful. The antitrust laws were based on the Commerce Clause of the Constitution, which allows Congress to regulate activities in or affecting interstate or foreign trade or commerce.

What constituted interstate commerce was still an open question in the decades after the enactment of the Sherman Act. By the late 19th century, everyone agreed that this included railroads whose very business involved transporting goods and people across the country. While odd to a modern reader, the Supreme Court also held in 1895 that the Sherman Act did not cover manufacturing, since the act of manufacturing by itself was local, rather than interstate in nature.[8] There was no definitive ruling whether live touring theater was more like the railroads in traveling from state to state or more like manufacturing since each performance took place in a fixed location in a particular city or state.

The Syndicate, and the rest of the theater industry in the early 20th century, had good reason to believe that the antitrust laws did not apply to them and they acted accordingly. In 1907, a New York state judge held that live theater was not even trade or commerce, let alone interstate commerce subject to the federal antitrust laws. That case began when a New York state grand jury heard from Syndicate rivals Lee Shubert, David Belasco, and others and indicted the Syndicate and its members for "criminal conspiracy in restraint of trade," under the New York state equivalent of the federal Sherman Act.

Later that year, Judge Otto Rosalsky dismissed the indictment holding that: "plays and entertainments of the stage are not articles or useful commodities of common use, and that the business of owning, leasing, and controlling theatres, and producing plays therein, is not trade, and that, therefore, the defendants did not commit acts injurious to trade or commerce."[9]

The judge continued: "The defendants were engaged in a private business and hence were not obliged to aid a business rival by permitting him to use their private premises. They had the undoubted right to book or refuse to book any production that they saw fit and to maintain and close any of their theatres at their option."[10]

The trial judge further found that the Syndicate competitors had successfully presented and booked shows despite their lack of ability to access Syndicate theaters. The judge also found that the Syndicate had not acted with an improper purpose, engaged in any illegal means, or committed any illegal acts by lawful means. He described the motive of the agreement as "self-help" and ultimately concluded that "theatrical amusements" could not be considered articles of trade or commerce covered by the law of restraint of trade. This is legalese for holding that the antitrust laws didn't apply to the Syndicate and even if they did, the Syndicate had done nothing wrong.

Texas, Indiana, and Massachusetts introduced legislation that would have barred self-preferencing and other anticompetitive abuses in the legitimate theater industry, but none of these bills were ever enacted into law. In the Massachusetts State Senate, future President Calvin Coolidge was the sponsor of a similarly unsuccessful bill that would have prohibited discrimination by booking agents "against any particular man's attractions."

Judge Rosalsky's 1907 opinion was based on New York state law. The question of whether legitimate theater or vaudeville was subject to the federal antitrust laws was more nuanced. By 1914, the Supreme Court held that the licensing of motion pictures was interstate commerce. That same year a federal trial court in New York found that the interstate commerce aspects of the national vaudeville circuit were "essential" to its operation.[11] However, a New York state appellate court found that a smaller tour of opera productions with United States and international performers was not trade or commerce at all, and thus not subject to the New York state antimonopoly laws.[12]

In the 1920s, The Federal Trade Commission (FTC) was the first federal agency to investigate the vaudeville industry on antitrust grounds. The FTC investigation focused on whether the vaudeville monopolies in the eastern and western halves of the United States had engaged in unfair methods of competition in forcing all performers to join an association called the National Vaudeville Artists, Inc. (NVA). The NVA allegedly was a management-led organization (masquerading as a labor group) that took high fees from the performers, forced them to advertise in *Variety* magazine, and blacklisted any performer who had the temerity to join the real unions – the colorfully named White Rats Actors Union and the Associated Actresses of America.[13]

The FTC held extensive hearings spanning thousands of pages of testimony and documents, only to conclude that vaudeville, even touring vaudeville, did not constitute interstate commerce and therefore was not subject to the federal antitrust laws. Despite grave abuses in the vaudeville industry harming competition, performers, managers, and booking agents, there was nothing that could be done. While the FTC took the unusual step of referring the matter to the Justice Department for its own review, the Justice Department also declined to bring either criminal or civil proceedings.

The Justice Department had already declined to bring a similar complaint relating to the vaudeville industry. That complaint was brought by William Morris, then a leading vaudeville talent manager and later founder of the famous Hollywood talent agency bearing his name. He complained to the Justice Department in 1907 (after the Rosalsky decision) that the Syndicate, the Shuberts, and the two main operators of big-time vaudeville had conspired to prevent Morris and other competitors from booking vaudeville performers.

Morris had been the booking agent for as many as five thousand different vaudeville acts. He was primarily concerned about the demise of a failed joint venture by the Syndicate and the Shuberts to take over vaudeville. Advanced Vaudeville, as it was called, hired Morris to book the talent for their new vaudeville circuit but failed to ever turn a profit. Advanced Vaudeville and its Syndicate and Shubert owners settled with the vaudeville circuits they sought to ruin by agreeing to exit the vaudeville market and stay out for ten years in return for a paltry payout of $250,000.[14]

This decision to divide the market between the Syndicate/Shuberts theater owners and the Keith-Albee/Orpheum vaudeville circuits harmed competition, performers, and consumers. But the most immediate and direct victim was William Morris, who was now unemployed, and possibly out of business as a vaudeville talent agent.

In a display of both bravado and chutzpah, a representative of Klaw and Erlanger, the leaders of the Syndicate, publicly stated that the settlement arrangement was "obviously in no manner a trust or merger."[15] Lee Shubert offered what today would be a confession, rather than a defense: "The new association is only an association for arranging certain troublesome matters among ourselves. It is more a meeting or convention of men in one business. . . ."[16] There is no evidence that the Justice Department ever took any action against this agreement between the leading competitors in the legitimate theater and vaudeville industries.

***

In the landmark 1922 *Federal Baseball* case, the Supreme Court held that professional baseball was immune from the Sherman Act, because that sport also did not constitute interstate commerce.[17] According to Justice Oliver Wendell Holmes, the games themselves were local exhibitions, even though the players (and some of the fans) travelled from other states. The opinion compared professional baseball with lawyers traveling to argue a case in another state, or a speaker on the Chautauqua lecture circuit traveling to speak in another state, and scoffed at the notion that any of these types of enterprises constituted interstate commerce.

The next year the Supreme Court reached a different conclusion about the nature of interstate commerce in an antitrust case involving the big time vaudeville industry and its national tours. Max Hart, a manager and agent for vaudeville performers, sued the two big time vaudeville circuits, the Keith-Albee Circuit in the East and the Orpheum Circuit in the West. He alleged that the circuits blacklisted him and his performers in violation of the Sherman Act. The lower court had found (like *Federal Baseball*) that the interstate transportation of people, scenery, and props was incidental to the inherently local vaudeville shows.

Holmes again wrote the unanimous opinion for the Court.[18] Surprisingly, this time the Court held that touring vaudeville was indeed interstate commerce for reasons the Court struggled to explain in a brief three-paragraph opinion.

Holmes noted that Hart had argued in his complaint that touring vaudeville involved the transportation of a large number of performers, scenery, music, costumes, and animals and "in the transportation of vaudeville acts the apparatus sometimes is more important than the performers. . . ."[19] The Court held that at this early stage of the case otherwise valid complaints should not be dismissed unless the case was "wholly frivolous." The Supreme Court sent the case back to the trial court for further proceedings.

If the Supreme Court was trying to send a hint to the lower court that the *Federal Baseball* case should not be extended beyond the unique setting of professional baseball, it failed. After hearing all the evidence in Hart's case against the vaudeville circuits, the trial court concluded as a matter of fact that the inherently local nature of the performances predominated over the railroad travel and freight necessary for the performance, particularly for many of the acts like jugglers and comedians who needed few costumes or props to perform.

Hart appealed, but the United States Second Circuit Court of Appeals upheld the trial court's decision for the defendants. In a brief opinion, the appellate court stated that the large volume of scenery, costumes, props, and countless performers crossing state lines did not change the inherently local nature of the vaudeville performances themselves.[20] The Supreme Court declined to rehear the case, effectively leaving unresolved the question of whether live entertainment was subject to the federal antitrust laws.

Whether the legitimate theater and its many "direct from Broadway tours" were more like professional baseball, the movies, or the vaudeville circuits did not reach the Supreme Court again during this era. Both the Syndicate, and later the Shuberts, took full advantage of the ambiguity in the existing cases and acted as if the antitrust laws were at most a minor irritant. Both organizations treated any cases brought against them as a mere cost of business, to be settled on the cheap whenever possible. They also exploited the legal ambiguity to occasionally sue each other and other businesses when it suited their interests. Any resulting settlements never involved admissions of guilt or any definitive resolution of whether the antitrust laws applied at all.

This legal loophole unleashed the Syndicate (mostly through Klaw and Erlanger) to use its full economic muscle to coerce, control, and crush the independents who tried to defy them. The uncertain reach of the antitrust laws also defined the Syndicate's complex relationship with the Shubert brothers who, by the dawn of the 20th century, dared to compete with the mighty Syndicate on its own turf.

5

The Price of Independence

The Syndicate created some efficiencies. An example was the 1897 tour of the otherwise long forgotten *A Midnight Bell*. The producer of the show, Duncan Harrison, testified that it took a mere seven minutes for Erlanger to book a twenty-seven-week tour covering all the principal cities in the United States.[1] Even David Belasco conceded that the nation-wide booking system was in principle a good thing.[2]

Charles Frohman's brother, Daniel, gushed in his memoir:

> It marked a real epoch in the history of the American theater because within a year a complete revolution had been effected in the business. The booking of attractions was emancipated from curb and café; a theatrical contract became an accredited and licensed instrument. The Syndicate became a clearing-house for the theatrical manager and the play-producer, and the medium through which they did business with each other.[3]

The Syndicate also created push-back from a diverse group of producers, performers, writers, and publishers deemed the Independents. The actor Richard Mansfield routinely denounced the Syndicate from the stage after his performances.

The other leading independent voice from the stage was Minnie Maddern Fiske, one of the most famous actresses of the time and a pioneer of a more naturalistic acting style. For nearly fifteen years, Mrs. Fiske was the only actor, producer, or presenter of note who consistently opposed the Syndicate and refused to work on the Syndicate circuit.

Minnie Fiske was married to the businessman and publisher Harrison Grey Fiske, who owned the *New York Dramatic Mirror*. The offices of the *Dramatic Mirror* were deliberately surrounded on both sides by Syndicate houses once the Syndicate built its Empire Theatre on Fortieth Street and Broadway in addition to its existing property on the other side of the *Dramatic Mirror*.

The *Dramatic Mirror* became the principal voice for the independent movement, denouncing every aspect of the Syndicate on a weekly basis for more than a decade. In response, the Syndicate posted signs in its theaters forbidding actors from advertising, buying, or reading the *Dramatic Mirror*.

When Minnie performed outside of New York City the price was heavy. Her husband was able to lease a first-class theater in New York City where she could perform. On the road, things were very different. She frequently performed in smaller, and often dingy, theaters that remained independent of the Syndicate.

When nothing else was available, she performed in any public space that could be adapted for a play, including second-rate theaters, public halls, former movie houses, ex-churches, ice skating rinks, tents, and other outdoor spaces. Sometimes nothing at all was available in some cities that fall outside of Syndicate control and some of her tours covered only one-third of the country, with little or any profit, given the power of the Syndicate and its blacklist.

Harrison Fiske published fifteen separate supplements, between November 1897 and February 1898, promising to expose all the shady practices of the Syndicate until the trust "shall vanish like a bursted bubble." He later published the full contents of the Syndicate agreement itself.[4] Shortly thereafter, Joseph Pulitzer's *New York World* joined the fight with an editorial reading: "The Theatre Trust is a peculiar abomination. It aims not only to compel the public to pay what prices the trust pleases for its entertainment, but to decide arbitrarily what plays and what actors the public shall see."[5]

The Syndicate fought back through its control of the *Morning Telegraph*, its mouthpiece for pro-Syndicate propaganda. The Syndicate canceled its own advertising in the *Dramatic Mirror* and refused to book any production that advertised in Fiske's paper. Nixon and Zimmerman pressured hotels in Philadelphia to stop selling the *Dramatic Mirror* in their lobbies, on pain of not providing theater tickets to the hotels for their guests.

Meanwhile Mr. Fiske hurled insults at each of the members of the Syndicate by name, gleefully reporting on every attempt to silence him or the handful of other Syndicate opponents. The Syndicate eventually responded by filing a libel case against Mr. Fiske and the *Dramatic Mirror*. Mr. Fiske replied by publishing extended verbatim copies of the testimony and exhibits of the trial. Things got so bad that Harrison Fiske and Erlanger got into a fistfight on Broadway, leading to the two gents being taken to the police station before being released without charges.

The libel case lingered until 1900 when the Syndicate dismissed the case hoping the whole matter would just go away. Instead, Fiske took the occasion to review the entire case and denounce the dangers the even larger and more powerful Syndicate now posed.[6]

Fellow travelers in the Independent movement included the producer David Belasco, and some of the leading actors of the time such as Richard Mansfield, Nat Goodwin, Francis Wilson, and James Herne. Another noted critic of the Syndicate was James O'Neill, famous for his performances in the long touring *Count of Monte Cristo*, better known today as the father of the famed playwright Eugene O'Neill. The combined prominence of the Syndicate and the Independents, and the many stars and celebrities taking sides, made the ongoing struggle front-page news in mainstream newspapers all over the country for many years.

The actor-producer-manager David Belasco was a particularly vocal and public critic of the Syndicate. The press was eager to publish his every word on his on-again off-again feud with the Syndicate. Although he had begun his career working with Charles and Daniel Frohman, he later told the New York Times:

> The simple fact [is] that six men, imbued with no other spirit than commercialism, have gained control over the drama. They are uncultured, unlettered men, without the slightest interest in art, with no care for its advancement or its future; yet they dictate to the stage as would the Czar to his subjects. . . . You cannot make a trust of art. Commercialism and art are incompatible. . . . A few years ago some of these men were advance agents, some of them were opera glass sellers. Today they are rolling in wealth because they have cheapened the drama and profited thereby.[7]

Belasco went on to criticize the Syndicate (in this case Frohman, but not identified by name) for bringing over theatrical failures from London and Paris and passing them off as great successes, solely because of the cheap prices for the rights to such shows.[8] Within a month of the publication of his comments, he wrote a letter to the editor claiming that the *Times* had published his comments without his knowledge and consent, but that he was only too pleased to say that he was "correctly quoted" and that he "made no assertion not capable of the most absolute proof. . . ."[9] He also complained bitterly that the Syndicate sometimes took between a third and a half of his total profits.[10]

Things got so bad that Belasco had to rent a dilapidated convention hall in Washington, D.C. for one of his 1904 productions. On a night with heavy rains, Cabinet Secretaries and Navy Admirals sat through the final act holding umbrellas.[11]

***

In 1905 Belasco went to trial in a complicated lawsuit about whether Klaw and Erlanger and/or the Syndicate were secret partners in a production called *The Auctioneer*. The trial was a *cause célèbre* in the theater world and widely followed in the press. At different times, Belasco, Erlanger, Klaw and David Warfield (the star of the show) took the stand to assert or deny that Klaw & Erlanger muscled its way into a behind the scenes stake in the production, who owed whom money for the booking fees, and who controlled the right to produce the show going forward. The courtroom was packed as colorful counsel argued and feisty witnesses took the stand while the judge did his best to keep things civil and moving along.

After court adjourned for the day following a particularly contentious cross-examination of Erlanger, Belasco threatened to fight Erlanger until the lawyers separated their clients and hustled them down the elevator and the staircase to the street. Belasco ultimately lost the case, further cementing his relationship with the rival producing faction of the Shubert brothers who welcomed him with open arms.[12]

Nevertheless, by 1909, Belasco was again working with the Syndicate. Belasco became increasingly concerned that the Shuberts were even worse than the Syndicate (and more powerful) by this point. He uncharacteristically made peace when Klaw and Erlanger agreed to a rare exception from their blacklist to bring Belasco back into the fold without insisting on exclusivity.

***

None of the serious attempts to oppose the Syndicate before the Shuberts were successful. An early boycott in 1898-99, organized by the star actor Francis Wilson, sought to organize an "alliance" to fight back against the "trust" of the Syndicate. Wilson wrote to the press that while the Frohmans were not so bad: "Klaw & Erlanger are the 'despotic' trust fellows. They are the real geniuses in the 'trust,' and devise the ways and schemes to bear down on the profession with an iron hand."[13]

The actors' alliance failed, despite an agreement establishing a $5000 penalty for any members who defected from the boycott. The Syndicate picked off most of the group one by one with threats and promises. The actor Nat Goodwin went back to working with the Syndicate in return for a promise of shows where and when he wanted them, including a long engagement at the Syndicate's New York Knickerbocker Theatre.[14] By the end, only a small number of the actors' alliance stood firm, including Minnie Fiske and the aging star of an earlier era, Joseph Jefferson, whose stature in the industry meant he could pick and choose his engagements without regard to the battle among the booking circuits.

The independents and their supporters were not helped by the highbrow elitist tone of many of the objections to the Syndicate. Most of the criticism came from concern over the artistic quality of commercial theater, rather than harm to the ticket buyers. Some of the critiques seem more concerned about the commercial and social gaucheness of the new barbarians in the industry who cared more about money than art. Some of the discourse veers close to old WASP elite objecting to the growing power of uncouth newcomers crashing their former more socially restrictive enclaves.

For example, literary giant William Dean Howells opined: "Not merely one industry, but civilization, itself, is concerned, for the morals and education of the public are directly influenced by the stage. Every one who takes a pride in the art of his country must regret a monopoly of the theatre, for that means 'business' and not art."[15]

Thomas Bailey Aldrich, a noted writer, critic, and long-time editor of *The Atlantic*, wrote: "The inevitable result of a Theatre Trust would be deterioration in the art of acting and discouragement of dramatic literature. Certainly that is not a consummation devoutly to be wished."[16]

The star actor Richard Mansfield thundered: "Art must be free. I consider the existence of the Trust or Syndicate a standing menace to art. Its existence is, in my opinion, an outrage and unbearable."[17] Even if these critiques were true, they often seemed more like the concerns of fading out of touch elites, rather than any serious concern for the harms of monopoly and cartels of the Gilded Age.

The actor Francis Wilson came the closest to linking the Syndicate's growing power to the real harms affecting the public at large. He published a cartoon where the Syndicate was an octopus strangling all who opposed it. He gave fiery speeches to audiences from the stage after his performances. He frequently published letters in *The World* and other newspapers that opposed the Syndicate.

In one of his pieces in *The World* Wilson made the most direct case that the Syndicate was bad for the real world, and not just lofty concerns for art. He wrote:

> The Trust cajoles where presently it will command. Once it succeeds in accomplishing its present purpose, there will be nothing but the Trust. Ambition will be futile. The independent actor-manager will have to disappear. The public will be obliged to take what the Trust gives it. Actors will be able to obtain employment only through the Trust. Playwrights will be dependent upon the Trust. Theatrical advertisements, since there will be no competition, will be limited to two-line announcements, and also the dramatic critic's occupation will be gone. This is not fiction. It is truth. Shall actors be beggars at the door of the Trust? It is the artist that the people go to see, him and his work. It is the artist in whom the people are interested, not the members of the Trust."[18]

By the end of 1898, Mansfield had defected, and even Wilson sold a half interest in his business for fifty thousand dollars to Syndicate members Nixon and Zimmerman. Wilson sheepishly told friends that the opposition was losing its stalwarts and not gaining any new converts. He felt that the Syndicate was continuing to grow in strength, and his own followers were slipping away because of the quality of the theaters he was forced to perform in. Wilson said he had lost income and incurred increased expenses in order to circumvent the Syndicate, and he was concerned for providing for his family.[19]

In 1902, Harrison Fiske organized a competing booking group called the Independent Booking Agency (IBA). The IBA handled his wife, a few other actors, and originally thirty different theatrical ventures. The IBA represented as many as 450 theaters, but the vast majority of those venues were substandard venues suitable only for one-night engagements, and too insignificant to bother the Syndicate.

By 1904, the IBA folded, with the Syndicate picking off the few first-class theaters on the IBA roster of clients. A similar revolt on the west coast covering a dozen or so second-class theaters had little impact on the Syndicate growth or dominance of the touring market.

Over time, the Syndicate bought off, blacklisted, or threatened almost everyone, except Mr. and Mrs. Fiske. She continued as an independent performer, backed by the daily vitriol hurled by her husband at the Syndicate by the *Dramatic Mirror* and protected in a long-term lease of the Manhattan Theater in New York City, so she could continue to perform in an appropriate venue.

Even the Fiskes had their limits. By 1910, they reached their own accommodation with the Syndicate. The attacks in the *Dramatic Mirror* stopped, and by 1911, Harrison Fiske had sold the *Dramatic Mirror*. Although Minnie Fiske hailed her new-found ability to play Syndicate houses as a victory over the Trust, even this arrangement reflected more the Syndicate's power and influence.

***

Actors and critics blamed the Syndicate for destroying the artistic merit of the American theater, a charge much harder to sustain than attacking the rough edges of their business tactics. The Syndicate was described as an "incubus" and its principals as an "absolute dictatorship or tyranny."[20] Much of this criticism was overblown hyperbole and included a great deal of cultural snobbism and poorly remembered nostalgia for a past era combined with more than a hint of outright antisemitism.

Fiske relied on innuendo and relatively subtle anti-Semitic tropes, but *Life* magazine led with straight up bigotry with drawings labeled "Theatrical Trust. Of the Jews. For the Jews. By the Jews." and text stating "In their veins runs the blood of Fagin, Shylock and the money-changers who were scourged from the temple. . . ."[21] Other publications called the Syndicate "the Incubus" and the "Sheenee Theatrical Trust."[22]

Frohman and Klaw responded in such mainstream magazines as the *Saturday Evening Post*, *Harper's Weekly*, and *Cosmopolitan*. Klaw defended the Syndicate as having brought "order out of chaos" and claimed they only responded to the laws of supply and demand and did not create or tamper with them.[23]

Frohman responded in *Harper's* denying that the Syndicate applied to anything other than the booking segment of the industry. He claimed that the members of the Syndicate actively competed to acquire scripts, hire actors, and mount productions. He topped this off by asserting that "[t]he difficulty with the stage of today lies with the playwright" and claimed that the playwrights of the U.S., France, Germany, and England produced less than six genuine plays a year.[24] Frohman conveniently ignored how control of booking effectively controlled the industry, and how he benefited financially and artistically as a founding member of the Syndicate.

Monroe Lippman's 1940 analysis showed the Syndicate produced a substantial number of successful productions of the classics, quality new plays, performances by the leading actors of the time, and the first African American performers on Broadway.[25] Another theater historian more broadly characterized the artistic critics of the Syndicate as "a cultural aristocracy rooted in nineteenth-century values."[26]

While the Syndicate's priority was filling seats, they still had the incentives to produce new dramas and quality productions to create long-term relationships with new playwrights. However, It had an even bigger incentive to revive the classics, which had some built-in audience appeal, and more importantly, did not involve having to pay royalties to long-dead authors like William Shakespeare and Edmund Rostand.

The Syndicate had the herculean task of filling tens of thousands of theater seats every day in a world where every production could not be an artistic gem. They needed stars and plays that would appeal to mass audiences in every part of the country. One observer bluntly noted: "if a play was not considered practical it would not be produced."[27]

The limited successes of the independents only served to demonstrate the difficulties of standing up to the Syndicate. Lesser-known actors, and more poorly resourced producers and managers did not dare to risk a blacklist and agreed to book, perform, or present exclusively through the Syndicate for close to a decade without serious challenge.

Still, the Syndicate was of value to many of the theaters and producers that were its clients. The Syndicate usually delivered on its promise to book a season-long tour with all the paperwork and contracts completed within forty-eight hours. For theater owners, the Syndicate promised not to book any new competing theater in the same city as a Syndicate client, without the consent of that owner.[28]

At its founding, the Syndicate owned or managed only thirty-three theaters but they controlled the booking of more than five hundred. It quickly grew and by the turn of the century, the Syndicate acquired dozens more theaters in key cities and controlled booking for approximately two thousand venues. But the total number of theaters owned or operated by the sinister six always underestimated the power of the Syndicate's booking operations, which were the key to its dominance.

The Syndicate controlled for a time the critical bottleneck for the entire industry and was the first true national theater trust. This cartel and monopoly lasted until a new force in the industry, started far from the glitz of Broadway and quickly challenged the Syndicate on its own turf.

6

The Shubert Challenge

The Syndicate never really recognized the biggest threat they would face until it was too late. The Shubert brothers who supplanted the Syndicate came from humble Jewish immigrant backgrounds. Levi, Sam, and Jacob were the three sons of David and Katrina Szemanski. The Shubert brothers and three of their sisters, Fanny, Sarah, and Dora, were all born in the town of Shervient, in what is now Lithuania. The records are so garbled that it is difficult to determine whether the youngest daughter, Eva, was born in Europe or the United States.

David and the family fled anti-Semitism and the frequent pogroms of Czarist Russia. They came to the United States in 1881, via Hamburg, Germany and England. In the United States, David struggled with alcoholism and barely made a living as a peddler.

They first lived in New York City with relatives on the Lower East Side. Shortly thereafter the family made their way upstate to Syracuse and moved into a small three-room rented house. The money and drinking problems never really ended; the family of nine relied heavily on the charity of the Jewish community and the meager incomes the older children brought in to add to their father's erratic earnings.[1]

Along the way, the family name changed from Szemanski to Shurbent, Schurbart, Shobart, and finally Shubert. The rest of the family history is subject to many myths, fables, and outright inventions as the brothers became more assimilated, affluent, and famous. Names were changed; Levi became Lee, Jacob became J.J. Middle initials were added; ages and birth orders were often changed as the situation dictated.

The oldest brother was Lee, although he frequently referred to Sam as the oldest. Lee started shining shoes, selling newspapers, and running errands for tips in downtown Syracuse in front of the Wieting Opera House. He soon became the personal errand boy for John Kerr, the manager of the theater, bringing him his daily paper and carrying a pot of soup from Kerr's home to the theater for his dinner. By the time Lee was 12, the 9-year-old Sam joined him, and they worked together as a team.

The story goes that in 1885, while Lee was out bringing Kerr's dinner to the theater, Kerr saw Sam outside trying to sell his pile of newspapers coughing strenuously while huddling around a bucket with a charcoal fire. Kerr invited Sam into the theater to warm up and gave him permission to watch the show on a night where they were many empty seats.

The show was, of all things, *The Black Crook.*[2] By this point the show had been on tour in some form for nearly twenty years. The production Sam saw that night was "a third-rate, cut-down version, playing a tired performance."[3]

According to Shubert legend, that's when Sam knew how he would spend the rest of his life. Sam's first paid job in the theater was as an extra in a forgettable David Belasco production of *May Blossom*. He was paid one dollar for one week of work, plus free passes for the family.

Sam Shubert soon began his business career in the theater selling programs and candy for a weekly salary of $1.50. His younger brother Jacob was by now working outside selling papers, shining shoes, and running any errands that were likely to result in a tip from grateful customers. By the age of twelve, Sam was promoted to assistant treasurer at the Grand Opera House. While this was a lofty title, in reality he sold tickets at the box office. He had to stand on an actual box so he could see over the counter of the ticket window.

He soon impressed the owners with his work ethic and earned their trust. He was promoted within two years to treasurer and put in charge of the cash drawer and the nightly statements. By the time he was fifteen, Sam was the treasurer back at the Wieting Theater, then Syracuse's finest. By the time Sam was eighteen, he was charming and clever, but just over five feet tall, and always looked much younger than his true age.

If Sam was captivated by the art of the theater, Lee was principally captivated by the fact that people paid good money to see the plays and musicals at the handful of theaters in downtown Syracuse. Lee eventually worked at a series of jobs including cigar roller, shirt cutter, and a clerk in a haberdashery. He then became a partner in the clothes store with Jesse Oberdorfer, who later became a key financial backer for the Shuberts. Jacob later joined Lee at the store as a clerk. Their sisters Sarah and Dora worked there as well.

In 1894, while still a teenager, Sam bluffed his way into acquiring the rights to tour *A Texas Steer* by Charles Hoyt. Hoyt was a successful millionaire playwright of the day specializing in satires of current events. The limited tour of popular priced second tier theaters was successful enough that Sam also profitably toured a second work by the same playwright.[4]

In another piece of luck, an insolvent producer named Charles Lederer had a hit show called *The Belle of New York* that had already played in New York City and London. The belle of *The Belle* happened to be a Syracuse actress and a close friend of Lee Shubert's business backer Jesse Oberdorfer. The producer needed cash and the Shuberts needed a property to tour so they made a deal.

While Sam focused on touring, Lee took his place in the Wieting box office. Lee recalled that even then the Syndicate closed their theaters to Sam's tour, forcing him to cobble together a route using convention halls, auditoriums, independent venues, and the handful of Shubert theaters in upstate New York.[5]

In both cases, Sam relied on loans from a partnership of contacts from the Jewish community in Syracuse. The early tours were profitable enough that Sam began to aspire to loftier ambitions. Even in these early days, Erlanger and the Syndicate used their muscle to prevent the tour of *A Texas Steer* from opening in Boston by offering the presenter other productions for that year in return for canceling the Shubert engagement. While Sam and Lee kept their day jobs and Jacob became an assistant at the Wieting Opera House, more and more of their time was devoted to the presentation of vaudeville and plays in Syracuse and the surrounding region.

The first theater Sam leased was the Barnstable in Syracuse. Soon he acquired the Opera houses (which played almost everything except actual grand opera) in nearby cities. Once working together, the three brothers began to construct or lease theaters in Utica, Syracuse, Rochester, and Troy, New York, creating a mini-circuit of five theaters where plays and musicals could tour upstate New York with limited travel expenses.

In the early days, the Shuberts were highly dependent on the Syndicate for booking attractions into the few theaters they owned or operated. From the Syndicate's perspective, the Shuberts were useful small customers with troublesome ambitions and delusions of grandeur.

Eventually the Syndicate tried to block Sam from presenting shows in Rochester. The Shubert brothers again encountered the Syndicate when they tried to buy land in Syracuse to build their own theater. In a turnabout, the Syndicate briefly gave them the exclusive rights to all Syndicate shows in Syracuse to punish a competing theater that was not cooperating with the Syndicate's demands. When the larger Lyceum Theatre finally agreed to the Syndicate demands for 50% of show profits, the Syndicate switched back. The Shuberts were left with the dregs of the independent or second-rate productions that the Syndicate had not bothered to control.[6]

By 1900, Sam and Lee had leased the Herald Square Theatre in New York City, near the site of today's Macy's department store, leaving J.J. to operate their theaters in upstate New York. There was already talk in 1900 of the Shuberts as "another antitrust combine."[7] But this was wildly premature. The three brothers had no practical ability to fully book any of these theaters on a year-round basis. This meant presenting plays from stock companies in some theaters, vaudeville in one house, and paying substantial booking fees up to twenty-five percent of net profits to the Syndicate for everything else. At this stage they barely controlled their own destiny let alone the theater industry.

The first Shubert show in Manhattan was *The Brixton Burglary*, a farce featuring Lionel Barrymore in one of his first major roles. *The Brixton Burglary* opened in May 1901 and played only 48 performances. Because the theater was fully booked for the next year by the prior operator, Sam went to London to scout new productions to bring back to the states, beginning a profitable two-way relationship with the West End for decades to come.

The Shuberts made waves by booking the British star Richard Mansfield for their newly leased Lyric Theatre in Manhattan. At the time, Mansfield was so popular that he was effectively independent of control by the Syndicate. He had no idea who the Shuberts were but assumed they were experienced (and older) producers.

It took three telegrams before Mansfield would even meet with Lee and Sam, summoning them to his private yacht in New London, Connecticut. Even then, he was more amused, than impressed, with the two youngsters who appeared on board in lieu of the veteran producers he had expected. Inexplicably, he said yes to starring in a play with unknown and untested producers.

Mansfield was so pleased with his initial run with the Shuberts that he returned for a second season in a revival of Shakespeare's *Julius Caesar*. The Shubert brothers also booked the leading actress (and Syndicate foe) Minnie Maddern Fiske for a production in Syracuse, in competition with a Syndicate production down the street with its own star attraction, the equally popular Maude Adams.

Sam and Lee expanded in New York by obtaining control of the Madison Square Theater (once the center of the Frohman operation), remodeling a decrepit burlesque house, and beginning construction on the Lyric, their first completely new theater. They also had a great success in 1902 at their newly acquired Casino Theatre with an imported English musical called *A Chinese Honeymoon* coproduced with Nixon and Zimmerman of the Syndicate, during a period when these Syndicate partners were in a feud with Erlanger over their share of Syndicate revenues.

During this period, Sam was the point person pushing for expansion with Lee following his lead. J.J. was relegated to minding the upstate New York operations and other out of town ventures. This was the first of many slights, both real and imagined, that would shape his testy relationship with his brothers and the rest of the theater world.

From the moment Sam entered the New York City theater scene, the Shuberts were watched carefully by the Syndicate, which was beginning to recognize the growing threat to its power. Klaw and Erlanger refused to provide the Shuberts with any productions or to book Shubert shows in Syndicate theaters. They warned Syndicate associates and clients not to do so either.

Sam contemplated presenting vaudeville as an end-run around the blacklist but was stymied outside of Syracuse by Keith's control of vaudeville bookings through what would become the United Booking Office (UBO). In his unpublished memoir, Lee claimed decades later that Sam gave Keith and Albee the idea for a national booking circuit.[8] Most sources indicate this is fanciful, and that the Syndicate itself was the model for the UBO and its eventual monopoly over vaudeville booking in North America.

As late as 1902, Erlanger imperiously dismissed the Shuberts saying: "If I squeezed my hand . . . I would put them out of business in two weeks." Erlanger continued "Why should I bother? It's always good to have one independent for the people to throw rocks at. . . . The Shuberts are mosquitoes and I'm too busy to swat them."[9]

By the fall of 1902, Erlanger decided it was finally time to deal with the Shuberts. The Shuberts now owned or leased ten theaters. Erlanger arranged a meeting with Sam and Lee where he laid it on thick. He proposed a marriage of the two organizations and an arrangement where the Shuberts paid 25% to the Syndicate going forward. In return, they would have access to Syndicate theaters for their productions and Syndicate productions available for their theaters.

After much consultation among the brothers and their advisers, the Shuberts signed on the dotted line the first of many truces between the two warring factions. Less than a week later, Erlanger "requested" a small amendment where the Shuberts would agree in writing that they would not expand their circuit, whether by purchase, lease, or construction of new theaters. In effect, they would not only be stuck with the current confines of their small circuit but, even worse, would lose existing theaters as the existing leases expired.

The Shuberts politely declined to change the existing agreement and Erlanger shortly informed them that Klaw and Erlanger could no longer book Shubert attractions in Syndicate houses because of their "breach of contract." Out of necessity Lee and Sam began to build, buy, or lease their own theaters in upstate New York, then in New York City, Chicago, St. Louis, Philadelphia, and eventually around the country. The competition for shows, talents, and venues eventually included a profitable relationship with London, which was both a fertile source of shows and talent for the Shuberts, and eventually also a market for their New York hits. By 1905, the Shuberts controlled more theaters upstate, plus first-class theaters in Philadelphia, Chicago, Pittsburgh, Boston, New Haven, and London.

Sam also had ties to the producer David Belasco, the Fiskes, and access to capital back home in Syracuse from wealthy individuals in the Jewish community such as the clothier J.W. Jacobs and Lee's former business partner, Jesse Oberdorfer. Later, Sam was able to tap similarly influential and wealthy individuals in Cincinnati.

Erlanger responded with the now usual threat to blacklist any producer, playwright, manager, or actor who did business with the Shuberts. The Shuberts survived by continuing their strategy of building or buying theaters and using outside capital from backers to finance new productions, including an increasing number of shows brought over from London. According to Lee Shubert, the Syndicate was responsible for the Shubert's loss of the lease of the Herald Square Theatre, their initial foothold in New York City.

Erlanger arranged, through Syndicate partner Sam Nixon, a meeting with Lee. Rather than squashing the Shuberts, Erlanger proposed closer ties and a discount on fees paid to the Syndicate.[10] The Shubert brothers conferred and agreed to hear more, but also continued to refurbish, acquire, and build more theaters including a new site on 42nd street, near the new Belasco Theatre and the Syndicate theaters in what is today's Times Square, the heart of Broadway.

Daniel Frohman, the producer and brother of Syndicate heavyweight Charles Frohman, wrote of this period:

> A warfare developed that was almost as bitter and costly in its way as was the old disorganized method in vogue before the business was put on a commercial basis. It naturally led to over-production and to a surplus of theaters. Towns that in reality could only support one first-class playhouse were compelled to have a "regular" and an "independent" theater. Attractions of a similar nature, such as two musical comedies, were pitted against each other. In dividing the local patronage both sides suffered loss.[11]

In an audacious act of defiance of the Syndicate, the Shuberts also booked one of the many U.S. farewell tours of Sarah Bernhardt, the leading French actress of her generation. Sensing opportunity, Bernhardt demanded $1,800 per performance (about $64,000 today), payable in gold in advance.

The farewell tour was still profitable despite her astronomical salary. In cities where the Syndicate had theaters and the Shuberts had none, they did their best to creatively present and publicize their star attraction in tents, ice rinks, town halls, and once even outdoors on a hillside.[12] In Austin, Texas,

Bernhardt performed in the Syndicate-controlled theater, only after the Attorney General of Texas threatened to prosecute the Syndicate for antitrust violations if they continued with their blacklist.[13]

***

The war between the Syndicate and the Shuberts led the Shuberts to adopt and trumpet their "open door" policy, both out of principle and necessity. The open door meant that any producer, author, actor, or theater could book with the Shuberts, whether or not they did also business with the Syndicate. But the reverse was hardly true, and the Syndicate would blacklist any production or person who did business with their rivals. Over time, the Shuberts persevered, prospered, and more and more theaters booked through the Shuberts once they were convinced that the Shuberts were in it for the long haul.

As late as 1903, the Shuberts entered into an exclusive booking arrangement with the Syndicate for their theaters in New York, Boston, and Chicago. The Shuberts paid 25% of net profits under the contract and were prohibited from booking any attractions into their own houses without the consent of Klaw & Erlanger.

There was a tacit understanding that the Syndicate would reciprocate by booking Shubert shows into Syndicate theaters, which Nixon and Zimmerman did for a time in their theaters in Philadelphia. This continued until Erlanger again demanded that the Shuberts cease building, buying, or leasing any additional theaters on their own. When the Shuberts built the Garrick Theater in St. Louis, Erlanger insisted that they book the theater exclusively through the Syndicate. After the Shuberts refused, Erlanger supposedly boasted that the brothers would be out of business in sixty days.[14] Instead, the Shuberts cut a deal to present the work of renegade producer David Belasco who was having his own feud with the Syndicate at the time.

The Shuberts, led by Sam, entered into their most fervent period of expansion. Their expansion followed the route of the New York Central Railroad through central and western New York into Cleveland and then Chicago.

Chicago at the turn of the 20th century was typical of the fight for theater space between the Syndicate and the growing power of the Shubert brothers.

Most of the legitimate theaters were located on Randolph Street at the north end of the Loop, the downtown area roughly bordered by the elevated train tracks circling the business district.

Randolph Street was lined with restaurants and theaters. The Syndicate already had the Illinois and the Powers theaters and were building the Iroquois Theatre which eventually opened in November 1903. The main vaudeville theater was the Majestic, the Midwest anchor of the Orpheum Circuit located a few blocks south of Randolph (purchased much later by the Shuberts).

The Shuberts initially did not have a theater on the row of theaters called the Randolph Rialto but found a true architectural landmark that was available. One block west of the Iroquois was the old German opera house that later was known as the Schiller Theater. The building was one of the first steel skyscrapers built in 1892, designed by the firm of Dankmar Adler and Louis Sullivan with the able assistance of their young draftsmen and assistant Frank Lloyd Wright. When Wright left Adler & Sullivan, he set up his new office near the top of the Schiller.

The Schiller Theater was a soaring seventeen-story, highly ornamented building with offices and meeting rooms on the upper floors and a beautiful crown at the top of the building. The office space was intended to subsidize the theater space on the first floor. Unlike many of its neighboring theaters, the Schiller had no traditional marquee but instead had a recessed covered entryway that drew in the curious and the dedicated theatergoer.

The Schiller theater was built as a home for German language opera and other cultural programming for Chicago's growing German Jewish population. However, there was never enough demand to fill the theater throughout the year. The theater was used for English language shows and debates featuring Eugene Debs and Clarence Darrow on such topics as socialism, evolution, and the existence of God.

Over time, Anson Temple, the ambitious general manager, added English-language theater productions. Temple reached out to Charles Frohman to book productions that were quite successful. When Temple unexpectedly passed away, the Schiller was used for vaudeville shows, and later a stock company that produced a successful musical comedy called *The Burgomaster* that had an extended run and a lucrative tour.

Everyone expected the stock company to retain the lease, until Sam Shubert swooped in to lease the theater as part of its growing circuit. Chicago was both a lucrative market and the key to building a nation-wide circuit to book lengthy, efficient, and profitable tours from coast to coast. The Shuberts changed the name to the Garrick and operated the theater for hundreds of road productions until the depths of the Great Depression when they leased it for use as a movie theater.[15]

***

The Syndicate had its own larger nationwide circuit in place but soon suffered a tragedy in Chicago that made national news. The Iroquois was a brand-new luxury theater and boasted in its advertising as being "Absolutely Fireproof." The Iroquois opened with a Klaw and Erlanger production of a lavish musical comedy with aerial ballet and an enormous cast of over four hundred called *Mr. Bluebeard. Mr. Bluebeard* starred the popular Chicago-raised song and dance comedian Eddie Foy whom Charles Frohman had imported from the Drury Lane Theatre in London. The play and the theater opened after many delays on November 23, 1903 with box seats being auctioned off for $225, ten times the weekly salary of the reporter covering the opening that evening.

The opening of the Iroquois attracted broad national and local coverage with the *Chicago Tribune* describing the new theater as a "virtual temple of beauty – a place where the noblest and highest in dramatic art could fittingly find a worthy home."[16] The brochure for the new theater crowed: "The American public now, more than ever before, demand elegance of environment for their amusements, as well as provisions for comfort and security."[17] Most of the reviews of the opening night of *Mr. Bluebeard* were more about the spectacular new building than the performance itself.

The play was a mediocre pastiche of songs, comedy routines, aerial stunts, hundreds of cast members including many children, and a very loose plot drawn from European folk tales with a vague similarity to *The Black Crook*. Foy got generally good reviews, but most of the reviews were similar to the *Chicago Tribune* that noted: "Of story there is little or none. . .the music of the piece is hopelessly common, save bits here and there which are filched from the classics. . . ."[18] One critic went so far as to blame Erlanger himself for the miserable book.

Mr. Bluebeard was still running on December 30th, despite mediocre ticket sales. There was stiff competition in the Chicago Loop theater district from a very successful production of *Babes in Toyland* near the Iroquois. A streak of early bitter winter weather also hurt ticket sales, as did a lengthy and sometimes violent transit strike affecting patrons getting to and from the theater.

Sparks from a high temperature spotlight caused a muslin curtain to catch fire during Act Two of a rare sold-out matinee with over 1,600 people in attendance on December 30, 1903. The fire quickly spread to the curtains, sets, and draperies as the stagehands struggled to put out the flames. Bits of burning fabric began to descend onto the stage.

The cast and musicians began to falter. The asbestos fire curtain jammed and could not be lowered. The blaze continued to spread. The flames soon became visible to most of the audience who panicked and rushed chaotically for the exits. The fire then knocked out the power in the theater.

The only cast or crew members who died were two women in the rafters in harnesses preparing for a spectacular aerial number swinging out over the audience on the main floor. One slipped to her death, and the other was unable to escape from the harness and burned to death. The rest of the cast and crew were able to escape through backstage and side exits, including the large doors in the rear of the stage used to load in and out the scenery.

The audience was not so lucky. Only a few doors in the auditorium opened from the inside, most were jammed shut, and a few were locked. Over 600 people died, almost entirely audience members in the gallery and balcony sections most from burns, suffocation, and the crush of frightened audience members trying to flee.

Many suffocated in their seats. Others were burned to death or trampled. The crowds in the upper levels surged down two flights of stairs that merged into a single pathway down to the main floor. Others leaped to their death from the unfinished fire escapes far above the pavement in the alley next to the theater.

The death toll was more than double the fatalities from the city-wide Chicago Fire more than thirty years before. Hundreds more were injured from burns or injuries from the crush of people trying to flee the fire.

One of the reporters on the scene observed: "The bodies extended about one hundred yards on either side of the theatre's entrance. A long line of horse-drawn vehicles waited to haul the dead or dying to hospitals, morgues or funeral parlors."[19] The stores in the Chicago Loop donated hundreds of blankets used to both protect the living and shroud the dead. A paint store across the street and the Thompson restaurant next door became first aid and triage stations. Thousands of people began to gather to search for relatives and friends who had been at the theater. The Iroquois disaster remains to this day the single deadliest theater fire in the history of the United States.

Accusations came fast and furious that the Syndicate had built a death trap, paid off the Chicago fire inspectors, and even that they had set the fire deliberately for the insurance proceeds. Shortcuts abounded in the rush to complete the theater, and in many ways the Iroquois was never completed.

Nor was it up to code. There was no fire alarm system or telephone at the theater. One of the fire escapes was never completed and led to a high metal platform with no steps or ladders down to the alley below. The fire curtain, which was supposed to be pure asbestos, was in fact made in part of cheaper materials which eventually caught fire during the conflagration.

The tragedy may have been the result of negligence or indifference but certainly was not deliberate. The fire became an occasion for another round of national attention and criticism of the power and cruelty of the Syndicate. The press was merciless, and cartoons depicted the Syndicate as the literal angel of death.

Sam Shubert reached out to Erlanger to offer him the use of the Shubert's theater in Chicago following the Iroquois fire. This was both an act of kindness and self-interest. Erlanger originally accepted but changed his mind two weeks later without explanation. Regardless of motivation, any chance for another truce between the two competitors ended, and both circuits continued to present at their other theaters in town.

***

The accusations of wrongdoing continued to hound the Syndicate but produced little concrete legal action. One of the accusations was that fire inspectors had been bribed with free tickets to overlook code violations. It was more likely political clout, rather than bribery, that allowed the Iroquois to open with inadequate fire safety precautions. The main accusations against Klaw and Erlanger were that they had scrimped on safety in a rush to open the Iroquois before the holiday season.

The mayor of Chicago, Carter Harrison II, was indicted by the coroner's jury and detained briefly when it was discovered that the City Commissioner of Buildings had not inspected the building nor enforced regulations regarding fire escapes and extinguishers. Klaw and Erlanger, despite owning twenty-five percent of the Iroquois, and controlling much of its operations, were never indicted. Nor were Harry Powers, the President of the Iroquois, Ben Marshall, the architect, or the Fuller Construction company.

Will J. Davis, the general manager of the theater, was prosecuted criminally and there were numerous civil suits for damages. The criminal and civil suits were based on the failure to comply with Chicago ordinances relating to fire prevention and building safety.

Klaw, Erlanger, Powers, and Davis were represented by Levy Mayer, a preeminent Chicago trial attorney, who later represented Klaw and Erlanger and other Syndicate members in less fraught matters. He defended the suits with intelligence, tenacity, scorched earth tactics, and endless delays.

The judge in the Circuit Court of Cook County eventually quashed the criminal indictments and dismissed most of the civil lawsuits. The refiled criminal case later was moved out of Chicago and eventually went to trial in a downstate Illinois courtroom in March 1907. After three years of delays, changes of venue, procedural motions, and arguments, Mayer convinced the judge that the Chicago municipal codes that were the basis of all the claims were unconstitutional and beyond the powers delegated to the city by the State of Illinois.

No case ever reached a jury. A few of the cases were settled for nominal amounts. While building codes were changed for the better, no one was ever held individually accountable for the tragedy. Klaw and Erlanger, and the Syndicate, however, continued to suffer in the court of public opinion. *Mr. Bluebeard* was never performed again anywhere in the world.

Because the exterior of the Iroquois largely survived intact, the Syndicate rebuilt the theater and reopened it as a vaudeville house. In 1904, the theater was sold to Powers and Erlanger and renamed the Colonial. It reopened with a pre-Broadway try-out version of George M. Cohan's *Forty-Five Minutes from Broadway*, featuring the classic showstoppers *Give My Regards to Broadway* and *You're a Grand Old Flag*.

The Colonial was demolished in 1924 to make room for the highly ornate Oriental Theatre. The Oriental Theatre eventually became a downscale movie theater, and finally a vacant eye sore, until it was lavishly restored as a legitimate theater in 1998. It is still in operation today, now named the Nederlander Theatre, part of the Nederlander chain that came to national prominence after the eventual forced antitrust divestiture of the Shubert road holdings.

The fallout from the Iroquois disaster affected the theater industry across the country. Theaters all over the world were shuttered for months for inspection and required changes. A number of theaters eliminated standing room tickets entirely. Many cities revised their building and fire codes. Theaters had to be retrofitted across the country and abroad. All exits had to be clearly marked. Doors had to be openable from the inside, even if they were locked from the outside to prevent non-paying customers from sneaking into the theater.

***

By the summer of 1904, the Shuberts owned, leased, or booked approximately fifty theaters and were already the principal competitor to the Syndicate. Sam and Lee began to rationalize their business operations by incorporating Sam S. and Lee Shubert Inc., but conspicuously did not include J.J. That same year Sam "wrote" and produced a musical comedy called *Fantana*, and in December Lee and Sam produced a musical called *Lady Teazle* starring the great Lillian Russell.[20]

The Syndicate blacklist and the ongoing theater war indirectly led to the death of Sam. The spring of May 1905 saw the end of the long-running litigation between Belasco and the Syndicate in New York state court. Just days after the end of that trial, the Shuberts had a court date of their own against Klaw and Erlanger.

Sam was desperate to obtain the lease for the Duquesne Theater in Pittsburgh out from under the clutches of the Syndicate. The Syndicate tried to block the transfer of the lease and Sam sued for restraint of trade. Now freed up from his own trial, David Belasco originally planned to join Sam, presumably to watch him inflict more distress on the Syndicate, who had tortured him in his own case. Belasco's plans changed and he backed out, having no idea of the ordeal that lay ahead.

Sam's train raced through the night towards Pittsburgh the evening before court. Well after midnight, the passenger train crashed into a freight train carrying Army munitions. The freight train exploded and the passenger train caught fire. While rumors abounded that something more nefarious had occurred, with the Syndicate perhaps being involved, it turned out to be the tragic, but purely accidental, end for the most talented, intelligent, and sophisticated of the brothers Shubert.

Sam was badly burned in the ensuing fire and was taken from the accident to the Commonwealth Hotel. Sam's legal counsel William Klein was in the upper bunk and survived his less serious burns and wounds. Klein did his best to help Sam out of the wreckage. Lee and J.J. were grateful to Klein, employing him and his law firm for the rest of his life to represent the brothers in their endless array of business and courtroom disputes.

Sam died the following day, on May 12th. Rumors of murder and mayhem circulated in the press and the theater community, until it became clear that the incident was a horrible and tragic accident. Few who knew of his accomplishments could fathom that he was only thirty years old.

J.J. arrived in Harrisburg shortly before Sam's death. Two different versions exist of Sam's last words. In one, he praised the man who pulled him and Klein out of the train wreck, and another that accused Erlanger of murder as if Erlanger had actually shot him to death.[21]

The news of Sam's death reached Lee in London, who was supervising the opening of the Shubert's new Waldorf Theatre. Ironically, Lee was staying at the same hotel as Charles Frohman from the Syndicate. Putting aside for the moment business rivalries and jealousies, Frohman conveyed his genuine sympathies to Lee and was visibly shaken by the tragic news.

Lee idolized Sam and continued to honor his memory for the rest of his own life, naming new theaters after him and hanging his portrait in the lobbies of many of the growing Shubert national circuit. Even late in life, he remained in awe of Sam's accomplishments long after he and J.J. had built an empire beyond whatever Sam had envisioned. Lee gushed in an unpublished memoir: "His breadth of vision, his poise at moments when lesser minds would have cowered, his impeccable honesty, his acceptance of financial hazards that would have daunted seasoned financiers, his organizing ability, his deep understanding of the problems of showmanship – all of these qualities, astonishing if possessed in full by a man in his fifties, were incredible in a youngster."[22]

Sam's mother and father eventually sued the Pennsylvania Railroad with future U.S. Supreme Court Justice Benjamin Cardozo as co-counsel. They were successful in proving negligence, but awarded only $25,000 by the jury.

Civility briefly was restored on the business front between the Syndicate and the surviving Shubert brothers. Lee went through a lengthy period where he withdrew from all day-to-day business. J.J. eventually moved to New York City from upstate and became more involved in the national aspects of the enterprise. Erlanger told Lee Shubert that he wanted to attend the funeral but was so shaken that he remained home. Erlanger also refrained from aggressive action for most of the spring and early summer of 1905.

Lee eventually asked for a meeting with Erlanger and indicated that neither he nor J.J. wanted to expand their operations any further. He further said he would consider selling some theaters *if* Erlanger would honor contracts Sam had struck with David Belasco to book upcoming Belasco productions through the Shuberts. According to Shubert biographer Jerry Stagg, Erlanger snarled back, "I don't honor contracts with dead men." Lee reported the insult to J.J., who replied, "We'll kill the son of a bitch."[23] The war was back on.

7

War, Peace, and Dirty Tricks

The Shuberts had a strategy to break the dominance of the Syndicate through rapid growth. After Sam's death, Lee and J.J. Shubert combined forces with Belasco and the Fiskes to form a credible new circuit. The new venture consisted of the Shuberts' fifteen theaters, Belasco's three New York theaters, the Fiske Theater, Fiske's stock company, the *New York Daily Mirror*, and the star power of Minnie Madern Fiske.

Lee eventually recognized J.J.'s expanded role and changed the name of the principal corporation from "Sam S. and Lee Shubert" to "Lee and J.J. Shubert Enterprises" in 1907. However the old stationery remained in use until the 1920s, more a result of cost consciousness than a deliberate insult, but another of the many irritants that poisoned the well between the two brothers now in charge of a growing national business.[1]

By 1910, the Shuberts advertised a total of fifty-nine theaters.[2] Lee and J.J. bought entire blocks of New York City real estate to build their new theaters, purchased existing theaters, and expanded into the newly chic theater district in what is now Times Square, eventually including the famous Shubert alley. Many of the theaters were bought by the two brothers in their individual capacities, rather than by any of the Shubert business entities. They expanded their theater empire in major cities like Chicago, Philadelphia, and Boston, as well as smaller ones like New Haven; all of which became key sites for out-of-town tryouts of new shows before they opened on Broadway, and later part of any national tour.

While the open door booking policy was key to the early expansion after Sam's death, the booking operation over time became the key to the Shubert Organization's eventual dominance of the industry and their conquest of the Syndicate. Once dominant, the Shubert booking organization required exclusivity, just as the Syndicate had done and enforced its dominance with the same threats and blacklists. As a prominent economic historian observed:

> "Once the Shuberts achieved the position they sought, they conducted their enterprises in essentially the same way as the Syndicate conducted its. They devised nothing new in the way of circuits, booking offices, theatrical systems. They followed a model; they enlarged its scale; they did not alter its proportions."[3]

At the same time, the surviving Shubert brothers ran a highly dysfunctional business model. While both Lee and J.J. idolized Sam's memory, they detested each other. Neither had Sam's sense of diplomacy, and neither had much of a sense of humor. Lee had a sentimental side and J.J. had a towering temper, a propensity for outright violence, and a lingering sense of grievance of not being given the respect that Lee received as the older, and presumably wiser, of the surviving brothers.

The business thrived despite this tense relationship but eventually required separate offices in separate buildings across the street from each other. Terse communications were conducted through intermediaries, relatives, or memos, and only rarely face-to-face discussions of the most pressing matters. This unusal arrangement began when their offices were on the same floor of the same building and eventually led to J.J. moving across the street to offices in the penthouse of the Sardi building (owned by the Shuberts personally) requiring the messengers to cross 44th Street back and forth to deliver any communications or documents.

The brothers similarly developed separate spheres of influence that made their physical separation more manageable with Lee handling most dramas and J.J. responsible for most musicals and revues. Lee managed New York theaters and other real estate; J.J. supervised real estate on the road. Lee was in charge of booking and signing stars, with J.J. hiring the chorus and ensemble, dancers, composers, and crew.[4]

They also had vastly different styles for selecting which shows to produce. J.J. read the plays that he worked on, although he leaned heavily toward musical revues with no plots to speak of, but with plenty of chorus girls to cast. Lee preferred more serious dramas with moralistic messages. However, Lee relied on trusted assistants who prepared summaries for him. When he met with playwrights, Lee often dozed off. How he ultimately chose which works to produce will never be known.[5]

Despite this personal animosity that never abated, the Shuberts' business and finance methods differed significantly from the Syndicate in two important ways that made it harder for the Syndicate to keep up with the increasingly successful and more nimble Shubert organization. First, the Shuberts over time developed into a vertically integrated set of firms. The Shubert organization was a version of a modern integrated family of corporations controlling the selection and development of scripts, financing, physical production, booking, marketing, and presenting. In comparison, the Syndicate remained an agreement between three separate partnerships that focused on different aspects of the theater business and partially shared profits. As a result, the Syndicate had few incentives to better integrate their operations or become more efficient.

The other significant advantage the Shubert Organization had over the Syndicate and independent producers and presenters was access to capital. The Syndicate depended on the internal generation of funds, or borrowing, for its productions, making it more vulnerable to booms and busts in the economy, such as the panic of 1907.

The Shuberts, in contrast, had ready access to outside investors who funded (and bore most of the risk) of new Broadway productions. Much of the early capital came from friends from the Jewish business community in Syracuse, and later Cincinnati. Initially, these financing arrangements were highly informal verbal agreements memorialized, if at all, on notes on scraps of paper.

Later, the Shuberts became the first theatrical producers to create a publicly owned corporation selling share to the public, but retaining control in the family.[6] Going public allowed the Shuberts to enrich themselves, raise capital, and issue bonds, in effect borrowing money from the public at attractive interest rates, without surrendering control or profits from the productions the bonds helped finance.

The individual partnerships for any particular production also evolved into more detailed legal agreements that created a limited partnership for each new production with outside investors lacking any control over the production itself. On a show-by-show basis, the outside investors were limited partners providing specific amounts of money, sharing in net profits if the show succeeded, but without any control over the artistic or business aspects of the new show.

The Shuberts (or legal entities they controlled) were the general partners having full operational control over the new play or musical. If the show failed, the limited partners bore no risk beyond the amount they invested. If the show succeeded, the producers paid back the limited investors first from net proceeds and then split net profits, usually on a fifty/fifty basis. A substantial investor might be listed as a "producer" in the playbill but normally had no more creative or business control than the person buying seats in the balcony for a matinee.

Different Shubert-controlled entities also typically received fees and shares of profits for various roles played and services provided to the show partnerships. The producers, as general partners, received fees for office management and booking fees that came off the top. There were also fees for costumes, scenery, and scripts, all products of the many different Shubert entities. These fees were paid as costs before the production went into profits that were shared with the outside investors.

The different entities were difficult to keep track of. The accounting was opaque, and the fees charged to outsiders often exorbitant and comical, such as an invoice reading "Glue $1900". As a result, highly successful shows rarely generated net profits as promised to the stars, outside producers, or investors, often generating litigation that could be settled for pennies on the dollar. The many excesses of this system became known as the Shubert way.

The modern version of this system continues to this day with most producers, other than the Disney Corporation, following the first and second rule of producing a Broadway show as described in the hit film and Broadway musical *The Producers* in which Rule 1 is "Never invest your own money," and Rule 2 is "NEVER INVEST YOUR OWN MONEY!"

Along with the many Shubert advantages over the Syndicate came one big downside: Lee and J.J. detested each other. Lee and J.J. increasingly relied on a business model based on confrontation and hostile relations with any perceived or real opponents including each other. This also included producers, playwrights, performers, unions, suppliers, theater critics, and politicians. Lee generally had a smoother style than J.J. (and never punched anyone), but both Shubert brothers delighted in provoking unnecessary disputes often ending in litigation as the years passed.

**

When the Syndicate and the Shuberts were not at peace, they were fierce competitors. They competed for productions, bookings, talent, and for theaters. This competition was a gift to actors, particularly the stars, as well as theater owners and operators. The public benefited from an unprecedented amount and variety of legitimate theater available in both New York City and on the road.

The competition for talent was brutal. The Shuberts created *The Passing Show*, a big budget review rivaling the *Ziegfeld Follies*, which booked exclusively through the Syndicate. The Shuberts recruited Al Jolson from vaudeville to compete with the *Ziegfeld Follies* and headline *The Passing Show*. His salary grew to total $1,500 per week, a $10,000 bonus, and ten percent of profits.[7] Both productions competed to lure, and retain, their top talent from raids by their rival and from the vaudeville circuit.

The real competition was for the theaters to book their growing array of productions. The Shuberts built several gorgeous theaters in key markets, always with a portrait of the late Sam Shubert prominently displayed in the lobby. They also lavishly renovated theaters when they could buy or lease them. The demands of building this type of national circuit of luxury theaters was out of the reach of the Syndicate. Klaw and Erlanger, and their partners, frequently had to buy or lease older theaters, converted opera houses, and poorly located buildings that often required substantial investments. When theater owners switched their booking operations from the Syndicate to the Shuberts, they rarely switched back.

The battle continued in England, where Frohman and the Shuberts controlled theaters to both present their existing shows and find new shows to produce and tour in the United States. The distinguished playwright, and noted socialist, George Bernard Shaw routinely pitted the Shuberts and the Syndicate against each other to extract the best terms possible when his plays were presented in North America. On one occasion, he wrote that "the agitation against the Syndicate is all nonsense"[8] as Shaw continued to switch between Syndicate and Shubert booking for most of his career based on which group presented "the most generous terms."

**

The Syndicate and the Shuberts also fought in the press. They fought for the best publicity for their own cause and to heap the most negative coverage of their competitor. They fought for the public's attention and loyalty in the general press and the trade publications like *Variety*, which had started as a vaudeville publication but quickly expanded to cover the legitimate theater industry. Local newspapers covered the struggle between the Syndicate and the growing Shubert empire with front page stories and quotes from Klaw, Erlanger, Frohman, Belasco, Lee, and J.J.

Every New York City newspaper, and most papers in the larger cities, had their own theater writers, critics, and gossip columnists covering the wins and losses as theaters signed up or switched between the Syndicate and the Shubert camp. Even the 1896 obituary for prominent Chicago theater owner James McVickers speculated what his death meant for the Syndicate cause.

In addition, each camp owned its own newspapers to spread its versions of the financial and artistic developments. The Syndicate's voice was the *Morning Telegraph* in New York City. By 1905, the *Morning Telegraph* was full of anti-Shubert stories, editorials, and cartoons. The independents had the *New York Dramatic Mirror*, until the Fiskes made their peace with the Syndicate. Most of the less reputable dailies were either Team Syndicate or Team Shubert at any particular moment.

The Shuberts eventually withdrew all their advertising from the *Morning Telegraph* and created their own magazine and newspaper. They briefly published a magazine called *The Show*, and switched to a more lasting weekly newspaper, the *New York Review*.

The first issue of the *New York Review* appeared in August 1909. Most copies of the *Review* were distributed for free in the theatrical district to tout Shubert shows and trash Syndicate productions. The officers of the *New York Review* were a Shubert in-law and the brother of the Shubert's long-time attorney. The Shuberts remained in the background but pulled the strings of what would appear in their newspaper.

Lee and J.J. solicited advertising from theaters that were part of the Shubert theater empire and suppliers that did business with those theaters. The paper also traded ads for free show tickets or ad space on the drop curtains at Shubert productions. They even used what amounted to early product placements in song lyrics.

Shubert productions were lauded and Syndicate productions panned weekly in the Shubert paper. Anti-Syndicate cartoons were a staple of the paper, as were anti-Syndicate articles and editorials detailing scandals and misdeeds of Syndicate members and their lackeys.

Stories and headlines were not subtle. One article opened with the wordiest antitrust headline ever read:

> "Competition has Given Authors, Acts, Managers Opportunities They Never Could Have Had Under Monopolistic Conditions –the Young Playwright Now Gets Hearing – The Actor Can Select His Own Part and Name his Own Salary – Both Can Look Managers in the Eye and Tell Them Where to Go."[9]

The *New York Review* was an actual news source in addition to a public relations vehicle. The paper covered an enormous number of plays and vaudeville shows in New York City and the road. Independent shows generally were reviewed on the merits. Anything associated with Erlanger, Flo Ziegfeld, or David Belasco (after he broke with the Shuberts) were panned mercilessly. For whatever reason, Charles and Daniel Frohman were treated with more respect. The *New York Review* also editorialized for allowing theatrical performances on Sundays, decried the growing clout of the movie industry, and even included coverage of automobile racing, professional sports, and the women's movement.[10]

***

Both the Syndicate and the Shubert assiduously cultivated the general public and the newspapers they did not own or control. The Shubert's not-so-secret weapon in this campaign was a press agent with the surreal and superbly appropriate name of A. Toxem Worm.

Born in Denmark in 1866, Conrad Henrik Aage Toxen Worm immigrated to the United States prior to the turn of the century. He adopted the contraction A. Toxen Worm, a name which seemed to perfectly communicate his willingness to get down in the dirt in service to his clients. In less sympathetic company, he was known as the Great Dane, due to his fifty-inch waistline.[11]

Worm was eccentric, suspicious, and prone to joke at someone else's expense. He was often an acquired taste, with *Variety* calling him "one of the most unpopular publicity producers in the history of the craft."[12] But none could dispute his talent for both hyperbole and disparagement.

It was precisely these characteristics that drew the Shubert brothers to Worm in 1909. Worm worked for them as press agent, frequent contributor to the *Review*, and later manager until his death in 1922. The announcement of Worm's representation of the Shuberts was controversial, with two papers refusing Shubert advertising so they would not have to work with Worm.[13]

Worm became famous for extravagant, bizarre, and off-color publicity stunts that helped build the growing narrative of the Shubert inevitable ascent and diminish the Syndicate in the process. For example, when white pigeons could not be obtained for the 1912 show *Broadway to Paris*, Worm had a solution. He issued a press release explaining that the market for white pigeons was cornered by China, where they are bought "to accompany the flight . . . of their souls into kingdom come." Toxen assured the Shubert brothers that he would simultaneously advertise for pigeons *not* employed presently in Chinese funerals.[14]

Worm also represented French singer, dancer, and pantomime Gaby Deslys, who worked for the Shuberts from 1911 to 1914. Worm's representation was itself a selling point, with a Chicago theater manager noting that "it is the ultra-sensational A. Toxen Worm stuff which will bring in the money. For instance we could make much out of the carrying about of her pearls – have the police appoint special detectives just to guard them. If necessary we might even have a false robbery."[15]

At different times, Worm linked her with the deposed King Manuel of Portugal, invented a passenger on the boat that brought Deslys to America who was so in love with her that he had the baker imprint her name on his daily bread, and had Deslys dine with a baby elephant onstage at the Hippodrome. When J.J. worried that other stars might get jealous of Deslys's publicity, Worm simply reasoned that if "Gaby were not sensational, you wouldn't be paying her the salary that you are paying her."[16]

Worm proved particularly useful to the Shuberts in positioning them as the David to the Syndicate's Goliath, long after the Shuberts had acquired rough parity with their older rivals. Worm would publish article after article in the Shuberts' *New York Review*, attacking the Syndicate as a corrupt monopoly, with "Little Abie" and his associates always in the crosshairs.

One 1910 headline read "C.F. now stands for Complete Failure" detailing how "Charles Frohman has been an upright and industrious man according to his own mistaken lights. . . . While canny little Aby was raking in the coin from all sides and risking practically nothing, Charley Goat risked much and has little. . . . He's a well-meaning dupe. . .. It is high time for his friends put him in some safe barnyard."[17] The *New York Review* played a vital role in destabilizing the Syndicate's hold on the industry, leading to the revolt of theatre managers against Syndicate domination and eventually to the formation of the National Theatre Owner's Association favoring the Shuberts.[18]

Worm was present when the Shuberts decided to observe tryouts for Florenz Ziegfield's *Follies of 1909* at the Atlantic City Apollo Theatre, along with their chief of press Lew Fields, and Field's wife, Rose. Unfortunately for the Shuberts, Abe Erlanger was also in the house, presumably watching from his backstage peephole. When Ziegfield sent the theatre manager to eject the Shuberts from the Syndicate-allied Apollo, the Shuberts refused, having paid for their tickets. Ziegfield himself attempted to eject the party but could not succeed. Only when two stagehands arrived (presumably on orders from Erlanger) and Rose Fields became visibly embarrassed, did the Shuberts relent and leave.

Even in periods of détente between the Syndicate and Shuberts, J.J Shubert couldn't resist setting Worm loose to taunt Erlanger. In August of 1918, J.J. ordered Worm: "My dear Worm, I want an article dealing with the fact that Erlanger, like the leopard, never changes his spots."[19]

While J.J. specified he wanted the article clean, and without referencing Erlanger's personal life, Worm also could not change his slash and burn approach. Worm's draft claimed that back in 1900, Erlanger "tried to induce

[George] Lederer to start a fist fight with the late Sam. S. Shubert [who] only weighed ninety pounds and was scarcely five feet high." The proposed draft went on to detail Erlanger's court battles with a nurse and an actress, writing that "Miss Judd has filed with the court a bill of particulars . . . describing her relations with . . . little Abie."[20] The piece was excessive even to J.J., who called it "a little too fiery" and directed Worm to tone it down.

Faithful to the Shuberts to the end, one of Worm's last acts in his tenure was suing *Variety* in 1919 for stating that as the Shubert's press agent, Worm embroiled them in an unprecedented series of battles with the press. Worm did not collect any of the $100,000 in damages that he sought.[21]

The tirades of bile and outrageous stunts continued until January 13, 1922. While on vacation in Paris, A. Toxen Worm died of apoplexy. Never one to miss a chance at a dig, he wrote in his will: "In conclusion, I wish to voice my affection for this country . . . I consider New York to be the most wonderful city in the world, and I hope that its prosperity, uninterrupted, may be forever continued by Providence. In this connection I also express the earnest hope that God may take care of Chicago in the future, so as to enable it to live down its miserable past and wretched present."[22]

***

The Shuberts, like most producers, had a rocky relationship with theater critics. Favorable reviews were a vital part of making a show a hit on Broadway and setting the stage for successful national tours. However, critics who panned a show could single handedly doom a production from even making it to Broadway or to close a show after a disastrous opening night.

This led to much litigation relating to the common practice of barring critics who wrote unfavorable reviews. This practice had started long before the Shuberts perfected the art of barring critics who dared to be critical. The critic for *Life Magazine* in 1905 was barred from a group of theaters connected to Klaw and Erlanger after his negative reviews (as well as his virulent anti-Semitism). He responded by swearing out an unsuccessful criminal complaint for conspiracy against the theater owners and managers.

The Shuberts even banned Channing Pollock, a former writer for their magazine *The Show*, who switched to the Syndicate *Telegraph*. At first, they feted his departure and gifted him with a diamond-studded gold cigarette case hoping they would have a friendly face in the enemy camp. Instead, their former friend had a mixture of positive and negative things to say about Shubert shows, so they banned him for life. Pollock retaliated by adopting various disguises, wigs, fake noses, and dark glasses to sneak into Shubert productions. Over the years, Lee and J.J. each banned for life a substantial circle of esteemed critics in New York, Chicago, Boston, Kansas City, and elsewhere, only to relent when bad publicity or litigation dictated.[23]

In 1916, Lee Shubert in a fit of pique, barred the prominent critic Alexander Woollcott from the theater following several negative reviews of Shubert productions. Woollcott sued, arguing that the ban threatened his livelihood, but lost. The Shuberts continued to ban, and eventually make up, with critics who published negative reviews depending on the importance of the reviewer and their publication. Over the years, the Shuberts banned and reinstated other leading critics of the day including George S. Kaufman and Walter Winchell.

This pattern lasted until the late 1930s, when a critic banned by the Shubert family successfully lobbied for a New York statute that guaranteed admittance for anyone over 21 to legitimate theaters absent abusive or offensive behavior. The bill passed over the strenuous objections of Lee Shubert, who lobbied against the bill including writing directly to the governor.

***

The bad blood and dirty tricks between the Syndicate and the Shuberts seemed destined to go on forever. But by 1907 there was a sense that the Shuberts were on the rise and would eventually catch up to the Syndicate. Instead, the Shuberts and the Syndicate joined forces to take on the one live entertainment monopoly bigger than both of them combined.

8

The First Vaudeville War and Dreams of Global Domination

The first grand alliance between the Shuberts and the Syndicate pitted them against a common rival – big time vaudeville. Vaudeville was a well-established nationwide business but still had the reputation of being more down market and more working class than the "legitimate" theater. What attracted the Shuberts and the Syndicate was profits, not prestige.

In the first decade of the 20th century, vaudeville was dominated by two circuits—the Keith-Albee circuit in the east and the Orpheum circuit in the west. Chicago was roughly the dividing line, functioning as the easternmost edge of the Orpheum circuit, and for a time, housing its headquarters.

Both circuits formalized this market division and cooperated through the formation of the United Booking Office, the Combine, and eventually a full merger. A shrewd observer of vaudeville noted: "They [Keith-Albee] made . . . entertainment a specialized, regimented industry; were products of their time – in organization and development for financial gain this pair was to vaudeville what Frick and Carnegie were to steel, the elder Rockefeller to oil, the elder Morgan to banking."[1]

Early on, B.F. Keith studied Klaw & Erlanger's operations and saw how booking was the key to the Syndicate's power in legitimate theater. He established the United Booking Office (UBO) in 1906 to organize vaudeville "intelligently and logically" and to consolidate his power.[2]

The UBO was intelligent, logical, and chaotic all at the same time. Bookings for big time vaudeville took place on the sixth floor of the Palace Theater building on Broadway and 47th street in Manhattan. The Palace Theater was the pinnacle of the vaudeville circuit and the reason that making it to the top of show business became known as "playing the Palace."

The *Saturday Evening Post* described the operation of the main booking floor on six as an:

> open market, with all the elements that constitute a trading place. To anyone who comes upon this scene uninitiated, it all seems quite wild and incomprehensible, much as the operations on the stock exchange or the old curb market must appear to a newcomer unversed in financial trading. Considerable noise, a great deal of excited gesticulation, many strange phrases, mark the proceedings.[3]

Bookings for small time vaudeville took place on the fifth floor in even more informal surroundings. The UBO could book a lengthy and profitable tour of up to eighty weeks for proven talent and a yearlong calendar of shows for the vaudeville theaters across the United States and Canada.[4] In return, the UBO took a five percent booking fee, plus another five percent for the talent agent's fees, which were remitted directly to the agent, rather than passing through (and possibly staying in) the performer's hands. The sheer number of vaudeville houses across America, and the gradual decline of the touring market for Broadway musicals and drama, meant that vaudeville was immensely more profitable than the legitimate theater, even if ticket prices generally were much lower.

In 1906, the members of the Syndicate were hard at work seeking to expand the Syndicate to encompass both legitimate theater and vaudeville on a national scale. In April, representatives of Klaw & Erlanger and the Keith-Albee/Orpheum circuits met to try to hammer the details of a new mega-Syndicate. Apparently, the initiative for the venture came from the vaudeville side but was eagerly embraced by the theatrical bookers. Albee, on behalf of Keith and his allied vaudeville managers, told the *New York Times*:

> "This combination, which will represent an aggregate of fully $30,000,000 is not designed to crush any of the independent theatrical firms now doing

business. We are simply organizing to gain greater economy and efficiency in handling the enormous volume of business detail connected with managing and booking."[5]

This proposed doubling of the Syndicate, to include vaudeville, appeared to be an attempt to crush the independent agents, performers, and presenters who still represented some competition depending on the city or region of the country. This agreement ultimately fizzled, leading to an all-out war that would forever change both industries.

After the failed attempt to merge with the vaudeville combine, Erlanger saw easy pickings and vast new profits in the adjacent vaudeville market. He thought vaudeville offered the "largest profits for the smallest amount of work" with virtually no risk.[6] But for his scheme to work, Erlanger now needed the Shuberts to create a combined nationwide circuit of theaters to enter the vaudeville business on a massive scale.

News of the proposed vaudeville invasion leaked to the industry and press by February 1907. At the same time, the UBO continued to grow absorbing several of the remaining independent vaudeville presenters and managers.

Meanwhile, the Shuberts needed product to fill their growing circuit of theaters, particularly during the years when the Syndicate blacklist was still taking its toll. Vaudeville represented a potentially lucrative way to fill Shubert theaters with a popular product. The Syndicate also needed shows to fill its theaters and needed more presenting theaters in cities where the Shuberts were strong and the Syndicate partners less so.

Klaw and Erlanger proposed a deal with the Shuberts to cooperate in the vaudeville space, while presumably continuing to compete less vigorously for Broadway and touring Broadway productions. The press assumed correctly that the Shuberts would curb their theatrical expansion as part of the deal with the Syndicate to jointly enter the vaudeville space.[7] As theater historian Jack Poggi notes: "In the legitimate-theater field, the Shuberts and the Syndicate remained separate, but it is likely that they had an informal agreement to limit Shubert expansion, to respect certain territorial rights, and to compete on a friendly basis."[8]

The United States Amusement Company (USAC) was incorporated in April 1907. Fifty-one percent was controlled by Syndicate interests, another forty-two percent by the Shubert brothers, with the remaining shares held by a number of other industry investors. It created a new vaudeville circuit called Advanced Vaudeville to challenge the Combine and the UBO.

This was not an outright merger of the two organizations, but rather a joint venture that combined personnel and capital to create a new vaudeville circuit in direct competition with the long dominant UBO. Erlanger was President, Lee Shubert was Vice President, Marc Klaw Treasurer, and Levy Mayer served as outside general counsel. The directors included J.J. Shubert and Al Hayman among others connected with the two theatrical entities. USAC was capitalized at $20,000,000 with heavy money from both Wall Street and the movie industry. The first Advanced Vaudeville show was set for April 1907 in Philadelphia.[9]

The USAC was almost entirely an Erlanger & Klaw project with the active assistance of the Shuberts in providing theaters for the new circuit. USAC productions were normally billed as "Erlanger & Klaw" productions.

Frohman was not even in the United States for virtually the entire existence of Advanced Vaudeville and appeared to have little to do with the project. There is not a single mention of the USAC in the nearly daily cables and letters Hayman sent Frohman in 1907.

This was typical for Frohman. Throughout his career, Frohman routinely distanced himself from the Syndicate, telling anyone who would listen that all he ever got out of the Syndicate "was trouble."[10] Putting aside the immense amounts of money he received, he certainly had plenty to keep him busy separate from the machinations of Erlanger and Klaw. Unlike Erlanger, Frohman dreamed of hits, glowing reviews, and profits, not monopolies and bigger syndicates.

***

To line up the talent for the new venture, Advanced Vaudeville turned to William Morris, the same William Morris who later formed the famous Hollywood talent agency in Los Angeles. At this stage of his career, Morris was the leading independent vaudeville booking agent and avowed enemy of the UBO, claiming to represent as many as five thousand vaudeville acts.

William Morris was born Zelman Moses in Schwarzenau, Germany in 1873. He came to the United States at age eleven. As a teenager, he worked as an ad salesman and in publishing. Morris quickly found work through his uncle (a theater manager) with a prominent booking agent in the early 1890s.

Morris began to sign his own clients and negotiate lucrative deals for the existing clients and was quickly promoted to partner. As his client list and reputation grew, he opened his own agency. The newspapers began to refer to him as the "Napoleon of Vaudeville," around the same time Abe Erlanger held down that nickname in the legitimate theater space.

For Morris, the real nemesis was the vaudeville monopoly—the Keith-Albee Circuit, its collusive arrangement with the Orpheum Circuit, and the combined might of the UBO. In his early days, Morris had booked talent for Keith and Albee.[11] But by 1907, much of his client lists, including many of the best-known managers and performers, deserted him for the UBO.[12] Morris was more than eager to assist the Syndicate, and their Shubert partners, to set up United States Amusement Company, break the existing Keith-Albee-Orpheum trust, and enrich himself in the process.

The legitimate theater producers, actors, and venues who staked their financial lives on the success of the Shubert open door policy were not thrilled by the peace deal between the Shuberts and the despised Erlanger-led Syndicate. One shrewd observer concluded:

> "[W]ith one clever stroke, the Syndicate accomplished several things. First, it effected at least a truce with its most dangerous opponents, for although there was actually no agreement the Syndicate and the Shuberts as to their legitimate productions, the members of the Syndicate guessed rightly that the Shuberts would lose their enthusiasm in fighting them in the legitimate field as long as the vaudeville partnership existed."[13]

The dominant vaudeville chains were faced by the prospect of well-funded competitors with an enormous national network (actually two such networks now being shared) now presenting big time vaudeville. The vaudeville Combine responded by announcing that they would begin presenting legitimate theater in a circuit of thirty of their own vaudeville houses.

***

Neither the Syndicate nor the Shuberts (or their combined might) were able to establish much of a foothold, let alone success, in conquering vaudeville. There is no evidence that either the Orpheum or the Keith-Albee vaudeville circuits ever seriously attempted to become legitimate theater producers. The legitimate theater and vaudeville combinations sometimes competed fiercely for talent, but each had loyal audiences with somewhat differing demographics and price points.

The Shuberts had an advantage on the talent side. They were already a powerful theatrical circuit and booking enterprise when they made their initial inroads into vaudeville and could offer the UBO performers a better deal, both for their new vaudeville circuit, and the implied prospect of even more lucrative work down the road on the theatrical side.

New theaters had to be leased or built in cities where the combined Shubert-Syndicate theaters could not handle full schedules of both legitimate and vaudeville productions. For example, in Chicago, the number of vaudeville-only theaters expanded to roughly equal the number of vaudeville houses in New York City.

Performers jumped to Advanced Vaudeville (or stayed with UBO) for more lucrative contracts and increased status as headliners. William Morris and other Klaw & Erlanger bookers deliberately recruited a horde of new talent for Advanced Vaudeville from England and Europe, where they did not have to contend with existing UBO contracts. Advanced Vaudeville stars from the United Kingdom included famed Scottish comedian Harry Lauder and top English music hall star Vesta Victoria.[14]

By Labor Day 1907, Advanced Vaudeville was presenting weekly programs in seventeen theaters in major markets in the eastern half of the United States including Boston, Philadelphia, Hartford, Kansas City, Chicago, St. Louis, Milwaukee, Buffalo, and Brooklyn.[15] Headliners included some of the best and most famous vaudeville and music hall acts from around the world.

The problem was that many of these new headliners were unknown in the U.S. Even when embraced by U.S. audiences, these top acts only filled one or two of the slots on the average vaudeville bill. The quality of many of the rest of the acts was questionable and often disappointed the audiences willing to give the new venture a try. Despite headlines in *Variety* reading "Klaw and

Erlanger Enter Vaudeville Successfully," unnamed sources in the Shubert camp were saying by July of 1907: "the whole thing seems like a joke."[16]

Advanced Vaudeville's main tactic appeared to be overpaying for competing U.S. and international talent to headline their programs. Its weekly payroll was estimated to be twice that of the UBO typical lineup.[17] The UBO's main tactics were to match salaries for certain headliners, blacklist any performer or theater who signed up for Advanced Vaudeville, and sit back to watch the new competitor bleed money on a weekly basis.

Lee Shubert recalled that the losses mounted for both sides of the war until the head of the UBO offered USAC three million dollars in ten annual installments to call off the war. According to Shubert, Erlanger angrily rejected the offer shouting "I'll take $7,000,000 to call it off or else I'll drive him out of business."[18]

The combination of high talent costs, and the difficulties in establishing a new brand that appealed to a sufficient number of loyal UBO vaudeville audiences, made USAC a financial sinkhole of epic proportions. One prominent exception was the enormous Auditorium Theatre in Chicago where Advanced Vaudeville played to mostly sold-out crowds in the thousands throughout its run. Overall, the Advanced Vaudeville losses were estimated to be well over a million dollars.

Peace negotiations began again in October 1907 between Advanced Vaudeville and the UBO.[19] By year's end, the Shubert-Syndicate venture struck a face-saving deal with the Combine. The Shuberts and the Syndicate abandoned vaudeville and agreed to not reenter for ten years, all in exchange for a paltry $250,000 payment and an agreement for the Combine to assume the contracts of the existing artists of the USAC.[20] Equally important, the UBO was no longer a threat to enter the legitimate theatrical field, perhaps the real reason for the vaudeville wars in the first place. In total, two hundred-forty acts appeared in Advanced Vaudeville shows and the UBO took over one-hundred ninety of the contracts. The last Advanced Vaudeville show occurred in New York City on February 1, 1908.

In the end, Lee Shubert put a brave face on his surrender in the first vaudeville war. He told Ed Sullivan years later that in addition to recouping most of their outlays in Advanced Vaudeville, "we were relieved of over a million dollars' worth of contracts which Erlanger had made with the vaudeville headliners. Never again was I in awe of Abraham Lincoln Erlanger."[21]

***

The failure of the attempt to take over vaudeville in the United States had other lasting consequences. Erlanger had boasted of trying to combine all the theatrical interests and the vaudeville managers. The Shuberts and the Syndicate together dreamed even bigger. They hoped to parlay an Advanced Vaudeville monopoly into a true world theater trust controlling the United States, Germany, Austria, France, Switzerland, and England involving both "legitimate" theatrical and vaudeville houses.[22]

Klaw and Erlanger dispatched their legal counsel Levy Mayer to sail to Europe to work on these negotiations. Mayer was an inspired choice for the project. He was a brilliant attorney and prominent Chicago practitioner who started Yale Law School at sixteen. He graduated second in his law school class but was too young to sit for the Illinois bar until he turned twenty-one. He came to the attention of Klaw & Erlanger through his successful defense of the President of the Iroquois Theater in both the criminal and civil litigation following the 1903 fire that killed nearly 600 people in the brand new centerpiece of the Syndicate theater empire in Chicago.

Over his illustrious career, Mayer became an antitrust expert, representing the Whiskey Trust and a key company in the Beef Trust. He also engineered the merger of most of the grain elevators in the Great Lakes region, as well as a combination of steamship companies owned by different railroads. He also represented numerous banks and large corporations fighting the antitrust laws and the growing array of governmental regulations in the early 20th century. For Klaw and Erlanger, he would play the role of cartel ringmaster for a proposed theatrical combination spanning the globe.

Mayer also developed a thriving theater practice, representing Klaw & Erlanger in key struggles with Actors' Equity and the other growing theatrical unions. He later represented the Shuberts, the producer of the *Ziegfeld Follies*, Florenz Ziegfeld, and Charles Frohman in a key copyright case in the United States Supreme Court.[23] His name lives on today in the ivy-covered older wing of Northwestern University Law School known as Levy Mayer Hall and as the founder of what is now known as Mayer Brown, one of the largest law firms in the world.

Emboldened by their 1907 New York state court victory where the court ruled that live theater was not interstate trade or commerce subject to the antitrust laws, Erlanger happily confirmed to the press the plans for worldwide domination. He bragged that the proposed new global combination would be capitalized at $100 million, becoming the largest entertainment syndicate the world had ever seen.

Most U.S. newspapers reacted in horror at the thought of such a global Syndicate. *The Cleveland Plain Dealer* wrote:

> "It is difficult to believe that Klaw & Erlanger will succeed in their attempt to combine all important theaters of Europe and America in one big trust. But is is possible, for these men have brains and money and audacity, and are flushed with their victory in the New York court, which, by declaring that their trust in not a trust, has made them supreme in the United States.' Such a merger, it goes on to say, would be the greatest misfortune that has befallen the stage."

Mayer confirmed from London that he was negotiating what the *New York Times* called a $100,000,000 theater trust, but claimed he acted only on behalf of Klaw and Erlanger and United States Amusement Company.[24]

The vaudeville barons also had their own dreams of world domination. In the summer of 1907, Martin Beck sailed to Europe to try to establish an International Booking Syndicate uniting the vaudeville theaters in the U.S. with "38 of the best known theatres of the Continent and a large number of in England."[25] One of Beck's partners bluntly told reporters that the ongoing vaudeville war had driven up the cost of vaudeville talent and that a "powerful combine . . . might be able to obtain artists at far cheaper rates."[26]

The financial panic in the fall of 1907, indifference by the foreign theater owners, and the ensuing dissolution of the USAC effectively ended all such dreams of a global entertainment trust. Beck's attempts to enter the English market prompted the head of the largest English music hall circuit to briefly consider entering the U.S. in cooperation with William Morris.[27]

Advanced Vaudeville failed to dislodge the Combine from its dominance of big time vaudeville in the United States. The Shuberts and the Syndicate closed their Advanced Vaudeville tours, and converted their vaudeville theaters back to legitimate stages.[28] The stars of the Advanced Vaudeville, including the magician Hardeen (Houdini's brother), had to make their peace with the Keith-Albee Circuit, which normally meant taking out ads pledging loyalty in *Variety*, or groveling apologies from the stage, before being allowed back into the good graces of (and employment by) the UBO.

***

After the collapse of Advanced Vaudeville, William Morris was out of a job, but not bound by the truce and non-compete agreement between the theatrical and vaudeville trusts. Morris turned down an offer from Keith to run the UBO. Instead, he presented his final bills to Klaw & Erlanger and embarked on a round of litigation to preserve his access to theaters and continue an independent vaudeville operation.

He incorporated a new vaudeville company to commence operations on January 1, 1908, offering contracts to performers for a twenty-week tour. He continued to book vaudeville acts in the United States for the shrinking number of independent houses and continued to import talent from Europe where the vaudeville trust was never active. The Morris circuit offered a program of up to twenty-two acts for a budget price to compete with the Combine's skimpier and pricier offerings. Even when the talent was free from the clutches of the Combine, the theaters where they would perform were not. His efforts were often stymied by the exclusive contracts and blacklists of the now supreme UBO, which made it impossible in many cities for competitors to lease a theater or book top-flight performers.[29]

Morris also filed an unsuccessful antitrust complaint with the Justice Department demanding that the Attorney General prosecute both the theater and vaudeville owners for their agreement ending the vaudeville wars. While President Theodore Roosevelt's personal intervention was enough to allow Morris's acts to perform in Washington, D.C. at the Belasco theater, it wasn't enough to keep his independent mini vaudeville circuit afloat. Eventually, Morris sold out to Marcus Loew, a Shubert ally who at the time operated a small time vaudeville circuit.[30]

Morris eventually returned to booking vaudeville acts, both on his own, and on behalf of the Paramount movie chain, which used a few vaudeville acts to supplement its early feature films in its own growing movie palace empire. Morris correctly predicted that the growth of the movie industry would absorb the talent and the audience for vaudeville. He soon moved his remaining business to California and formed the talent agency that made him internationally famous and wealthy.[31]

The Syndicate's foray into the vaudeville space produced a continued taste for monopoly and collusion in the vaudeville industry. Keith used the peace to take over a number of vaudeville houses in the Midwest, and increase his cooperation with Martin Beck and the Orpheum circuit. He amplified the scope and power of his grip on big time vaudeville, and limited the ability of Morris, and other independents and mini-chains, to book acts for any upstart competing circuits.

***

The *New York Times* and *Variety* reported in the summer of 1908 that Erlanger (assisted by Mayer) had convened a meeting with Lee Shubert, Keith, Beck, and other notables on both the legitimate theater and vaudeville sides. They discussed how best to address the excess capacity in both industries, due in part to the rapid expansion of the number of theaters during the Advanced Vaudeville skirmish.[32] As a result of having two competing vaudeville circuits, there were now many more theaters on the road than could be profitably booked for either vaudeville or legitimate theater.

The *New York Times* reported that the object of the meeting was to keep some theaters permanently closed and create a fund that would subsidize those theaters taken out of circulation. It noted: "Thus independents would find the road harder and the organization's power would be absolute."[33] Once again, the Syndicate did out in the open what most conspirators did in the shadows to avoid the antitrust laws and other litigation.

1908 featured another brief respite from the rigors of competition in legitimate theater. The Syndicate and the Shuberts came together to form the National Association of Theatrical Producing Managers (NATPM), an arguable trade association, intended to arbitrate contract disputes and blacklist performers who "jumped" their contracts. For a brief time, most of the independents joined as well. Disputes over production rights, and a perceived bias in favor of the Syndicate, led to the quick demise of the Association and the war was back on.

Whatever good feelings, or at least subdued hostilities from cooperation in vaudeville and the NATPM, quickly ended. For the next four years of the new war, there were the usual threats, blacklists, and recriminations, both private and public. Theaters, producers, and actors shifted between the Shubert and Syndicate camps. The Syndicate began presenting the *Ziegfeld Follies* to great acclaim and profit.

The Shuberts countered with their own musical revues. They also began their signature European style light operettas, first with *The Merry Widow*, and followed by numerous other productions in the same style, many of which succeeded on Broadway, toured the country, and were revived frequently for decades to come.[34]

All the while, the Shuberts continued their steady growth in theaters, productions, and bookings in New York City and across North America. By 1910, the Shuberts and the Syndicate controlled roughly the same total number of theaters in the U.S., with the Shuberts starting to pull ahead. However, each circuit still held stronger positions in different areas of the country and the Syndicate remained particularly strong in many smaller markets necessary to create the longer, and more profitable, national tours.

Entire chains of theaters, including the National Theater Owners Association, switched to the Shuberts' open door policy and effectively broke the Syndicate's monopoly power for good. Lee Shubert estimated that these defections cost Klaw & Erlanger close to $1 million a year in booking fees.[35]

The Syndicate unsuccessfully tried to counter this news with a multi-pronged strategy. They first organized an alliance with leading producers including both Frohmans, the newly returned Belasco, Ziegfeld, and many others who agreed to book exclusively through Klaw and Erlanger. Second, they trumpeted plans to build, buy, or lease new theaters throughout the country, particularly on the West Coast. Marc Klaw toured the west coast and other key markets announcing the new acquisitions to much fanfare and media coverage.

A few key managers and presenters reaffirmed their ties to the Syndicate, now believing the Shuberts were a bigger threat to their happiness and profits.

Francis Wilson, the actor who once led the independent opposition to the Syndicate, now opined that the Shuberts were "no better and, in some respects, worse."[36]

The press was soon reporting a possible buyout of Klaw & Erlanger by the Shuberts with the help of outside financing. No buyout ensued, but instead the two sides negotiated a more comprehensive formal truce agreement in 1913.

Ruinous competition was again a thing of the past. The two sides reached the kind of agreement that in today's terminology would be per se illegal and normally send all the principal participants to jail for several years. In those simpler times, the parties did not hide their agreement but instead discussed it openly with the press including an agreement to raise top prices in New York from $2.50 a ticket to $3.00.

J.J. Schubert described the arrangement to the press:

> "We have agreed to eliminate the ruinous competition that exists to the detriment of both. It is very expensive to fight . . . That sort of thing will now be eliminated, and it will be a fine thing for all concerned."[37]

Lee speculated publicly that perhaps actors would be paid less, but work longer a season, and thus come out ahead. That only hastened the movement to unionize the actors who correctly interpreted this comment as a threat to cut pay and increase workloads.

Under the 1913 agreement, both sides would be allowed to book each other's shows. They tried to avoid booking directly competing types of productions in the same city at the same time. In some cities, they pooled and shared profits. Subsequent agreements involved showing films in legitimate theaters that would otherwise remained dark at different times of the year.

This highly formalized (but unnamed) arrangement expanded to include price fixing for theater tickets divided into first-class and popularly priced categories. Lee described the arrangement, apparently without irony: "its civil war ended, the theatre entered a free, competitive existence."[38]

A dispute over alleged Shubert poaching of a lead actor from a Klaw & Erlanger production led to a falling out, litigation, and an uneasy settlement. The final straw was a separate lawsuit where the Syndicate and its allies successfully enjoined the Shuberts from presenting first-class attractions at the Chestnut Theater in Philadelphia (Erlanger's home territory) as a violation of the 1913 agreement. Almost immediately, the pooling arrangement dissolved, and the two sides returned to being competitors, rather than partners.

***

The urge to collude remained strong while the Syndicate soon became little more than just Klaw and Erlanger. Hayman, Zimmerman, and Nixon all retired by the end of 1913. Frohman passed away in 1915. There was still a vast oversupply of theaters across the country. It was good news and bad news for the Shuberts. The more theaters they controlled, the more they earned, but also required even more shows to fill the ever-increasing number of seats in the theaters now part of the Shubert "open door" sphere of influence.

In 1914, Klaw led another unsuccessful effort to create a new nationwide organization combining all managers of live entertainment from circus, opera, theater, and film. Like the Syndicate itself, these meetings took place in the proverbial smoke-filled room, this time in the Hostel Astor. Some of the activities of this proposed group, like lobbying for helpful legislation were benign and probably legal, but statements that the "intention is not to fight any one" suggested more nefarious goals as well.[39]

The continued oversupply of theaters led to 1915 talks about an outright merger between the two sides. Lee Shubert and Erlanger continued negotiating as business slowed down with the beginning of World War I in Europe. A new era of theatrical prosperity was announced as part of yet another working arrangement between the Syndicate and the Shuberts where all booking decisions would be made through one general office.

Erlanger would be the president and managing partner; Klaw was treasurer; Lee Shubert was vice-president, and J.J. was secretary. Eighteen months of negotiations resulted in the elimination of many competing houses on the road and a world where many smaller towns would only have one first-class theater going forward.[40] The often-reported merger never took place, with the two factions continuing to cooperate and bicker, until Erlanger angrily broke off talks claiming the Shuberts had cheated him and issued fraudulent financial statements where Erlanger attractions played in Shubert houses.[41]

The next round of the theatrical wars, i.e. actual competition, was on. This time, it would be Erlanger and Klaw, and not the Syndicate itself, who would continue the fight, following the formal dissolution of the Syndicate in 1916.

Newspapers reported every aspect of the battles, peace treaties, resumption of hostilities, and the collateral damage on the lives of producers, writers, actors, managers, and stagehands in a way that is unimaginable today. Papers from the *New York Times* down to the mouthpieces for the Syndicate and Shuberts, reported minute victories of the tactics, strategies, and outcomes of the seemingly endless war for control over legitimate theater. Publications like *Billboard* and *Variety* began to cover the battle for Broadway and the road. The next phase of that battle quickly spread to an open conflict between producers and the unions representing the actors and crew who made the shows possible.

9

Labor and Monopoly

Organized labor had an ambivalent relationship with the monopolies, trusts, and cartels of the Gilded Age. Some labor leaders believed that unrestrained competition required companies to cut costs to the bone preventing them from paying labor a living wage. To them, trusts and monopolies may well charge higher prices but were better positioned to share some of the profits (ill-gotten or not) with their workers.

Other parts of the labor movement welcomed the antitrust laws as a way to counter the power of monopoly capitalism and the robber barons who sat atop the economic pyramid. They saw the brute force monopolists used, including armed violence and even government military power, to break strikes and stop union organizing.

It turned out that both sides were wrong. Workers in monopolized industries fared no better than in competitive ones. In almost every labor dispute, industry used the courts, as well as violent self-help, to break or slow the union movement.

The antitrust laws often were used by business, rather than against them, to attack the unions on the theory that unions and strikes were unlawful restraints of trade by the workers. For example, the very first antitrust case filed after the Sherman Act was against labor and not capital. The Justice Department sometimes brought criminal and civil antitrust cases against the unions and their leaders. Businesses opposing the strikes frequently sued in state and federal courts to seek injunctions against the strikes, and then contempt of court penalties against union leaders if they continued their organizing and strike efforts. In fact, Eugene Debs, the labor leader and five-time Socialist candidate for President, was jailed for defying a court injunction relating to the Pullman railcar strike of 1894.

It took three separate Congressional statutes and a series of Supreme Court cases lasting into the 1940s to make it crystal clear that the work of a human being was not trade or commerce that could violate the antitrust laws, and that normal union organizing, collective bargaining, and peaceful strikes were lawful conduct. Only secondary boycotts against firms that did business with the company being picketed were subject to the antitrust laws. It has been the rare (and only recent) antitrust case that helped, rather than harmed, the interests of workers and unions.

***

Despite the massive legal, economic, and physical risks, live entertainment had a strong and early union movement. The union movements in both vaudeville and legitimate theater came about because of the mistreatment of the performers and crew at the hands of the cartels and monopolies that controlled the stage.

Actors and stagehands lived in a world where the contracts they held (when there were contracts) often paid nothing for rehearsal time or the load in or out of a production on the road. Performers usually supplied their own costumes and paid for their own transportation. The producers and managers had near total discretion to fire them for any reason, or no reason at all. To compound matters, the performers and stagehands normally were paid only at the end of a weekly engagement. There were numerous instances where no one got paid because the production failed or because of outright embezzlement. Cast and crew often were stranded in a distant city (or country) with no easy way home or the money to get there.

***

The predecessor to the International Alliance of Theatrical Stage Employees (IATSE) was formed in 1888 (before the rise of the Syndicate and Shuberts) to address the miserable working conditions for stagehands in New York theater.[1] Daily wages were 50 cents at best and the producers often used unpaid child labor in exchange for free tickets. Experienced stagehands walked out of key theaters in New York City, demanding a dollar per show and 50 cents for each load in and load out (a key issue on the road where shows often traveled from city to city on a daily or weekly basis). The producers tried to bring in strikebreakers, but the actors sided with the striking stagehands.

Five years later, in 1893, IATSE itself was born at a convention in New York City with seventeen delegates of previously independent local unions from across the eastern half of the United States. By 1896, IATSE expanded to the West Coast. In 1898, it added local chapters in Montreal and Toronto. As an alliance, IATSE gave substantial home rule powers to each local chapter as it expanded in size and scale.

IATSE quickly expanded into the movie industry, first organizing projectionists and the larger production staff as studios moved to the West Coast. IATSE grew rapidly as movies replaced burlesque, vaudeville, and legitimate theater as America's principal form of live entertainment. IATSE's growth in the movie industry cushioned the effects on membership of the eventual decline of touring theater in smaller towns.

***

There were several early unsuccessful attempts to create a union for actors in 1849 and then in 1896, just prior to the creation of the Syndicate. The formation of the Syndicate only exacerbated the exploitation of the actors.[2]

The average actor experienced low pay and abusive working conditions. There were no standard contract terms. Actors were unpaid for rehearsal periods that often exceeded the run of the show itself. They risked not being paid and left stranded on the road when a show on tour closed.

Cast members paid their own transportation to the show's opening destination and their way home after a show closed on the road. They paid for their own costumes, endured numerous layoffs and pay cuts without warning, and were not given advance notice of closings. Actors received only half pay during holiday weeks even with full schedules and were sometimes forced to play fourteen performances a week without any pay increases. Producers often terminated actors pursuant to so-called "satisfaction clauses," often on pretexts. Once a production closed, actors also had no practical ability to get back pay.

The average actor in the early twentieth century worked thirty weeks a year at a nominal salary. A 1907 article in *The Worker* blamed the worsening conditions on the Syndicate and its control over most of the leading theaters in the country.[3] One particularly heinous example involved the Shuberts, where an actor rehearsed without pay for fifty-seven weeks and performed with pay for only twenty-two weeks over a two-year period.

Actors' Equity Association (Equity) was the first theater union to successfully confront the Syndicate and the Shuberts. In late 1912, a committee formed for what would become Equity. The six-man organizing committee consulted and negotiated with a group of producers and managers considered fair-minded, including Daniel Frohman. In May 1913, Actors' Equity Association was created at a meeting at a hotel at the site of what is now the Time Warner Center on Columbus Circle on the west side of Manhattan.

Equity began negotiating with the National Association of Theatrical Producing Managers and the United Managers' Protective Association. Equity first sought to enforce the existing standard minimum contract and to prohibit companies from using actors who were eligible to be in Equity but had not joined.

After four years of negotiations, both sides held a ratification dinner at the Hotel Astor in November 1917, during one of the lulls in the war between the Shuberts and the Syndicate. When the conflict resumed less than a month after the dinner, neither set of producers honored the new minimum contracts.

Many of the managers formed a new, more anti-union organization called the Producing Managers' Association (PMA) and refused to negotiate with Equity. In 1919, the PMA even refused to agree to binding arbitration before former President William Howard Taft and Justice Charles Evans Hughes of the United States Supreme Court.

***

The first successful theater strike in U.S. history began in July 1919. By this point, Equity had more than 2,500 members and confronted a deeply divided community of producers. Within thirty days, the strike closed more than three dozen shows in eight different cities and forced the cancellation of another sixteen productions. Losses totaled an estimated three million dollars (approximately $56 million today). The strike ultimately was successful because most of the theater unions, from stagehands to teamsters, supported the strike and walked out in support of the actors.

Lee Shubert blustered that he would rather shut down his theaters or convert them to motion pictures, but in the end he was more concerned about the losses from empty theaters than any anti-union sentiments. Lee played a pivotal role for the theater owners in their negotiations. He even unsuccessfully sued Equity for $500,000 in lost profits due to the strike. Lee was accused by even more strident owners of selling out to the union. But he simply had too much money at stake not to settle.

On the plus side, the Shuberts would benefit from unionization to the extent that smaller competitors would be disproportionately hurt by the higher costs. As landlords, the Shuberts would also benefit from rents and percentages of profits once production resumed.

The producers ultimately agreed to a five-year contract. The core provision established what is known as a closed shop, which meant that if a theater company had one Equity member, the entire company must be Equity members, subject to some agreed exceptions. Much to the irritation of Equity, the Shuberts continued to flaunt union rules on certain productions.[4]

There was one unwritten exception for the legendary producer and actor George M. Cohan. Cohan was a former vaudevillian and a beloved performer. He authored more than fifty shows and composed more than three hundred songs, including *Yankee Doodle Dandy* and *Give My Regards to Broadway.* He was an early member of the American Society of Composers and Performers (ASCAP) to protect the rights of composers.

Cohan remained a staunch lifelong opponent of unions on the performing side. He never signed an Equity contract and, in a lengthy career that continued until 1940, was the only non-union actor allowed to perform in an Equity production.[5]

The minimum contract limited performances to eight shows per week and unpaid rehearsals to no more than four weeks, required producers to provide costumes and transportation, and established a two-week notice period for either firing an actor or an actor resigning from a production. There were separate rules for actors hired for the run-of-the-play, chorus members, stock company productions, and tent shows.

Only male actors were covered by the original collective bargaining agreement, but female performers were quickly included. The collective bargaining agreement was ratified by nearly 97% of the voting members.

Equity was aided by the continuing feud between the Shuberts and the Syndicate. In general, the Shuberts were more willing to implement the closed shop provisions, since they had more to lose than the declining Syndicate. In addition, the higher costs of a new labor contract would disproportionately harm what was left of the Syndicate and its smaller base of operations.

Disputes, arbitrations, and litigation continued throughout the life of the first five-year Equity agreement. Equity's demands for a closed shop remained a significant issue. Another smaller, less contentious strike ensued after the expiration of the agreement in June 1924. Only seven productions closed, although the strike lasted almost twice as long as its 1919 predecessor. The PMA broke up in the aftermath of the strike mostly because of the continued difference of opinion between the Shuberts and the other producers, including the remaining Erlanger faction.

Equity was not the only actors' union during this era. There were separate unions for "Hebrew" Actors, a Hungarian Actor's Union, and one for German-speaking performers, none which have survived into modern times.

Over the decades, Equity eventually agreed on different rules and lower pay for performers depending on the size of the theater, and the nature of the touring production. More controversially, later agreements created certain tiers of productions that required a minimum number of Equity performers, but allowed a certain number of non-Equity actors. In modern times, the Broadway League has taken over the negotiation and arbitration of labor disputes with Equity and the many other unions and guilds that represent playwrights, musicians, stagehands, company managers, box office personnel, teamsters, press agents, costume designers, directors, and set designers.

***

The dramatic decline of the road by the late 1920s led to the creation of a new relatively small union, the Association of Theatrical Press Agents and Managers (ATPAM).[6] This tiny union (now part of IATSE) covered press agents who publicized the shows on a city-by-city basis, the company managers who took care of the traveling company on the road, and the house managers who ran the theaters themselves.

In addition to Equity, IATSE, and ATPAM, unions, guilds, and associations grew to include musicians, playwrights, directors, and other skilled craft persons who could not otherwise achieve economic security in an industry dominated by the Syndicate and then by the Shuberts. The producers fought each union tooth and nail, because every pay increase represented money out of their pocket. Each union bargained separately for the interests of each member, but they cooperated with each other in the timing of contract negotiations and potentially walking off the job in support of each other, to create maximum economic pressure on the dominant producers.

***

Playwrights were the only segment of the theater world that never unionized. This is in marked contrast to writers in the movie and television industry who formed the Writers Guild of America in 1933 and engaged in a high-profile strike in 2023 that shut down most movie, television, and streaming productions for many months.

Playwrights were always leery of unionizing because unionization generally required being an employee, rather than an independent contractor. Only employees could unionize, although the line between employees and independent contractors was always blurry for such theater professionals as press agents and managers.

Playwrights did not want to be, or be seen, as employees for several reasons, beyond just ego. Playwrights generally owned and controlled the copyright to their works. They licensed, rather than sold, their work to the producers.

Controlling the copyright also meant that changes to the script could not be made without their permission. This differed from writers working on movies and later television (which included some playwrights), where the writer produced a "work for hire" that the producers owned and could modify as they wished.

As a result, the playwrights formed the Dramatists Guild of America (DGA) as a trade association, rather than a union. Unfortunately, setting up a trade association provided no protection from the antitrust laws nor provided any clear legal right to strike or agree on prices, boycotts, or other working conditions. This created an uncomfortable dynamic where most producers eventually agreed to an ambiguous Minimum Basic Agreement (MBA) with playwrights in 1926. The Shuberts did not agree and tried to negotiate their own separate agreement with the DGA.

When the playwrights refused to work for the Shuberts, Lee and J.J. embarked on a different course of action. In 1927, the Shubert Theatre Corporation, with the help of their long-serving legal counsel William Klein, brought its own antitrust suit against the president of the DGA.[7] Lee opined, without any visible sign of irony: "Monopoly is bad for the public and bad for the little fellow who is the backbone of American business."[8]

The suit alleged that the Guild controlled the price and supply of plays and playwriting and had illegally coerced producers and managers into signing the MBA. Two prominent scholars described the case as a "win-win for the Shuberts" because "[t]he Guild could contract with producers as employees which meant the Shuberts would finally acquire control over the copyright as employers. Alternatively, if the dramatists continued to operate as independent contractors, and wanted to associate, they faced antitrust liability."[9] The only real downside for the Shuberts, as antitrust plaintiffs, was the tacit recognition that the production and presentation of live theater was indeed trade and commerce also subject to the antitrust laws.

The Shuberts eventually withdrew their lawsuit and signed the Minimum Basic Agreement. Industry insiders suggested that the litigious and bellicose Shubert brothers backed down primarily because of the fear that DGA members (if they became employees) threatened to join the more powerful American Federation of Labor.

This pattern would be repeated each time as the MBA expired. The Shuberts (and other producers) challenged the new version of the MBA as an antitrust violation. Each of these lawsuits settled, or was withdrawn, without any definitive ruling on the merits of the antitrust claims or the ability of playwrights to act together without becoming employees.[10]

***

Labor conditions were even worse on the vaudeville side, particularly after the failed 1907 alliance between the Syndicate and the Shuberts to take over vaudeville, and a later equally unsuccessful attempt by the Shuberts. On both occasions, the number of vaudeville theaters and employment opportunities briefly doubled and then crashed. The Broadway barons retreated to their side of the live entertainment industry and vaudeville actors encountered a smaller number of theaters under the control of a united and empowered Combine.

Attempts to organize a union for vaudeville performers began in June 1900, when performers met in the café and suites at the Parker House Hotel in New York City. It was an era when all attempts to stifle competition, or form unions in response to the lack of competition, seemed to take place in smoke-filled hotel rooms and restaurants.

Nine well-known vaudeville performers eventually banded together to form the "White Rats of America," named for, and inspired by, an earlier association in England. Keith and Albee sought to crush the White Rats using their go-to tactics of exclusivity and blacklists. A 1901 strike was unsuccessful. Out of fear, many vaudevillians never struck and others accepted slots relinquished by the striking White Rats. The need for unionization only grew after the formation of the UBO by Keith and Albee in 1906.

The performers sought to push back against the fees paid to the UBO and having to pay most of their own expenses and travel. They were also concerned about various swindles by the managers and agents, the hardships of routes with long jumps, and the contract clauses that allowed the presenting theaters to fire an actor without recourse or for the slimmest of pretexts.

The lack of competition and the abysmal economic conditions following the Panic of 1907 left thousands of performers stranded in the hinterlands with no income and often no funds to return home. The number of vaudevilles theaters shrank and many of the foreign performers brought to the United States by Advanced Vaudeville faced dim prospects in the U.S., the U.K., or the Continent, if they could even afford to return home.

The White Rats welcomed women performers for the first time in 1910, but it wasn't enough. They were never able to break through against the stranglehold of the UBO. Much of the problem was a simple matter of supply and demand. Arthur Wertheim estimates that at vaudeville's peak there were twenty thousand performers competing for approximately nine thousand slots.[11]

The power of the UBO, which included virtually all the remaining East Coast independent booking agents other than William Morris, led to an alliance between the White Rats and another labor group, under the umbrella of the American Federation of Labor, to present a unified front of performers. By 1916, the White Rats had about 14,000 members, easily eclipsing Equity which represented only about 2,500 actors in the legitimate theater.

Unlike their brethren in Equity, the White Rats strike in 1917 was unsuccessful. The Keith-Albee tactics of exclusivity and boycotts of union performers and any venues who hired them, crushed the movement.

Within two years, a new, less combative union was recognized as the sole representative of vaudeville performers. Albee further weakened the White Rats and union organizing efforts by creating the Vaudeville Managers Protective Association (VMPA), essentially a company union to arbitrate disputes between performers and managers. This was a function that was normally the subject of collective bargaining between union and management.

The VMPA was wildly popular among managers and supporters who dubbed it "the Supreme Court of Vaudeville."[12] Albee patted himself on the back in *Variety* and stated that the VMPA "has resulted in eliminating many petty abuses, has placed the humblest artist in as strong a position for enforcing rights and just treatment as the headliner, and has instituted and maintained a reign of justice and square dealing throughout vaudeville."[13]

While never the force that Equity became, the real vaudeville union did support the Equity strike in the summer of 1919 and refused to perform in any theater where the Equity performers were on strike. In 1919, the White Rats and the Associated Actresses of America finally merged into Equity. This came at a time when vaudeville had reached its peak and entered a slow decline in the face of the advent of movies, radio, and changing tastes in popular entertainment. Equity's only real attempt to improve working conditions in vaudeville failed in 1923.[14]

There was never any real lasting success on the labor side in big-time vaudeville. Eventually new technology and the Great Depression destroyed vaudeville. This left performers to fend for themselves in a new world where their talents and skills were not readily transferable to the legitimate theater, radio, or the increasingly important movie industry. The stars did fine, and often prospered, as new technologies gave them the ability to earn more and reach larger audiences. The rest did their best to hang on, left show business altogether, or were forced to survive on charity and the help of friends and family.

***

The Great Depression brought another twist in the ongoing battle between labor and capital. President Roosevelt used the National Industrial Recovery Act (NIRA) to establish Codes of Fair Competition that essentially turned every industry into a planned cartel. The goal was to keep prices up so firms could afford to increase employment and pay workers a living wage.

The Act required every industry, big and small, to negotiate a code of fair competition with minimal representation from labor and consumers that worked out a schedule of fixed prices, wages, and penalties for firms that failed to comply. Businesses and their trade associations quickly drafted codes which the government then approved in over 400 industries, including cotton, oil, concrete, ice, and numerous retail products.

Competition was dead as a national policy. The antitrust laws were defunct. Lawful enforceable cartels were the law of the land. The Syndicate would have been delighted, had it survived.

In August 1933, President Roosevelt approved the proposed Code of Fair Competition for the Legitimate Full Length Dramatic and Musical Theatrical Industry in a process dominated by Lee Shubert. The report by the head of the National Recovery Administration (NRA) recommending Presidential approval noted that the code covered performances of full length dramatic and musical plays, including stock companies, and excluded grand opera, vaudeville, tent shows, wagon shows, Chautauqua, showboat, burlesque, and motion pictures.

The administrator touted that:

> For the first time in the history of the legitimate theatre minimum wages and maximum number of hours have been fixed by agreement for actors, press representatives, company managers, house treasurers, and other labor. Wages have not been reduced, and, indeed, have been raised. Hours generally have been reduced.

> The trade practices declared unfair have been especially designed to promote the production of dramatic and musical plays and to attract the investment of capital into this industry.[15]

The Code stated that the employers agreed that employees had the right to unionize and bargain collectively and that employers had to comply with the maximum hours and minimum wages set out in the Code. The Code then set out in mind-numbing detail a series of minimum wages depending on the actor's years of experience and the top price for the show in question. Wages for rehearsals were specified, and a maximum workweek of 40 hours was established except for rehearsals. Playwrights agreed to modifications of their basic minimum agreement. Separate maximum hours and minimum wages were set for musicians, stagehands, scenic artists, wardrobe attendants, company managers, press representatives, house treasurers, ushers, cleaning crews, and even bathroom attendants. The code banned child labor under the age of sixteen, except for actors in roles written specifically for children. Finally, there were rules and wage scales for stock companies.

A list of unfair trade practices was buried toward the back of the code. Article XVI prohibited any employer from aiding or assisting in any way the voluntary release or dismissal of any actor, author, dramatist "for the purpose of permitting such [person] to leave the cast of an attraction then playing in order to accept employment in motion pictures."

With the stroke of a Presidential pen, it became illegal for any producer to allow an actor or writer under contract to leave for a better deal in Hollywood. As a result, the Code destroyed any bargaining leverage for talent trying to win the best terms from Broadway and Hollywood producers.

Organized labor was at the table, but the unions did not have the clout to write the rules. Unions viewed with suspicion any code designed to promote the production of dramatic and musical plays and to attract capital into the industry. The recognition of unions and collective bargaining was welcome but had already been achieved by this point. Soon enough, the National Labor Relations Act passed as an additional part of the New Deal, enshrining the right to organize, collectively bargain, and strike.

The minimum wage provisions were also welcome, but in no way guaranteed employment during a national economic emergency where an enormous number of theaters were dark for months on end. Equity was also suspicious that the producers used the Code and the continued depression as an excuse to cut the size of the handful of shows still up and running.

The nuances of the theater code quickly became irrelevant. In 1935, the Supreme Court struck down this entire portion of the New Deal as unconstitutional[16] and the ongoing skirmishes between labor and management (now predominately the Shubert brothers) resumed, constrained only by the power of the strike.

The strikes, the wars between the Syndicate and the Shuberts, the separate war between Advanced Vaudeville and the Combine, and the NRA theater code, all left their marks on the performers, crew, producers, and presenters of live entertainment. But even unionization didn't fully protect the many skilled workers in the theater world from the growing power of the Shubert theater empire.

Act III

The Monopolist

10

Empire

The Syndicate began to collapse starting with a unexpected tragedy that shook the entire theater community. In 1915 Charles Frohman died on board the ocean liner Lusitania when it was torpedoed just off the Irish coast by a German submarine during World War I. The Lusitania sank in the icy waters within twenty minutes of the attack, killing over 1,100 crew and passengers including Frohman, the playwright Charles Klein, and one of the Vanderbilts.

Frohman had sailed on the Lusitania to obtain the rights to *An Englishman's Home*, the next of the many English productions he hoped to present in the United States. Supposedly, Frohman's last words were a paraphrase from *Peter Pan*, one of his first English imports: "Why fear death? It is the most beautiful adventure of life."

Charles Frohman's body returned to the United States on the American ocean liner, the New York, in May 1915. Ships in New York Harbor flew their flags at half-mast to honor him and the remains of eight other victims of the Lusitania disaster. Daniel Frohman and Al Hayman brought the coffin to Daniel's home for a private funeral.

The public memorial was held later that day at Temple Emanu-el on 5th Avenue. The New York Times hailed the memorial service as the greatest "assemblage of theatrical folks ever" and noted the large crowds that lined the sidewalks and streets outside the synagogue. Memorial services were also held simultaneously coast to coast, sharing the genuine sorrow over the passing of the man, who, along with Abe Erlanger and Marc Klaw, made theater a national and international business.

The toll on the theater and vaudeville industry could have been much worse. Composer Jerome Kern, later earning fame as the author of *Show Boat* and numerous other Broadway and movie musicals, was scheduled to sail with Frohman, but overslept following a late evening playing cards.

William Morris was also supposed to be on the Lusitania that fateful day. He had a plan to revitalize vaudeville by bringing over new talent from Europe (and earning new agent fees in the process). When he pitched his idea to Albee, who was running the Combine at this stage, Albee supposedly responded, "[t]o hell with your proposal. I am vaudeville." Morris then rushed to cancel his booking and avoided the fate of Frohman and the many other victims of the Lusitania sinking, living long enough to leave vaudeville entirely and remake the agent business in Hollywood.

***

By 1919, the Syndicate had one active member -- Abraham Lincoln Erlanger. By this point, Frohman had died and Hayman had retired. Nixon and Zimmerman were out of the business, and Erlanger and Klaw had a falling out relating to the position of Klaw's son in the firm. But in the public's mind, Erlanger and the Syndicate always were one and the same.

There was still much for the press to cover as the Erlanger-dominated Syndicate and the Shuberts continued as competitors and occasional partners. Both sides continued to present their hit musical revues that delighted the public and earned the producers and bookers large profits. Both sides still occasionally poached each other's theaters, producers, and stars.

The Syndicate had the *Ziegfeld Follies*, modeled after the *Folies Bergère* in Paris. Erlanger originally gave the little-known Florenz (Flo) Ziegfeld space in a rooftop summer theater for his revue, with a small budget and the title of production manager. There was also animosity between Ziegfeld and the Shuberts over Ziegfeld's alleged poaching of Shubert talent for his productions and his relationship with Erlanger.[1]

Ziegfeld had so little money at the time that he had no budget for stars and effectively made the elaborate (but inexpensive) chorus the focus of the show. It was only later he had the fame and the cash to hire or make stars from vaudeville and Broadway such as Fanny Brice, Billie Burke (later his wife), Bert Williams, and many more.[2]

The Shuberts' response to this phenomenon was acquiring *The Passing Show*, an existing revue that started in 1894. J.J. took the lead in promoting the show in New York and on the road. He also dated several of the starlets he auditioned and hired for the growing number of productions of this hit revue. By the 1920s, J.J. created a more explicitly risqué revue called *Artists and Models*, where any pretense of a plot took a back seat to the scantily clad chorus in outfits bordering on topless.[3]

***

When the Shuberts and the Syndicate weren't competing, they were partnering, and sometimes outright colluding. They also cooperated lawfully, but unsuccessfully, to oppose President Wilson's plans to restrict theater operations during World War I.

As Klaw and Erlanger began to quarrel, Klaw started to withdraw from the partnership and the Syndicate. The Shuberts saw this opportunity for the permanent end to the struggle. In late 1918, J.J. and Lee contemplated buying out Klaw's interest in Klaw & Erlanger for the modest sum of $125,000, mostly to cause trouble for Erlanger's remaining business interests. There is no record that any formal offer was ever made. However, the *Wall Street Journal* tantalizingly reported: "Levy Mayer, counsel for theatrical interests concerned[,] refuses to deny or affirm any report that Klaw & Erlanger and Shubert interests plan complete merger, which a local newspaper says, is a result of a quarrel between Klaw and Erlanger."[4]

After the Klaw & Erlanger partnership unraveled, Klaw worked informally with the Shuberts, scouting talent for them in England and booking his individual productions through the Shubert organization. Klaw retired in 1926 and moved to Europe for the final ten years of his life.

By 1921, the Shuberts were fully in control and the Open Door policy was little more than a marketing slogan for a new dominant force in legitimate theater. Lee and J.J. controlled more than two dozen theaters in New York City, dozens more in major markets, and more than 1,000 in the United States as a whole. That year, there were again public rumors of a merger between the two organizations. Once again, they came to naught.

Erlanger and the Shuberts created a new pooling agreement in 1922 that expanded on the 1913 agreement. The 1922 arrangement vastly enlarged the number of theaters in the pool and spelled out sharing of ownership and profits for more than a dozen major markets.

The following year, a new combination was announced, bowing to the inevitable rise of motion pictures as popular entertainment. This agreement created a new joint venture between the Shuberts and Erlanger to form a national circuit to "exhibit moving picture spectacles at first-class theater prices."[5] There was much speculation in the industry and the press that these agreements were merely the prelude to a full merger between the two competitors. Yet again, nothing ever ensued.

***

The second vaudeville war began in December 1920, this time without Erlanger. The ten-year non-compete agreement between the theater barons and Albee and the UBO had long since expired. Vaudeville was still an enormous enterprise. The Orpheum Circuit had gone public, profits were high, and there were hundreds of theaters still booking first class vaudeville around the country.

Lee created Shubert Advanced Vaudeville without the help of either Erlanger or William Morris. Instead, he hired a former UBO booker who had been friends with Sam. They tried the same strategy of raiding the UBO by paying top talent, building new theaters, converting existing Shubert theaters, and leasing dilapidated vaudeville and burlesque houses, to create a rival nationwide vaudeville circuit. They also mined existing Shubert theatrical productions to create abridged versions for inclusion in Shubert Advanced Vaudeville bills. However, the old and new tactics yielded the same dismal results.

Albee responded by blacklisting for life any actors who performed in Shubert Advanced Vaudeville. He further hinted that he planned to enter the legitimate theater business, but never made good on his threat.[6]

As sales sagged, Lee tried to innovate by offering Amateur Follies (akin to an early *America's Got Talent*), presenting sketches using local Boy Scout troops, and offering frequent benefits for local causes to bring people into the theater. When that didn't work, Lee added short seven-minute newsreel films to the bills. Out of desperation, he even used the Shubert Advanced Vaudeville theater in Pittsburgh to show full-length feature films from D.W. Griffith and Metro Films.

The only winners in the short term were the top vaudevillians whose pay again soared. Shubert Advanced Vaudeville signed star talent for top dollar, such as Will Rogers, Jack Benny, Eddie Cantor, Al Jolson, Mae West, and the Marx Brothers. Plenty of other talent either signed for big raises to switch circuits or bargained hard to stay with the UBO. For example, Will Rogers jumped from the *Ziegfeld Follies*, where he was making $1,500 a week, to the new Shubert vaudeville circuit for a whopping $5,000 a week (worth over $90,000 in 2025).[7] Al Jolson topped the list of big earners, making $10,000 a week ($180,000 in 2025) plus a percentage of the gross of his shows.[8]

Toward the end of 1921, Lee observed: "It seems to be the opinion of the exhibitors and everyone in the show business that we are paying more than double for our acts."[9] The long-suffering vaudeville performers even used the Albee-Shubert skirmishes as an opportunity to reinvigorate the White Rats.

Lee lost a reported $4,000,000, an even larger sum than in the 1907 raid. He retreated to the theatrical world within months of this ill-conceived vaudeville foray with even less to show for it than the 1907 fiasco. His last straw was to sue Albee and the Combine under the antitrust laws for $10.5 million for driving him from the market. That suit was later dropped without settlement or comment.

The Shubert withdrawal from the business may have been a blessing in disguise, but a very expensive blessing nonetheless. Vaudeville declined rapidly over the rest of the decade.

On Albee's end, he showed some grace. While this time he did not even bother to take over the vaudeville contracts of the performers in the doomed Shubert venture, he only blacklisted the defecting performers for one year if they apologized in print.

***

Lee hedged his bets in the vaudeville space in a more diabolical way. In 1914, Lee reached an agreement with Paul Keith, the son of B.F. Keith, to stay out of vaudeville in Syracuse, and not lease Shubert theaters to any vaudeville productions, in return for fifty percent of the Keith-Albee profits in that city.[10]

What the Combine never knew was that Lee also had been secretly buying up shares of the Keith-Albee Circuit since 1918. When B.F. Keith died in 1914, his son Paul inherited one-third of the company and operated the business with Albee.

Four years later, in 1918, Paul died of influenza at the age of 43 during the Great Spanish flu pandemic, throwing the UBO into further turmoil. Paul's death put his shares of the business up for grabs. The estate trustee was willing to sell the shares and eventually reached an agreement with an otherwise unknown individual, Harry Diamond, represented by a reputable New York law firm.

Harry Diamond did not exist, at least not the Harry Diamond who was purchasing the shares of Keith-Albee from the Paul Keith estate. Diamond was merely the pseudonym for Lee Shubert. All contact between Albee's vaudeville operation and Diamond was through the Wall Street law firm that received the dividends and profits, and more importantly also received a variety of confidential information as one of the largest shareholders in the business.

But Lee was not done. Ethan Robinson, the longtime corporate secretary of the Keith-Albee Circuit, also owned eighty shares of the Keith-Albee stock, amounting to one-twelfth of the business. Following Mr. Robinson's passing, Lee arranged to purchase those shares in the name of Milton Wolf, his brother-in-law, who was married to his sister Dora. The price was $600,000, with $150,000 down and nine later payments of $50,000 each. Albee had the chance to purchase the shares, but thought the price was too high.

No one appeared to have noticed the Shubert connection with the purchaser of record. Three days later, the shares were transferred to the same mysterious and non-existent "Harry Diamond."[11]

Combining the shares from Paul Keith and Ethan Robinson, Lee owned more than one-third of the Keith-Albee Circuit. Lee profited from the arrangement in more ways than one. Some money passed from Keith-Albee to "Harry Diamond" and then to Lee. More importantly, Lee now knew much of the financial information of the biggest live entertainment business outside of the legitimate theater industry. This arrangement continued for about ten years until "Harry Diamond" sold his shares at a substantial profit for $1.7

million when RKO Studios bought out Albee and the rest of the Combine. RKO, led by Joseph Kennedy, then folded what was left of big time vaudeville and its theaters into its movie empire.[12]

***

As the 1920s rolled on, the theatrical war was mostly over. The Shuberts and Erlanger "operated separately but peacefully, with the Shuberts retaining the upper hand."[13] At the same time, efforts to arrange a true national monopoly of all Broadway producers and theater owners never came to fruition because of the continued ill will between Lee Shubert and Erlanger.

Although rumors swirled of grand schemes to consolidate control of the industry, the competitive clash was dulled by less overt agreements. Simultaneous bookings of similar productions in the same city mostly stopped. The number of competing theaters dropped, with houses in some cities switching to vaudeville or the movies. Some theaters were jointly booked, and the two booking operations generally kept each other informed on a day-to-day basis.[14]

Though the theatrical war was largely over, Erlanger still controlled dozens of theaters on Broadway and the road. Independent producers existed, but typically had long-term, nearly exclusive relationships with either the Shuberts or Erlanger. Many had migrated to the Shuberts, but the Shuberts also had enemies who were more than happy to book exclusively through Erlanger.

1924 was an important year for the Shuberts. Lee and J.J. created a new single corporation, the Shubert Theater Corporation, taking over the interests of the various affiliated Shubert entities that had grown over the years. The new corporation was listed on the New York Stock Exchange, allowing the Shubert access to additional capital to fuel further expansion. All the while, the brothers continued to control its operations.

Legal constraints on public corporations before the creation of the Securities and Exchange Commission were few and shareholder rights even fewer. One of the only requirements was annual reports that by 1926 showed Shubert ownership of more than 90 theaters nationwide and booking rights controlling an additional 750 theaters.[15] The Shuberts had a daily audience of up to 130,000 people and box office receipts that often topped $1 million a week.[16]

The structure of the corporation meant that the shareowners participated in the profits (when there were profits), but Lee and J.J. remained in control of artistic and business decisions. Each brother maintained his own sphere of influence. J.J. continued to handle musicals, revues, construction and maintenance of theaters. Lee managed plays, finance, booking, publicity, advertising, and non-theatrical real estate. Even with the creation of the new publicly held corporation, the brothers still owned a bewildering array of real estate and other assets in their personal capacity.

***

Erlanger increasingly focused on the movie business, holding the rights to the successful theater production of *Ben-Hur*, which had been a mainstay touring theatrical property of the Syndicate. The long-awaited silent film version of *Ben-Hur* finally premiered in 1926 giving further life, publicity, and profits for the epic novel by Civil War General Lew Wallace and the still touring theater version.

In 1927, there were seventy-one legitimate theaters in New York City (up from forty-six in 1910). Thirty-one were controlled by the Shuberts and thirteen by Erlanger. Five other individuals owned a pair of theaters each, and seventeen theaters were owned by different individuals. Looking back at the heyday of the Shubert empire, Gerry Schoenfeld, later the CEO of the Shuberts, said that in 1927 the Shuberts "owned or operated 104 theaters, and they must have booked a thousand."[17]

1927 was also the high point for the industry. A record 264 new shows opened that year.[18] It was also the year the Jerome Kern-Oscar Hammerstein Jr. musical *Show Boat* opened, produced by Flo Ziegfeld. *Show Boat* was an immediate hit, and later was adapted into successful movies in 1929, 1936, and 1951 (winning an Oscar that year). *Show Boat* was also an artistic revolution in American theater, integrating the music and the book into a new form of American musical theater dealing with race and social issues.

This artistic revolution mostly bypassed the Shuberts. The same year that *Show Boat* appeared, the Shuberts countered with a series of lesser revivals at discount prices, using existing costumes, scenery, and props. From time to time, the Shuberts produced work by Eugene O'Neill, George Bernard Shaw, and Lillian Hellman, but these were almost beside the point. The point was to make money and lots of it. By December 1927, the stock price for the Shubert corporation hit a record high.

1927 also brought about the further physical separation of J.J. and Lee. Rather than just being separated and largely uncommunicative in the same building, J.J. moved to a penthouse in the building on the south side of 44th street across from Shubert Alley where Lee kept his office.

They naturally wanted to call J.J.'s new office the Shubert Building, but were concerned that this would drive away tenants, particularly those in the theater industry. So instead, they called it the Sardi's Building, after the legendary ground floor restaurant that is still operating today. This new arrangement lengthened the trip for the messengers and intermediaries when the two brothers needed to communicate.

***

It is hard to overestimate the continuing power and profit of the Shubert booking operation over the far less concentrated producers, who needed theaters in both New York City and on the road. The moderate competition in New York City did not reflect the fact that theaters in many of the major cities on the road were one hundred percent owned or controlled by either Shubert or Erlanger. Even the biggest New York hit needed both long-term bookings in major cities and a web of one-night and split-week engagements in smaller cities on the road to be profitable.

By the late 1920s, the Shuberts were more ruthless than Erlanger in enforcing the closed-door exclusivity of road bookings. Erlanger was barely either competing or colluding with Shuberts. Erlanger still controlled some fifty theaters, he was no longer much of a competitive threat to the Shubert empire. He remained both rich and successful, boasting of a net worth of more than $5,000,000 in a 1927 advertisement in the *New York Times* offering a mortgage on the New Erlanger theater in New York City.

***

The expansion of the Drama Guild into national touring caused one of the late-stage conflicts between the Shuberts and Erlanger, at a time when the battle was nearly over. The Drama Guild was one of a series of noncommercial theater companies experimenting with a repertory model, more serious artistic productions, and a subscription model to provide a steadier income stream. Unlike most of the other noncommercial producing groups, the Drama Guild also sought to tour the larger cities to capitalize on their more successful productions. The Drama Guild expanded to six key cities, including Chicago, Philadelphia, and Boston, in addition to its New York productions. The Shuberts booked all these cities for the Drama Guild.

The subscription model intrigued Lee Shubert, although it would be decades before the idea would catch on around the country as a model for presenting touring Broadway theater. The Drama Guild blindsided Lee in 1928 when it announced it was switching its booking operations from the Shuberts to Erlanger.

Lee responded with a two-prong attack reminiscent of the heyday of the earlier Shubert-Syndicate wars. First, he filed indecency complaints against two of the Drama Guild's road productions, including Eugene O'Neill's *Strange Interlude*. This gambit backfired when the local district attorney revealed that Lee Shubert was the source of the complaint.

The other prong of the attack was the tried-and-true strategy of the fighting brand. The Shuberts created their own "Dramatic League" to present more serious dramas on a subscription basis in Chicago and Philadelphia. Like most fighting brands, it was a money-losing proposition, but inflicted greater damage on the more fragile Drama Guild's operations by sowing confusion among ticket buyers.

After Erlanger's death, the Drama Guild subscription series merged with the Shubert Drama League into a new entity jointly managed by the Drama Guild, the Shuberts, and the remnants of the Erlanger operation. By 1933, the entire operation was taken over by the newly reconstituted United Booking Office, now controlled by the Shuberts, and the final battle with the Syndicate was over.

***

By the time Erlanger died in 1930 at the age of 70, the Syndicate was defunct as a result of a combination of factors. There were the ravages of the Great Depression, the deaths and retirements of key founders, the effects of the competitive battles with the Shuberts, the failed attempt to take over vaudeville, and the changing technology and tastes brought on by radio, silent films, and then the talkies.

For the Shuberts, commerce was the greatest art form. As the critic Brooks McNamara noted, "Lee and J.J. were America's principal *manufacturers* of theatrical productions."[19]

The Shuberts controlled about half of the Broadway theaters, as well as controlled the booking of the road through the United Booking Office, acquired during the later days of the Syndicate. They owned or operated 350 theaters across the country. They produced, invested in, or booked hundreds of productions ranging from classics to what one historian described as "witless comedies, noisy spectacles, and tasteless revues."[20] While they produced dozens of shows on Broadway, seventy-five percent of their shows began with outside producers in search of theaters on Broadway and on the road for the inevitable tours of the hits.[21] Overall, the Shuberts controlled about twenty-five percent of the plays in the United States and seventy-five percent of the theater tickets sold nationwide.[22]

For example, in Chicago, they owned or booked ten of the fifteen legitimate theaters.[23] The Shubert organization was now an vertically integrated monopolist, having its own in-house supply of composers, playwrights, set designers, costumes, props, publicists, and eventually lawyers.

***

Among the most prolific composers of all time was Sigmund Romberg. Romberg was an émigré from Hungary, where he had ushered at the Vienna theater. He was working as a conductor for a New York restaurant orchestra in 1914 when the Shuberts hired him to fill in for an absent rehearsal pianist at J.J.'s recommendation after seeing him perform at the restaurant.[24]

Romberg quickly became the Shubert staff composer, working mostly with J.J. He wrote his first nationwide hit in 1914 with the song *Omar* for the Shubert *Passing Show of 1914*.[25] For the next dozen years, Romberg churned out numerous scores for Shubert musicals, mostly in the form of similar and derivative light European operettas. But they worked.

Blossom Time was a big hit in 1921. It was revived five times in New York and toured for decades. For a time, it was so popular that it ran in separate theaters across the street from each other in New York City.[26]

Romberg's most famous score was *The Student Prince*. It was a massive hit on Broadway in 1924, playing for more than six hundred performances in New York, making it the longest running show of the 1920s, more than even *Show Boat*. The Shuberts revived *The Student Prince* on Broadway twice, once in 1931 and again in 1941. It toured the country for two decades. Profits from *The Student Prince* amounted to $750,000 ($14,153,000 in 2025) in the first year and many millions more in the years to come.

Despite these monster hits and many other successes, J.J. never treated Romberg very well financially or personally. As a result, Romberg left the Shubert orbit in 1926 and continued to compose hit shows with Flo Ziegfeld, Oscar Hammerstein Jr., and others. He briefly returned to the Shubert fold with considerably less success.

Independent producers found it difficult to mount commercially successful shows unless they did business with the Shuberts in New York City and on the road. Even not-for-profit entities like The Playwrights' Company still needed theaters for their productions and used Shubert theaters.

***

The Shuberts faced the same criticism as the Syndicate had in prior years – that they specialized in the lowest common denominator of live theater. The critics charged that they churned out musical revues and cookie cutter operettas to the detriment of the more refined theater arts.

Like these charges against the Syndicate, there was some merit to the accusations. The Shuberts were not against the fine arts, they were simply commercial theater producers with hundreds of theaters to fill on a nightly basis across North America.

Musical revues and operettas filled many of those seats for decades. The annual versions of *The Passing Show*, originally designed to compete with the *Ziegfeld Follies*, lasted for twelve years, and toured the country even while it continued to sell out one or more theaters on Broadway. During the 1925-26 season and beyond, the operetta *The Student Prince* had up to thirteen companies on tour in the United States and Australia, grossing as much as $250,000 a week.[27]

Shubert biographer Jerry Stagg described the five different ways to make money in the theater business:

1) Owning the real estate (the theaters) that are leased for a flat fee, a percentage of the revenues, or both;
2) Finding a play and a cast, renting a theater and hoping the public likes the play;
3) Providing the supplies that producers need to mount their play, including scenery, lights, props, costumes, etc.;
4) Booking a route for a tour and taking a fee from the producer, the venue, or both; and
5) Scalping tickets.[28]

The Shuberts had perfected the art of making money from each of these sources and looked forward to a period of high profits and little remaining competition.

***

The Shubert brothers faced new challenges after their lengthy struggle with the Syndicate. The first was the collapse of the road. The number of touring road companies plummeted from a high of 392 in December 1900 to a low of seventy-eight in the spring of 1928. The number of theaters outside of major cities on the road dropped by more than half from 1,500 in 1910 to 624 in 1925, and many of those theaters were not open on a regular basis.

This decline was in full swing even while most of the country were enjoying the boom times of the roaring twenties. Hundreds of small cities and towns that previously hosted one-night engagements of tours no longer had any live Broadway theater. The shows that did tour were frequently shabby productions often without recognizable stars. Most baffling, this was all during a period when the number of productions were increasing in New York City and holding steady in larger cities such as Chicago, Philadelphia, and Boston.

There is much debate as to why. One historian writing about the late 1920s noted, "a town with a population of from ten to fifty thousand which was formerly on the route of every attraction that hit its section of the country, now seldom, and some instances never, sees a legitimate road show."[29]

The plight of the road affected all segments of the industry: theaters, actors, authors, stagehands, advance men, and booking agents. In many cases, movies, amateur productions, and the return of locally based stock companies only filled part of this void.

One explanation for the dramatic decline (no pun intended) was simply oversupply from the on-again off-again warfare between the Syndicate and the Shuberts.[30] For example, Chicago grew from four legitimate theaters to over a dozen, and many smaller towns that could barely support one theater now found themselves with two or more struggling to survive. In addition to the actual quality of the show, the overcapacity led to concerns to the truthfulness of the advertising of "direct from Broadway" and other misleading ads and promotions.

Local theater owners and managers received much of the blame. In reality, they had little control over the product sent their way from the booking agents. Their degree of control or the quality of the production was unlikely to change if they made the occasional switch between the two barely competing booking circuits.

Producers and presenters were caught between higher costs and no real ability to raise prices for a diminished product. Consumers could spend their hard-earned dollars on the movies, what was left of vaudeville, or the free entertainment coming into their homes over the radio. The widespread sales of automobiles also increased the mobility of theatergoers, who could finally travel longer distances conveniently and cheaply to see better legitimate theater in larger neighboring cities. In many cases, the movie studios purchased or leased the former legitimate theaters and used them exclusively to show their own films, with no incentive to book legitimate theater.

A *Billboard* magazine survey in 1926 listed the top causes for the decline of the road as:

1) Movies;
2) High cost of admissions;
3) Control of suitable theaters by movie and vaudeville interests;
4) High cost in general, making theatrical productions unprofitable;
5) Available theaters not as attractive to public as movie and vaudeville houses;
6) High transportation costs making tours unprofitable;

7) Decline in quality of plays;
8) Misrepresentations by producers;
9) Change in public amusement taste;
10) Radio; and
11) Vaudeville.[31]

Coincidentally, Erlanger shifted his attention that year to the silent movie version of *Ben-Hur,* which had been one of his biggest theatrical attractions. Erlanger was hardly the only theater person to be lured to the increasingly lucrative movie industry. Successful plays could always be licensed to Hollywood as an additional revenue stream for producers like Lee Shubert or Daniel Frohman. Over time, playwrights negotiated through the Dramatists Guild for fifty percent of the income from the sale of movie rights.

Sometimes the stars of a hit would temporarily relocate to Hollywood to create a film version of their work. Less frequently, the entire cast would do so for a musical or a revue like the *Ziegfeld Follies.* Increasingly playwrights, actors, directors, and producers found Hollywood more lucrative and relocated there fulltime. These numbers increased dramatically after the advent of sound in movies beginning in 1927.

The small increases in stock companies, tent shows, amateur productions, and the rise of smaller more experimental theaters could not replace the monumental decline in touring Broadway productions. Many of these alternatives were largely a summer phenomenon. Outdoor summer stock still exists in many communities today.[32] At most, stock companies and little theaters were able to create mini circuits of a few neighboring towns to extend their runs and revenues, but never on a scale to replace the national Broadway tours.

Tent shows also faced a well-organized campaign by the movie industry at the state and local level to pass statutes and ordinances that would ban, highly regulate, or raise licensing fees that would make such attractions prohibitively expensive. In some towns, the movie studios would simply rent out all the suitable spaces where a tent show could perform. There was an accompanying propaganda campaign to stigmatize the shows as nuisances and criminal disturbances of the peace, all to prevent the siphoning of entertainment dollars from the movie theaters.

Touring Broadway, which increasingly meant Shubert touring Broadway, faced only limited competition from the Chautauqua and Lyceum lecture circuits that occasionally featured other types of performances, including magicians and dramatic readings. There were still occasional moderately priced legitimate theater in independent circuits, student productions, amateur community theater productions, and the innovative tours by the Theatre Guild Repertory Company in the late 1920s.[33] There was also widespread graft, theft, dishonesty, and what came to be known as "ice" (various forms of box office skimming) on the local presenting side that were additional contributing factors to the increasing unprofitability of the road.

The biggest threats were the high ticket prices of theater and the widespread appeal of the movies. This was true even before the advent of sound, that made going to the movies an even more effective substitute for the spectacle of live theater. Tickets for a "first class" production on the road (regardless of the literal truth of this assertion) usually were $2 or more. Movie tickets, in contrast, were usually between 25 and 75 cents, and sometimes included a double bill. Movie theaters often were luxury movie palaces featuring live music, occasional live acts (often magicians), and early types of air conditioning during the sweltering summer months.

The *Wall Street Journal* estimated that by 1925 movie attendance had soared to 130 million viewers for the year spread over tens of thousands of theaters nationally. The 1920s brought a wave of new movie house construction across the country as well as the acquisition or leasing of the dilapidated theaters and converted opera houses. The movie studios had no incentive to lease these new acquisitions to any competitors or to allow them to book legitimate theater.

It was the opposite problem in the larger cities, where there were too many theaters for the amount of quality product available through either Erlanger or the Shuberts. As the quality of the productions also declined, presenters and theatergoers grew wary of threadbare "direct from Broadway" shows and other dubious and misleading advertisements and promotions.

Broadway was in trouble. And it would get worse.

11

Survival

The late 1920s should have been the high point of the Shubert empire and the beginning of a long run at the top of the theatrical pyramid. The jazz age economy was roaring. The steady spread of the automobile gave theatergoers an additional option to attend live theater in their own towns or any nearby larger town or city.

Then came the Stock Market Crash of 1929 and the beginning of the Great Depression. This national tragedy nearly closed the entire American theater industry at the very moment the Shuberts had triumphed over all competitors. The Syndicate was essentially defunct, and vaudeville was at the verge of extinction.

Like the rest of the country, Broadway and the theater industry quickly felt the impact of the Great Depression. The number of operating Broadway theaters dropped by fifty percent from seventy-two to thirty-six with more than half of all theater staff unemployed. Most producers, actors, and crew didn't know if they would ever work again.

The Shuberts tried to cut costs and wait out the Depression. They hoped in vain for a quick turnaround that never came. They stopped production of new shows, closed most existing productions, discounted ticket prices, and dropped leases on theaters wherever they could.

They invested in some shows produced by friends to get them to Broadway, in a Shubert house of course. They experimented in bringing low-cost road companies back to Broadway as "revivals," but these rarely were profitable. Even an adaptation of a European musical starring Al Jolson at the height of his fame lasted less than ten weeks and lost money. To make matters worse,

Lee and J.J. still had hundreds of theaters they owned, or leased, that lost money because the audience could not afford a night at the theater or there wasn't even product to fill the theaters.[1]

Few shows, and even fewer hits, meant mounting losses. The Shubert Theatrical Corporation went into receivership in 1931. Receivership is an informal form of bankruptcy where a court appoints one or more neutral parties to run an insolvent business to maximize its profits and assets and pay off creditors to the extent possible.

The court appointed receivers for the Shubert Theatrical Corporation were the Irving Trust Bank, and most unusually, Lee Shubert. Two years later, there was an auction for the assets of the Shubert empire where Lee was the only bidder. He paid $400,000 to reclaim his old company and set up a new entity called Shubert Select Theatres. Those funds went to pay off the creditors of the Shubert organization, which included Lee and J.J. who personally owned much of the real estate and the theaters that were rented by Shubert productions.

***

The final act of the war between the Syndicate and the Shuberts ended with a whimper instead of a bang. Abraham Lincoln Erlanger died at his Manhattan home in 1930 of uremic poisoning. This left Marc Klaw as the only surviving original member of the Syndicate, although he remained retired in England until his death in 1936.

After the death of Erlanger and the decline of the Shubert organization into receivership, the two groups made one final attempt to merge when it largely ceased to matter. Both sides were a shadow of their former selves. Erlanger's brother, former Judge Mitchell Erlanger, was acting as executor for Abe Erlanger's estate. It was unclear what the Erlanger estate had that was of value to the Shuberts, except for the theaters it owned or leased. It was equally unclear what attraction the Erlanger booking office could hope to continue representing now that the Little Napoleon was gone.

The Shuberts were hardly in better shape. The future of live theater was in deep doubt. Live theater was at the mercy of the state of the economy and the ever-growing popularity of motion pictures which were priced to deliver an evening of drama, comedy, or a movie musical for a fraction of the cost of a live theater ticket.

The three-page draft merger agreement declared that the purpose of the merger was to "unify and organize the legitimate theater outside of the City of New York, that is to say "The Road" so as to serve the public more efficiently, to assure producers a profitable operation, to secure attractions for theaters more regularly and to eliminate an unwieldly or unnecessarily large number of theaters in certain cities."[2]

The agreement designated a number of formerly Syndicate or Shubert theaters as part of a unified road circuit in all the major markets. It established a new production, finance, and booking office to run the combined operation. The new circuit consisted of three theaters in Boston, three in Philadelphia, five in Chicago, one or two in Detroit, and one in each of St. Louis, Pittsburgh, Kansas City, Cleveland, Baltimore, Washington, D.C., Los Angeles, San Francisco, and Buffalo.

The proposed merger also created a new central booking office. Each theater selected for the new unified circuit would operate as a local company separate from the new central booking office. The new booking office would be called the United Booking Office (UBO) named after the booking operation of vaudeville in its glory days but not connected to the defunct Combine. The new UBO would receive one-third of the profits, plus fees, divided equally between the Shuberts and Erlanger groups.

The new UBO would be run by Marcus Heiman, a childhood friend of the Shuberts. Heiman had joined the Shuberts after a career with the vaudeville Combine. He would be the CEO of the new UBO and would manage all aspects of the unified circuit. Mitchell Erlanger would run the remains of his brother Abe's former operation.

The agreement called for a new company with at least $500,000 of capital and required the approval of Lee and the other receiver. Presumably, competition would continue within New York City but would cease on the road.

The proposed merger never took place, and the new company never came about. The death of Abraham Lincoln Erlanger and the failed merger effectively meant the death of competition in the booking space. Instead of a merger, the

Shuberts acquired the Erlanger Theatre (renamed the St. James) from the Erlanger estate and simply began to use the UBO name for their booking operations with Heiman in charge.[3]

Around the same time, any competition from the vaudeville Combine for audiences or talent ceased with the death of the industry. Martin Beck briefly joined RKO in an unsuccessful attempt to revive vaudeville at the Palace. The final two a day big time commercial vaudeville show took place at the Palace Theatre (then owned by RKO Studios) in New York City in late 1932. Beck returned to the legitimate theater world in 1933.

The Palace Theater struggled financially for three more years, presenting a hybrid program of a few live acts with a full-length feature film up to five times a day. By 1935, the Palace was a full-time movie house. It hosted a brief vaudeville revival from 1949-51 and occasional other live shows in the 1950s and 60s with Judy Garland and a few vaudeville-style opening acts.[4]

***

Despite the ravages of the Great Depression, the Shuberts continued to consolidate their precarious perch as the only national theater organization in a struggling industry in an ailing economy. After the death of Flo Ziegfeld in 1932, Lee Shubert licensed the rights to the *Ziegfeld Follies* from Ziegfeld's widow, Billie Burke, and began presenting the Syndicate's former star musical revue under the Shubert name.

Lee produced the Shubert version of the *Follies* himself, instead of deferring to J.J., who had traditionally produced the musical revues. This was another in the endless series of grudges and feuds that poisoned the relationship between the brothers.

The Lee Shubert version of the *Follies* proved a profitable attraction in New York City and on the road. It featured excellent casts including current and future stars such as Josephine Baker, Bob Hope, Bert Lahr, Milton Berle, and Gypsy Rose Lee, and lasted into the 1940s.[5] In 1935, Lee also produced a separate revue that ran 198 performances, a solid accomplishment given the decrepit state of the American economy.

***

Plate 1 *THE BLACK CROOK: Part of the cast of the 1866 extravaganza The Black Crook, the first nationwide hit. Photograph by Napoleon Sarony circa 1893; Courtesy of Library of Congress Prints and Photographs Division.*

Plate 2 *BENJAMIN FRANKLIN (B.F.) KEITH: The creator of big time vaudeville. Unknown photographer, New York Star (Mar. 27, 1909), via WikiMedia Commons.*

Plate 3 *EDWARD FRANKLIN (E.F.) ALBEE: Keith's partner and successor who made big time vaudeville a national empire. Unknown Photographer, New York Star (December 19, 1908 Vol. 1 No. 12), via WikiMedia Commons.*

Plate 4 *MARTIN BECK: The long-time head of the Orpheum vaudeville circuit, part-owner and booker of the Palace Theatre, and Broadway producer. George Grantham Bain Collection, Library of Congress, Prints and Photographs Division.*

Plate 5 *ABRAHAM LINCOLN ERLANGER: Mastermind of the American Theatrical Syndicate and "Napoleon" of American theater. Unknown photographer, New York Star (January 23, 1909), via WikiMedia Commons.*

Plate 6 *MARC KLAW: The lawyer and former advance man who was Erlanger's partner and enforcer. Courtesy of the University of Washington Libraries Digital Collection, J. Willis Sayre Photograph Collection.*

Plate 7 *CHARLES FROHMAN: The Syndicate member and producer of Peter Pan and dozens of hits for the Syndicate. Courtesy of the Miriam and Ira D. Wallach Division of Art, Prints and Photographs: Photography Collection, The New York Public Library.*

Plate 8 *HARRISON GREY FISKE: Fierce opponent of the Syndicate, and husband of leading actress Minnie Maddern Fiske. Courtesy of Billy Rose Theatre Division, The New York Public Library.*

Plate 9 *MINNIE MADDERN FISKE: One of the leading actresses of her time who continued to perform in New York City despite the best efforts of the Syndicate. Otto Sarony Co. Mrs. Fiske. 1907. Photograph. The Theatre 7, no. 78 (August 1907), 211, via WikiMedia Commons.*

Plate 10 *DAVID BELASCO: Producer, writer, theater owner and frenemy of both the Syndicate and the Shubert Brothers. Courtesy of the Shubert Archive.*

Plate 11 *COMPOSITE OF J.J., SAM, AND LEE SHUBERT: The Shubert Brothers who challenged and eventually supplanted the Syndicate as the dominant force in the theater industry. Courtesy of the Shubert Archive.*

Plate 12 *J.J. SHUBERT AND AL JOLSON: J.J. Shubert and the "World's Greatest Entertainer" Al Jolson, who wowed audiences in vaudeville, theater, and later the movies. Courtesy of the Shubert Archive.*

Plate 13 *J.J. SHUBERT AND SIGMUND ROMBERG: J.J. Shubert at the piano with his most successful in-house composer Sigmund Romberg who created many operettas that played for decades in New York and on the road. Courtesy of the Shubert Archive.*

Plate 14 *LEE AND J.J. SHUBERT: Lee and J.J. putting aside their many differences to pose for the camera. Courtesy of the Shubert Archive.*

Plate 15 *MARCUS LOEW: A leader in small time vaudeville, motion picture exhibition, and later studio head. Frequent partner but never direct competitor of the Shuberts. Unknown photographer. Marcus Loew, 1924, photograph, N.V.A. Souvenir 1924: National Vaudeville Artists Eighth Annual Benefit, p. 15 (New York: National Vaudeville Artists, 1924).*

Plate 16 *SHUBERT "MONOPOLY" MONEY: The Shuberts even had their own "money" used when money changed hands between the actors. Courtesy of the Shubert Archive.*

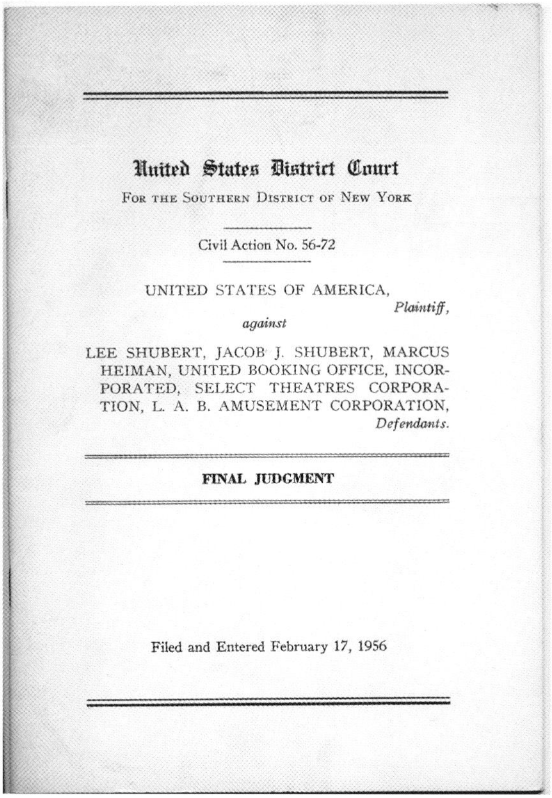

United States District Court

FOR THE SOUTHERN DISTRICT OF NEW YORK

Civil Action No. 56-72

UNITED STATES OF AMERICA,
Plaintiff,

against

LEE SHUBERT, JACOB J. SHUBERT, MARCUS HEIMAN, UNITED BOOKING OFFICE, INCORPORATED, SELECT THEATRES CORPORATION, L. A. B. AMUSEMENT CORPORATION,
Defendants.

FINAL JUDGMENT

Filed and Entered February 17, 1956

Plate 17 *TITLE PAGE OF CONSENT DECREE IN SHUBERT ANTITRUST LITIGATION: The 1956 settlement between the Shuberts and the Justice Department that required the sale of Shubert theaters to create more competition. Courtesy of the Shubert Archive.*

Plate 18 *LYCEUM THEATER ATTIC READING ROOM: The reading room atop the Lyceum Theatre that was the producing office of Charles and Daniel Frohman, an attic of a Shubert theater, and now the home of the Shubert Archives. Courtesy of the Shubert Archive.*

From 1935 to 1939, the Shuberts faced a new type of theater competition for the first time: a publicly funded Federal Theatre Project. Roosevelt's New Deal included an ambitious Works Progress Administration (WPA). The WPA was an attempt to get the United States back to work through massive public works projects such as roads, dams, bridges, conservation, and rural electrification.

The WPA also included the first serious federal commitment to support the arts. The WPA supported painters, photographers, musicians, and writers through programs that produced lasting works of art, music, and publications that enriched the country cultually and allowed the artists to practice their craft and earn a living in desperate times.

The WPA also created the Federal Theatre Project (FTP). The FTP was centered in New York City but had a regional staff of seven spread around the country. The FTP supported new works, revivals of plays from Broadway, children's theater, revues and musical comedies, vaudeville, circus, dance, puppets and marionettes, African American productions, and foreign language plays. There were units for a live theater newspaper based on current events, motion pictures, radio, research, publication, and municipal theater.[6] As historian James Shapiro noted: "Nobody had ever attempted to stage several hundred productions a year – from circus shows to vaudeville to classics to new American plays – in scores of locations, relying on mostly untried or rusty performers."[7]

The Federal Theatre Project was a very different model from the commercial theater world of the Shuberts. The FTP produced new and classic work with high artistic ambitions, at a scale even the Shuberts could not match. In 1936, a week before Roosevelt's landslide reelection, the FTP opened a theatrical adaption of *It Can't Happen Here*, Sinclair Lewis's ominous novel about the rise of fascism in a thinly veiled version of then contemporary America.

It Can't Happen Here premiered in eighteen different cities simultaneously from coast to coast, something neither the Syndicate nor the Shuberts ever considered in lieu of a traditional tour.[8] It was a lengthy melodrama with a cast of twenty-seven actors plus musicians on loan from the Federal Music Project. Regional productions were given permission to alter the location to suit local audiences and even alter the ending, often drastically changing the final message of the play. Sinclair Lewis himself appeared in one of the Vermont presentations.

It was a rocky road to opening night. Large changes to the script and the sets were made up to the very last minute, both for artistic reasons and to respond to the furious accusations of partisanship and politics. Despite all the changes, some cities dropped out of the production. The FTP imposed severe restrictions on publicity and promotion.

In the end, *It Can't Happen Here* was a success. More than 379,000 people attended a total of 584 performances. Attendance exceeded sales of the book itself.[9]

The FTP also toured some of its other more popular productions, but only on a regional basis. Two-thirds of the audience had never seen a play; others had not seen live entertainment on the stage since the death of vaudeville. Most of the productions were free. The ones that charged were priced well below the dollar that it cost for the worst seat in the balcony of a Broadway show.

The focus of the FTP was jobs and art, not profits. A twenty-year-old Orson Welles, in his theatrical directorial debut, directed an all-black cast of *Macbeth* in Harlem, produced by the English actor John Houseman. This version of *Macbeth* ran for six months at the Lafayette Theatre in Harlem and then moved to Broadway for a brief run. The production eventually toured the country, including some of the Jim Crow south, with an enormous 180-person integrated company, often playing to integrated audiences in otherwise inhospitable locations.

The FTP also gave a start to Arthur Miller, who became a Pulitzer and Tony award-winning playwright with such works as *Death of a Salesman* and *The Crucible*. The project also supported the work of Black playwrights, although Black writers complained bitterly of their treatment by Houseman, Welles, and many of their less famous white colleagues.

Over its four-year lifetime, the Federal Theatre Project staged "for a pittance, over a thousand productions in twenty-nine states seen by thirty million, or roughly one in four Americans."[10] Millions more listened to its productions on the radio. It employed more than 12,000 people, more than half of which were performers, including many former vaudevillians. The rest were crew, lighting and sound designers, scenery artists, electricians, stage managers, and even publicists. Over ninety percent of the FTP budget went toward wages.

There were new and classic works, with many of the productions focused on the social issues of the times including homelessness, poverty, and politics. Despite great caution to avoid the appearance of partisanship, there was an intense backlash to the progressive ideals of most FTP's productions. The FTP wanted "provocative American plays"[11] and rejected most of the more commercial fare that were the bread and butter of the Shuberts.

In the end, politics destroyed the FTP. By 1937, Congress was already cutting the budget for the FTP, and the WPA, forcing the firing of about twenty percent of the performers and other staff. More ominously, the House of Representatives expanded hearings accusing the FTP leadership of communist leanings. Other critics denounced the use of federal funds to support progressive theater pieces seen as propaganda for Roosevelt's New Deal agenda.

In 1939, Congress renewed funding for the WPA but cut all funding for theater despite the pleas of such show business luminaries as Al Jolson, James Cagney, Henry Fonda, and Orson Welles. Even the movie star Tallulah Bankhead could not convince her father, who was the Speaker of the House of Representatives, to continue support for the FTP. She was more successful with her uncle, who was a Senator from Alabama, but it was too late.[12] President Roosevelt signed the bill into law, continued funding for a much-reduced WPA, but failed to allocate any money for the FTP or any other form of national theater.

It would be more than twenty years before Congress created the National Endowment for the Arts that provided some funding for non-profit theater. To this day, there is no National Theater of the United States as is the case in most developed countries around the world.

***

Despite the substantial, but brief, impact of the Federal Theatre Project, it never really affected the Shuberts or the rest of commercial Broadway. The FTP was reaching audiences who often had never seen a Broadway show before, and mostly never would. It produced some plays and musicals that had been on Broadway or would eventually make it to Broadway. But overall, the FTP was aiming for an artistically and politically challenging type of play or musical that was never the bread and butter of commercial theater. It is telling that in the vast hordes of business records in the Shubert Archives, there are only a few references to the FTP, and nothing in writing discussing its effect on Shubert business.

The real competition the Shuberts faced during the terrible years of the Depression was from radio and the movies. Once families purchased radios, they did not have to leave the house for entertainment and the programs were free. The stations, and eventual networks, were controlled by large industrial corporations on a national scale with budgets beyond the scope of the Shuberts and their investors.

At the same time, the competition from radio was only limited. Comedians translated well to the radio, as did certain dramas and serials that could be altered to accommodate the need for sponsors and commercial breaks. While it is always hard to compete with free, the audio format of radio was only a partial substitute to an evening out of the house to take in the spectacle of a Broadway play or musical, if the family could afford the tickets.

The movies were different.

***

Lee had long been aware of the financial opportunities and threat caused by the movies. As early as 1908, he and J.J. allowed Adolph Zukor and Marcus Loew to show their films in Shubert theaters on Sunday evenings, when the theaters would otherwise be dark.[13] But it was Daniel Frohman, the Broadway producer and brother of Syndicate stalwart Charles Frohman, who made headlines and a tidy profit showing the full-length 1912 Sarah Bernhardt film *Queen Elizabeth* at the Frohman-controlled Lyceum Theatre on 45th Street.

The vaudeville barons had dabbled in the film business even earlier. Keith and Albee acquired the exclusive American rights to the equipment and films of Lumière Cinématographe from France. They presented their first movies in 1896 at their Union Square Theatre in New York City.

In 1905, Keith and Albee switched to Edison Studios to supply the films and projection equipment. They later flirted with one of Edison's early attempts to introduce sound to films and rejected a separate opportunity to invest in a competing sound technology. By 1926, they were investing in film studios, but mostly to guarantee access to short films for their traditional vaudeville programs.[14]

Despite being early adopters, Keith and Albee never actively entered the film industry themselves. They used short films as filler in vaudeville programs but quickly saw the motion industry invade the vaudeville space with so-called "unit stage shows." Rapidly growing movie chains like Paramount packaged a short program of two or three traditional vaudeville acts, often singers, dancers, musicians, and an MC, with a feature film, and routed this hybrid program through the more than fifteen hundred theaters it controlled in the late 1920s at prices below that of big time vaudeville. This invasion was more devastating than anything that Klaw & Erlanger or the Shuberts could ever devise.

As early as 1910, twice as many people in New York City were attending movies versus live vaudeville. Vaudeville profits began to plummet and turned to outright losses in the mid-1920s and the number of big time vaudeville theaters shrank for both the Keith-Albee and the Orpheum circuits. In 1923, Martin Beck left vaudeville and became a prominent Broadway producer building the Martin Beck theater which still stands today.

By 1928, the two flailing vaudeville circuits merged into one. Albee then sold the remnants of the Keith-Albee-Orpheum operation to Joseph Kennedy for 200,000 shares of Kennedy's Film Booking Office (FBO). For a time, RKO presented combination programs of sixty minutes of condensed versions of musical theater before and after feature films. Albee joined the senior management of the FBO, only to discover that Kennedy was interested in the former vaudeville monopoly for their theaters and land that they owned.[15]

Joseph Kennedy, the father of President John F. Kennedy, quickly eased Albee out of power. Kennedy, the consummate wheeler-dealer of his day, sold his stock to the Radio Corporation of America who formed its own studio giant with the name RKO, standing for Radio-Keith-Orpheum.

In the end, the Keith-Albee and the Orpheum circuits lived on only as initials in the name of the corporation that had bought and stripped them for parts. Albee retired to Palm Beach Florida, wealthy but bitter. He passed away in 1930 after living long enough to see almost all his beloved vaudeville theaters turned into movie houses.

***

The Syndicate also tried to profit from this new technology and mass appeal of the film industry. Klaw and Erlanger entered the film business in 1913, announcing that they were creating a new company to film the more than 100 theatrical properties they controlled. Only twenty-six titles were ever filmed, and none were successful artistically or financially.[16] By the 1920s, Erlanger would be drawn to Hollywood to produce the silent movie version of *Ben-Hur*, adapted from the long-running theater version the Syndicate had controlled for years.

Lee Shubert entered the film business in 1914 when it was still mostly located on the East Coast. Lee's original conception was to produce (and profit from) silent film versions of existing Shubert plays, as well as produce original motion pictures.

He began by investing with Lewis Selznick and a third partner in the World Film Corporation located in Fort Lee, New Jersey. There were a few minor hits along the way, but Selznick and the other partner both left by the end of 1915. Many of the star actors left World Pictures as the film industry began to relocate to the sunnier climate of southern California.

World Film only filmed a few of the Shubert theatrical properties because the typical Shubert musical comedies and lighter farces did not translate well to the silent screen. Nonetheless, the Shuberts made some money from film adaptations but film was never more than a side business in their theater empire.

Lee resigned as a director of the company in 1918, later joining the board of Goldwyn Pictures. World Films continued to make movies but remained unprofitable and closed for good in 1919. The Fort Lee facility eventually became the Shubert warehouse for scenery, costumes, and props, until it burned to the ground in a fire in 1958.[17]

***

A key ally for Lee Shubert was Marcus Loew. Loew was a serial entrepreneur who succeeded in both vaudeville and the movies, but never entered the legitimate theater industry. This made him a desirable ally and partner for Lee, but never a competitor.

Loew was born in 1870 on the lower east side of New York City. His father was a waiter who immigrated from Vienna. His mother was a young German widow who had two children from her first marriage. Marcus quit school at the age of nine. He worked at a map coloring plant, a printing press, operated a neighborhood newspaper, and worked in a men's clothing store.

By the age of eighteen, Marcus was working as a furrier in lower Manhattan. He partnered with Adolph Zukor, at the time also in the fur business, in a penny arcade business that featured coin-operated amusement machines and viewers for the early short moving pictures. Loew and Zukor built a growing group of penny arcades and nickelodeons offering short films and a handful of live variety acts.

From there it was a short jump into small time vaudeville, mixing one-reel films and such low-end acts as "animal impersonators, dancing bears, and mock hangings in which someone from the audience was invited to pull the rope."[18] Loew and Zukor merged their competing chains to form a growing empire of nickelodeon parlors and small time vaudeville theaters.

After the failure of the 1907 Shubert-Syndicate Advanced Vaudeville venture, Loew also bought out the William Morris booking operation. Morris sold out of desperation when he could not make money directly competing with the vaudeville UBO, and the Shuberts and Syndicate were bound by a multiyear non-compete agreement to stay out of the vaudeville business.

Loew thrived, where Morris had failed, because he never directly took on the Combine, who tolerated competition in small time vaudeville, but zealously defended their monopoly of the fancier big time portion of the business. Loew eventually expanded his business empire to include amusement parks and the movies.

Loew entered the movie business as an exhibitor. He rented short films to show in a room above one of his arcades in Cincinnati. Over time, he added more seats and showed short films and "scenic tours" simulating a train ride with films of majestic outdoor scenario, swaying seats, and recorded train sounds. In 1908, he refurbished a decrepit vaudeville theater in downtown Brooklyn, renamed it the Royal, and offered a combination of vaudeville and films.

Late in life, Loew claimed that his highly successful combination of film and vaudeville came about by accident after a friend:

> had recommended to me a pretty big actor who was out of work and wanted a position as a doorkeeper. I felt kind of sorry; I did not feel that was the position for him. I thought people would recognize him. So I said to him, "Can you recite?" He said, "Yes, of course." I said: "I have an idea. I will put on vaudeville with pictures." At that time we did not know what feature pictures meant. I had him recite "Gunja Din" twenty times a day.[19]

Loew would soon find that the higher-class neighborhood theaters were less interested in small time vaudeville. In those theaters, he dropped the live acts in favor of feature films, while the vaudeville-movie mix retained its more mass-market appeal.

Marcus Loew first did business with the Shuberts in 1909. He leased two of the Shubert theaters for his combination vaudeville-movie shows to great success. He later booked additional Shubert theaters in New England. The theaters provided a steady source of rent as the Shubert brothers expanded their theater empire in competition with the Syndicate and allowed Loew to expand his business to all five boroughs with his popular (and popularly priced) blend of vaudeville and film.

The Shuberts in turn invested $200,000 in Loew's rapidly expanding company. Lee was a preferred stockholder in Marcus Loew Enterprises and received quarterly dividends. Adolph Zukor signed on to serve as treasurer of what was now called Loew's Consolidated (Loew's) but soon left to pursue his own career in film production. By 1919, J.J. joined Lee on the Loew's board of directors.

The Shuberts also booked vaudeville acts from Loew for Sunday night "concerts" at several theaters as a work-around from blue laws that prohibited theatrical productions on Sunday evenings. Lee later acquired thirty-five percent in a new Loew's theater in Atlanta.

One of Loew's few missteps was the acquisition of the Sullivan & Considine theater chain. Loew hoped these thirty theaters would cement his presence in the Midwest and the West Coast. Instead, these theaters lost half a million dollars and Loew was forced to abandon the project.

Loew eventually created an integrated entertainment conglomerate headquartered at Broadway and 47th, just a few blocks north of the Shubert offices. By 1922, the Loew's motto was "theatres everywhere." The Loew's operation was far more diversified than the Shuberts, but they were never direct competitors. Loew was focused on vaudeville and the movies while Shuberts continued to stick to the legitimate theater and invest in Loew's more diverse businesses. Loew stuck with his format of mixed vaudeville and film, even as the film industry began to shift in 1914 to movie theaters showing feature length silent films, rather than short one-reel novelties.

His first venture in producing movies also involved his longtime associate, Adolph Zukor. Zukor had formed the Famous Player Film Company to create full-length films, rather than the short one-reel movies that were mostly novelties in the penny arcades, nickelodeons, and small time vaudeville theaters he operated with Loew. Zukor also teamed up with Charles and Daniel Frohman to produce feature versions of hit plays featuring the stars who had appeared in Frohman productions on Broadway.

In 1916, Zukor merged the Famous Players Film Company with the Jesse L. Lasky Feature Play Company and a small production and distribution company called Paramount Pictures to form the Famous Players-Lasky Corporation. Paramount became the exclusive distribution arm of the company. The new company was the first to combine movie production, distribution, and exhibition into a single movie studio. By 1917, it was the largest motion picture company in the world.

Famous Players-Lasky controlled many of the best-known actors in the U.S. film industry and was therefore able to raise prices for its films.[20] Because of his long-standing relationship with Zukor, Loew booked Famous Players-Lasky films for the Loew's theaters. Famous Players-Lasky soon faced its own competition from First National Pictures, itself a vertically integrated production and distribution company, featuring the movies of Charlie Chaplin and Mary Pickford, two of the era's biggest stars.

Loew took his company public in 1919, giving him the clout and the funds to buy a studio, and guaranteeing him a secure source of films for his theater chain. In 1920, Loew bought Metro Pictures (originally founded by Louis B. Mayer who had already left Metro to found Louis B. Mayer Pictures) through a mixture of stock and deferred cash payments, funded out of future studio earnings. It was essentially a no money down deal.

Loew now had his own vertically integrated movie studio covering production, distribution, and exhibition. This became a key feature of the Hollywood studio system that would continue until the 1940s, when the Justice Department broke up the major studios in a landmark antitrust case named after Paramount Pictures,[21] which had begun as the distribution arm of Zukor's first venture into film.

The combination of the roaring twenties and the rapid growth in popularity of full-length feature films meant good times and national prominence for the movie industry and its hold on the national imagination. Unfortunately, Metro Pictures languished. It made several hits starring Ramon Novarro and Buster Keaton but mostly made a small number of second-rate films with limited profitability.

Loew's ties with Lee Shubert provided a way out for Metro's woes. Lee served as a director of both the Metro and Goldwyn studios, today considered an antitrust no-no as an unlawful interlocking directorate of competing firms. Lee made the connection between Loew and the Goldwyn studios. The parties negotiated a complex deal exchanging stock (no cash changed hands) and a separate agreement to bring in Louis Mayer as studio head, creating the famed Metro-Goldwyn-Mayer, or MGM Studios (MGM), with Loew as the principal shareholder. Lee Shubert continued as a major shareholder and director of the new mega-studio.[22]

Loew ensured that his movie production remained profitable by introducing to MGM the practice of "block booking," which became standard in the industry. Block booking meant that a theater had to license (book) a number (or block) of a studio's films to get the rights to show the most popular films. This meant, as a practical matter, a theater had to license a bundle of pictures on a take it or leave it basis, taking the dogs to get the hits.

Zukor's Paramount Pictures first used this tactic, and Loew's MGM followed suit along with the other major studios. From the studios' perspective, this ensured a predictable revenue stream and made the bundles profitable overall.

Block booking was always legally suspect because it coerced movie theaters into showing movies they didn't want. The Federal Trade Commission unsuccessfully challenged Paramount's use of the practice back in the 1920s.[23] The investigation eventually revealed that after the MGM merger, Famous Players-Lasky and Loew's "gave each other preferential treatment when it came to releasing films."[24] Paramount ultimately prevailed, mostly because it held only twelve percent of the market at the time and the court was not convinced that the FTC had demonstrated any likely harm to competition since theaters could book films from other distributors and studios.

It was a different situation when **every** studio began to do business the same way. The Supreme Court finally outlawed the practice in 1948 in the *Paramount* case, and later banned blocking booking in the television industry in a case against Loew's in the early 1960s.[25] Eliminating block booking would prohibit an important selling channel that reduced the risk of any single film being a flop since it could be licensed to theaters (and eventually television) as part of a profitable bundle.

The success of *The Jazz Singer* in 1927 represented a major challenge to Loew's business. Talkies would be a boon to the movie industry but would quickly spell the doom of vaudeville that first brought Loew out of the arcade business and into the show business spotlight.

Loew never lived to see either of these developments come to fruition. He died in 1927, from complications from pneumonia, one month before the opening of *The Jazz Singer*. All Loews theaters closed for the day. Two thousand people attended a memorial service at the MGM Culver City studio and the "studio flag was lowered to half mast."[26] At the New York funeral, Lee Shubert, who reportedly was dry-eyed at the funeral of his own parents, openly wept.[27] Lee Shubert continued as serve as a director and shareholder of MGM for the rest of his life.

Lee Shubert played a critical role in the history of Hollywood and profited handsomely, but as an investor and corporate director at what became MGM, and also United Artists Studios. He never produced films or operated a studio. The Shuberts stuck to the theater business and rode out the Great Depression as the last national organization standing in the legitimate theater industry.

They outlasted vaudeville and continued to produce a product that radio could not duplicate. Movies would remain their principal competitor until the rise of commercial television broadcasting after World War II.

Theater became increasingly popular source material for the movies when sound became the norm, but those revenues were usually a welcome bonus, rather than a regular boon to the bottom line. The Shuberts were battered, but they had won. The real question was what would they do now?

12

The Quiet Life

The British Nobel winning economist John Hicks famously wrote: "The best of all monopoly profits is a quiet life."[1] As the economy started to improve in the late 1930s, the Shuberts had that quiet good life.

Lee approached his seventieth birthday as the elder statesman of Broadway. J.J. was truculent and aggrieved as ever, but still generated significant profits from the endless stream of revues and musicals that filled seats on Broadway and the road.

People finally again had money to spend on luxuries like a night out at the theater. Business was good, and existential threats were few.

Lee stepped up his charitable work, becoming chair of the theater division of the March of Dimes. He became increasingly involved in bringing live entertainment to U.S. troops abroad through the USO once the United States entered the war in 1941.

At this point in their careers, the Shuberts made most of their money renting theaters, owning real estate, investing in other people's productions, and operating ticket brokerage businesses in New York, Boston, Chicago, Philadelphia, and Detroit.

Many of their productions were old shows in new types of venues. During the late 1930s, the Shuberts began to produce familiar shows in open-air theaters in Jones Beach and Randall's Island in New York, and in the enormous outdoor suburban St. Louis Municipal Opera.

People in the industry noticed how the productions cheapened over time. Audiences might not notice unless they saw a show more than once or carefully compared the playbills from earlier Broadway or road productions. Recognizable actors playing minor principals were replaced by lesser-known actors once the show had been running for a while.

Once on tour, higher salaried actors were replaced, casts were smaller, scenes were cut, and the chorus would shrink, all to save money. Most of the costumes, scenery, and props came straight from the Shubert warehouses in New Jersey and Greenwich Village and had seen better days after decades of use in prior tours and Broadway runs.[2]

Lee and J.J. were now landlords and booking agents in an increasingly stagnant industry. They made a decent living, but took fewer risks, either financially or artistically. Producers still needed theaters to rent and tours to be booked. That was the sweet spot for the Shubert Organization that encountered only limited competition in either slice of the industry.

The real drama was within the Shubert family. In 1933, John joined the family business after graduating from Harvard Law School. He was by far the best educated of any Shubert to ever run a theatrical business. At the same time, he was an odd choice to join the "family" business since he had been estranged from J.J. for years following the bitter divorce between his parents when he was a young child. Throughout John's childhood, J.J. mostly denied paternity and frequently withheld financial support to John's mother. During the same period, Lee brought in his nephew, Milton Shubert, as his favored family member and future heir, ensuring that the family split in the business would continue for another generation.

1938 brought a true hit with *Hellzapoppin'*, a two-hour version of an earlier vaudeville-type sketch show where live entertainers performed before and after full length motion pictures. According to Shubert biographer, Foster Hirsch, it was "old-time variety with a touch of burlesque."[3] The show benefitted from relentless promotion and publicity from Walter Winchell in his newspaper columns and radio shows. Whatever its artistic merits, *Hellzapoppin'* ran for three highly profitable years.[4]

The increasingly thin line between a Broadway musical revue and an old-fashioned vaudeville show was mostly erased with sketch shows that had no discernable plot such as *Priorities of 1942* and *Keep 'Em Laughing*. The epitome of this trend was the show *Wine, Women, and Song*, which was billed as a "revue-vaudeville-burlesque show."[5] Several of these shows were priced more like old-time vaudeville than traditional Broadway fare.[6]

Besides relying on vaudeville type shows, Lee and J.J. still mounted revivals of increasingly cheap looking versions of old classics like *Blossom Time*, Gilbert & Sullivan operettas, *The Student Prince*, and the *Merry Widow*. In 1943, Lee Shubert produced another version of the *Ziegfeld Follies* which was successful largely because of the popularity of comedian Milton Berle. Agatha Christie's *Ten Little Indians* in 1944 was one of the last successful plays the Shubert brothers actively produced.[7]

They passed on investing in *Oklahoma!* which Lee dismissed noting, "Who wants a musical with a funeral in the second act."[8] In so doing, they missed out on one of the most artistically and financially successful musicals of all time. *Oklahoma!* played for more than 2,200 performances and continues to be revived and performed to this day on Broadway and around the country. The Shuberts' hard bargaining also lost them artistic and financial success in shows like *Guys and Dolls* and *My Fair Lady*.[9]

Former New York Times theater critic, Frank Rich, summed up the Shubert era: "Not a single one of the Shuberts' prolific productions – most of them vaudeville-centric revues and threadbare touring companies of tired European operettas – came anywhere near entering the canon of American entertainment, let alone American drama."[10] Instead, they continued to invest in shows, book tours, broker tickets, and lease theaters for the productions of others, but there were no new hit productions where either Shubert brother made the artistic decisions after 1946.[11]

They continued playing their old tricks when faced with new competition. The New Opera Theater had a production of *The Merry Widow*, which the Shubert-led United Booking Office (UBO) said could not be booked for lack of available theaters. The Shuberts promptly announced their own revival of *The Merry Widow*. When the New Opera Theater created their own four city tour on the West Coast and a New York engagement, the UBO now offered a route where the New Opera Theater production would follow the Shubert production in each city it would play.[12]

***

The 1940s also brought increased attention to one of the oldest hot button issues in live entertainment, then and now, ticket scalping. Scalping in the paper ticket era ranged from lawful licensed ticket brokers in a fixed location (often a hotel lobby) charging a regulated additional fee for their services to seedy characters standing on sidewalk in front of the theater selling tickets (often fake), for whatever the market would bear.

Sidewalk scalpers had been prosecuted in the larger cities as early as the 1870s.[13] Producers routinely denounced scalpers as pests who took advantage of the theatergoers.[14] By the 1890s, veteran producers like Daniel Frohman denounced scalpers as "nuisances" and kept close watch on the lobby and the surrounding sidewalks to bar any customer who purchased their ticket anywhere other than the box office.[15]

It was always hard to determine if the producers' complaints related more to the high prices being charged to customers, or the less noble concern that *if* higher prices were possible, that *they* should be the ones charging them.[16] Theater owners were suspected of collusion with the scalpers, since many of the worst offenders plied their trade inside the theater lobbies themselves.[17] New York City, and major markets like Boston and Chicago, responded by passing various ordinances barring sidewalk scalping and regulating where and when ticket brokers could sell and how much they could charge.[18]

The Shuberts were well established in the more legitimate end of the ticket brokerage business. Over time, they started, or acquired, licensed ticket brokerage businesses in key cities where they dominated the theater market. This way, they earned the full box office ticket price for their own hit productions, and whatever surcharges they were allowed by law as licensed ticket brokers.

About the only thing that could unite the Shuberts, the Syndicate, and the vaudeville kings were their loathing for ticket speculators that they did not control. Charles and Daniel Frohman routinely supported city and state attempts to limit ticket scalping. Erlanger declared war on ticket speculators in 1905. The Shuberts joined in by 1907 announcing that no tickets would be set aside for lobby agencies or sidewalk speculators. The war against scalpers was probably the only time Harrison Grey Fiske was on the same side as Klaw & Erlanger or the Keith-Albee Circuit.

This campaign could not prevail over the law of supply and demand. There was no market for ticket brokers for shows that flopped, but there remained great opportunity for profits for the hit shows.

Nonetheless, Marc Klaw vowed to fight scalpers to the "bitter end" in 1909.[19] Klaw worked with the Theater Managers Association (which did not include the Shuberts) to secure a New York City ordinance in 1911 barring ticket brokerage anywhere other than fixed business location. By 1918, Klaw claimed that speculators no longer existed.

***

The Shuberts were always suspected of more nefarious methods. Shady salesmen on the street weren't the only ones accused of taking a piece of the action when demand exceeded supply of the hottest tickets in town.

For nearly a century, the commercial theater industry was a cash business that sold paper tickets. Producers traditionally withheld a small number of tickets called "house seats" which could be given, or sold, to celebrities, politicians, friends of the producers, or anyone who was owed a favor. All producers relied on house seats to satisfy these sorts of last minute requests.

House seats play a legitimate role in ensuring the success of a play, but were also a recipe for bribery, embezzlement, tax evasion, or outright theft. The theatrical supply chain for house seats worked to raise ticket prices to the theater goer and to put money in the pocket of theater employees and owners.

The use of house seats to skim off additional profits became known as "ice." The term appears to derive from the financial settlement between producers and theater owners when producers were often cheated by extravagant deductions from gross income for "Incidental Company Expenses" or "ice".

One form of ice directly involved the producers who sold regular tickets or house seats well above face value to brokers or favored audience members, and simply pocketed the cash, and presumably never reported this additional income for tax purposes. Another version of the ice game involved box office personnel who did the same thing but shared some of the profits up the chain of command to their supervisors and further up the chain to the theater owners. By the 1930s, the higher ups were usually the Shuberts.

For decades, house seats meant a few tickets held back for emergencies. This grew over time, until in 1945, there were twenty-eight house seats reserved for each performance of the hit show *Harvey*.[20]

The Shuberts soon were demanding fifty or more house seats from the producers for hit shows like *South Pacific*. Congressman Emmanuel Celler denounced the Shuberts by name in 1950, noting that that this lucrative ticket allocation amounted to more than 20,000 tickets per year, over and above the rent paid by the producer. He announced Congressional hearings to explore how ice abused the public and amounted to tax fraud.[21] Celler thundered that the hearings were necessary because theater insiders were afraid to go public because of the fear of retaliation by the Shuberts.

The phenomenon reached absurd heights during the 1946 Philadelphia run of *Annie Get Your Gun* with Ethel Merman, when patrons at the box office were told that the first nineteen rows were sold out for all evening performances.[22] When the word got out, a furious Lee travelled to Philadelphia to dress down his nephew, Milton, who was in charge of operations at the theater. Miraculously the next morning, all seven thousand "missing" tickets were back in the box office and ready for sale to the public.

State and federal prosecutors investigated lower-level theater employees for ice, charging them with various combinations of theft, embezzlement, and tax evasion. The highest Shubert employee charged was the manager of Shubert central ticketing in 1963.[23] No Shubert family member was ever charged.

The real question was not just where did the tickets go but where did the money go? At one point, there was even a dedicated Shubert office in room 504 of the Sardi's building where the ice was collected and distributed.[24] A Shubert biography went so far as to suggest that Lee and J.J included periodic visits to Switzerland to hide and launder the ice that made its way to the top of the pyramid.[25]

The Shuberts also profited from the lawful ticket brokerage business, where tickets were resold by independent ticket brokers at a regulated profit in hotels or full-time brokerage location. At different times, they charged brokers a "license" fee to buy tickets for productions at Shubert theaters, a percentage of the proceeds the broker received, or both. Eventually, the Shuberts established their own ticket brokerage business, adding discrimination against independent brokers to the usual charges of profiteering when demand spiked for a hit show.

What Lee and J.J. did with their icy profits is not known. But when J.J.'s son, John, died in 1962, he left behind more than six hundred thousand dollars in cash in five different bank vaults, mostly in stacks of large denomination bills.[26]

***

By the late 1940s, Lee Shubert began to reflect on his legacy and started to think about publishing a memoir or an autobiography. He reached out to Ed Sullivan, the legendary entertainment reporter and radio-television host.

Sullivan got his start as a reporter in suburban Long Island New York doing local news and sports. He also worked in vaudeville as a producer and master of ceremonies of various shows in the 1920s and early 1930s.

Sullivan gradually evolved into a gossip columnist, becoming the chief rival to Walter Winchell in both print and on radio. In 1933, he wrote and starred in the film *Mr. Broadway*, giving viewers a behind the scenes view of the world of celebrities and performers.

In 1948, he began hosting the *Toast of the Town*, the television variety show that became *The Ed Sullivan Show* and ran until 1974. For more than a quarter century Sullivan made stars of Elvis Presley, the Beatles, and countless others who achieved national stardom.

Sullivan's on-air personality was stiff and awkward, but he was a major entertainment figure with a deep interest and background in live entertainment. Lee had met Sullivan while producing USO shows during World War II, and Sullivan had already recruited Lee to join several charity benefit committees for such causes as the New York Heart Campaign.

Sullivan, despite being a prominent entertainment personality, was an odd choice as a biographer or ghost writer. He had never written anything longer than a newspaper article before, or after, this proposed project. Sullivan also was extraordinarily busy with his many projects of his own. He wrote for the *New York Daily News*, worked many nights out of a booth in the El Morocco night club gathering show business gossip, appeared on radio and tv shows, and even made cameo appearances in movies. But he did have star power and great connections throughout the entertainment industry.

Lee paid Sullivan several thousand dollars in installments. They met on the project several occasions during the 1940s when their busy schedules permitted. Lee reminisced about people, places, productions, and battles from his past.

Sullivan produced the first two hundred sixty pages of a first draft by the summer of 1947. Most of the rest of the chapters of the eventual three-hundred-and-thirteen-page manuscript were finished by January 1948.

The book was titled *Mr. Lee* by Lee Shubert "as set down by Ed Sullivan", as if he had been the stenographer. Sullivan wrote a short preface, Lee wrote a separate introduction, and the rest of the book is set in Lee's first-person voice reminiscing about his lengthy career. The typescript copies of the unpublished manuscript that survive have handwritten edits, probably in Sullivan's hand.

Lee asked Sullivan to change the preface to indicate that Ed had suggested the book idea to Lee, despite the opposite being true. Lee also had delusions of grandeur and wrote to Sullivan about possibilities for a movie or Broadway musical production based on his autobiographical tale. He bragged to Sullivan that he couldn't give any publisher these ancillary rights and would handle those negotiations himself. By the summer of 1948, Lee was pushing his own publishing contacts, and increasingly asking Sullivan to use his industry connections, to find a newspaper or magazine to serialize the memoir and locate a friendly publisher to rush "Mr. Lee" into print.

Sullivan never produced a final text that pleased Lee. Lee complained repeatedly that Sullivan was evading his calls and messages. In an undated letter from late 1949 or early 1950, Sullivan finally wrote to Lee enclosing a completed copy of the manuscript: "As friends we certainly can work out a deal which will satisfy us both. . . . In the event that you wish to make other plans for the book, Lee – turn it over to somebody else. I'll appreciate learning of this from you directly."[27]

The memoir was never published, but manuscript copies survive in the Wisconsin (Madison) Historical Society and the Shubert Archives. It can charitably be described as episodic in nature. Lee is clearly the hero of his own story. He recounts the early family history, his saintly genius older brother Sam,[1] the feud with the Syndicate, labor issues, and an endless series of

[1]*Mr. Lee* perpetuates the fiction that Sam was older than Lee when he was in fact younger.

anecdotes about plays, musicals, stars, producers, and composers often with decades old dialogue of dubious accuracy.

While not actually good, and often factually incorrect, it accurately captures what was important to Lee reflecting on more than fifty years in the theater business. In Lee's mind, the Shuberts were always the good guys, the challengers, the up-and-comers who defied the odds and broke the Syndicate who previously held the industry in their thrall. According to Lee, business back in his youth was tougher, less genteel, and modern readers would be horrified at what was considered acceptable business behavior at the turn of the century.

Lee writes in his introduction of his early days in the theater business:

> "Many of the men who got in on the ground floor were hard. Many, too, were unscrupulous. All were ambitious for money and power. Their methods which would be shocking today were then merely routine. At the century's turn we were not as a people as sensitive of the rights of others, nor as sensitive to them, as we have grown to be in its middle years."[28]

Portions read like a 19th century melodrama where the villains (usually Abe Erlanger) roar lines like:

> "I'll drive you out of show business with Belasco. Stick with him, you fool, and every booking we've got with you is cancelled. From now on all your shows are barred from our theatres; and when you need attractions to keep going you won't get a single one – not if you get down on your knees and beg."[29]

Another chapter discusses the great vaudeville war where the Shuberts and Klaw & Erlanger failed to dislodge the vaudeville Combine and the UBO. Lee recounts how Erlanger's arrogance was fatal to the success of United States Advanced Vaudeville. In Lee's version, it was Lee who made the best of a bad situation and made peace with the Combine once he bought out Erlanger, ending the raid and the rivalry on lucrative terms.

Lee then turns his attention to Erlanger and, in his mind, finishes off the Syndicate with his open-door policy in the years that follow. Most of the rest of the book consists of feuds and friendship, long winded anecdotes about stars, shows, building, buying, and renovating theaters, as well as many conversations and quotes that no one can verify.

Recalling these tales and memories must have been cathartic for Lee and frustrating for Sullivan to set them down. Sullivan never succeeded in turning these recollections into a compelling read that met with Lee's approval. Lee characteristically finished his tale:

> "If you have enjoyed this book, I'm deeply pleased, because a lot of living, a lot of heartaches and a lot of happiness have gone into it. How much have I failed to tell? Surprisingly not very much. Some things can never be told."[30]

Regardless of the quality of the prose or the failure to publish the memoir, Lee and Ed Sullivan remained in touch socially and through charitable causes well into the 1950s. By then, Lee, J.J. and the Shubert Organization had to face more than memories and turn their attention to a new and existential crisis, the return of an old nemesis—the antitrust laws.

Act IV

The Breakup

13

Justice

The Shuberts faced their greatest legal challenge when the Justice Department began the antitrust investigation that led to the breakup of what remained of the Shubert empire. But first it was the movie industry's turn to feel the sting of the antitrust laws, setting the stage for theater's turn in the legal spotlight.

Hollywood was a prime target for the Antitrust Division of the Justice Department. In 1938, Thurman Arnold, a Yale Law professor and part-time adviser to the Roosevelt Administration, was appointed by the President to head the Antitrust Division with the mission to revitalize the Antitrust Division after decades of lethargy.

Arnold was already a minor celebrity in Washington circles for his surprise bestselling book *The Folklore of Capitalism*. At his confirmation hearings Arnold was grilled primarily about the parts of the book dismissing the antitrust laws as a fable to comfort people while the economy continued to evolve into industrial behemoths. The real surprise was that Arnold became the longest serving head of the Antitrust Division and achieved national renown for aggressively prosecuting cases against firms in the oil, automotive, aluminum, milk, tire, newsprint, steel, potash, publishing, and housing industries.[1]

During his time at the Justice Department, Arnold continued to publish books, give national radio addresses and interviews galore, as well as hold numerous press conferences every time the Antitrust Division brought a new case. He tirelessly promoted both himself and the cause of antitrust enforcement. He publicized how antitrust enforcement helped ordinary citizens get more for their money from the bullies and cheats who stole from them through illegal cartels and monopolies. Soon, this otherwise little-known law professor was the most prominent figure of the Roosevelt New Deal, with the possible exception of J. Edgar Hoover of the FBI.

The major Hollywood movie corporations owned the studios that produced the films, the distribution companies that licensed them to movie theaters, and often the movie theaters themselves. This made life difficult for an independent producer to get its films distributed or shown in theaters run by larger competitors. The studio system made it virtually impossible for an independent distributor to find the films or the theaters necessary to stay in business. Any actors, other than the very top stars, found they had very few options other than to stay put at the studio where they were under contract. And woe to the independent movie theater that wanted to show the most popular movies when their larger competitors owned a competing movie theater in that town or region.

Arnold brought a series of cases against the movie industry, challenging the very way the major studios did business. Four of Arnold's cases made it all the way to Supreme Court and resulted in landmark victories for the Government. The earliest case to reach the United States Supreme Court was the 1939 *Interstate Circuit* decision. In *Interstate Circuit*, the Court affirmed the criminal conviction of the leading studios for price fixing of tickets and colluding to stamp out independent theaters in the Southwest that competed with the studio-owned theaters.[2] The Supreme Court would hear a string of similar cases involving the movie industry in the 1940s and 1950s siding with the government, prohibiting different variations of these illegal cartels or schemes to monopolize at all levels of the studio system.[3]

The most important case against the movie industry was the *Paramount* litigation, named after the lead studio defendant, but included the eight largest Hollywood studios. For the first time, the government was trying to break up the studio system itself. The complaint sought to force all the so-called major studios (those owning production, distribution, and movie theaters), as well as the minor studios (typically lacking theater ownership) to divest their ownership of movie theaters and change their licensing practices to independent theaters.

The case made headlines because Arnold announced that he would personally lead the case. The complaint named all the major studies and over

130 individual defendants including stars such as Charlie Chaplin, Douglas Fairbanks, and Mary Pickford. The complaint also named numerous other Hollywood celebrities and business leaders who sat on the boards of the various movie studios, including James Roosevelt, the President's son.

The suit dragged on as the studios mounted both a scorched earth legal defense and elaborate public relations defense of the studio system. When the United States entered World War II in 1941, the *Paramount* case, like most of the other large antitrust cases, was put on hold in the name of national defense.

Long before the case would come to trial, Arnold left the Justice Department in 1943 for a federal judgeship. The quiet life of being an appellate judge did not suit him. After a few short, mostly unhappy, years on the bench, he entered private practice to found the quintessential Washington law firm, now known as Arnold & Porter.

His successors at the Antitrust Division continued to slog on with dogged determination after the end of World War II. The *Paramount* case went to trial without a jury before a three-judge panel of the United States District Court in Manhattan. The government won a smashing verdict with the District Court holding that virtually every part of the studio system was either an unlawful conspiracy or some form of unlawful monopoly.[4] In short, the Hollywood studios were both bullies and illegally ganged up on their smaller rivals.

Things didn't go any better for the movie studios on appeal in the Supreme Court. The Supreme Court affirmed the government's victory by a 7-1 vote.[5] Justice Frankfurter dissented, urging the Court to be even tougher on the studios than the majority opinion required.

For technical reasons, the case was remanded back to the trial court to determine whether the defendants were also guilty of creating a monopoly, and whether the studios should be broken up. In place of another trial that probably would go even worse for the studios, the defendants agreed to a group settlement, collectively known as the *Paramount* Consent Decrees. Under the *Paramount* Decrees, the defendants agreed to separate their exhibition, production, and distribution businesses. For Paramount itself, it agreed to divest at least 774 of its movie theatres and subject itself—and their now-separated distribution and exhibition businesses—to strict supervision to prevent future antitrust violations.[6] All the Hollywood studios agreed to similar changes that effectively destroyed what remained of the old vertically integrated studio system which had controlled the creation of motion pictures from their inception through the final version shown in the theaters.

The consent decree also prohibited the Paramount defendants from engaging in any of the unlawful practices described in the Supreme Court opinion. These practices include setting minimum prices, maintaining, granting, or enforcing exclusive contracts, making or performing any formula deal or master agreement, practicing block booking, or discriminating against smaller, independently owned circuits. Finally, the settlement allowed the Justice Department to monitor the defendant's records and behavior to ensure compliance with the agreement.

For over seventy years, the *Paramount* Consent Decrees continued to regulate the practices of the movie industry, ultimately leading to the dissolution (or merger) of most of the major studios. Over time, the industry began to question the necessity of the consent decrees in light of changing conditions, new technologies such as streaming, and the rise of the Disney studio, which was not bound by the decree.

In 2018, the Trump Administration Department of Justice launched an investigation to review the *Paramount* Decrees and determine whether the changing conditions in the motion picture industry warranted modification or termination of the Decrees.[7] This investigation culminated in a 2020 decision by the government to move to terminate the Decrees with a two-year sunset period in order to provide a smooth transition and avoid major market disruption.

The so-called *Paramount* Decrees did far more than just transform the movie industry. They also provided the antitrust handwriting on the wall for the fate of the Shubert empire.

***

Lee, J.J., and their attorney William Klein, carefully followed the *Paramount* case as it unfolded. Klein's younger partner, Milton Weir wrote to Klein as early as 1947 urging him to familiarize himself with the case and its potential to disrupt the live theater business.

J.J. Shubert was convinced that his antitrust troubles dated all the way back to 1940 with a complaint from Broadway producer Oscar Serlin to first lady Eleanor Roosevelt. Serlin was the producer of the 1939 Broadway smash hit *Life with Father*. *Life with Father* was a sentimental look at a strict, but loving, family in Victorian era Manhattan. Although quite tame by today's standard, *Life with Father* ran for 3,224 performances over an eight-year run. It became the longest-running non-musical play in the history of Broadway (then and now). It was adapted into a hit 1947 movie starring William Powell and Irene Dunne and featured the movie debut of a very young Elizabeth Taylor as one of the family's children.

Serlin was eager to tour *Life with Father*. However, he was not eager to pay the booking fees or share profits with the Shubert United Booking Office for what was expected to be a major hit on the road. He ultimately produced a tour that included eleven separate companies simultaneously touring across North America.

He complained vociferously about the Shuberts and the UBO to anyone who would listen, including in a published letter in *Variety* in 1941.[8] Whether or not he also complained to Eleanor Roosevelt is unknown, but there does not seem to be any correspondence between Mrs. Roosevelt and Thurman Arnold at the Antitrust Division or anyone else at the DOJ. Neither Arnold nor the Antitrust Division needed either Oscar Serlin or Eleanor Roosevelt to be interested in the Shuberts and the way their position in the theater industry strongly resembled the movie studios already under investigation.

Serlin was hardly the only person in the industry who had issues with the Shubert organization. Gerry Shoenfeld, the eventual co-head of the Shubert Organization always believed that the Nederlanders, who were partners with the Shuberts in the Detroit market, were the key instigators for the Antitrust Division's investigation.[9] Gossip columnists speculated that an unnamed Broadway "angel" investor had instigated the investigation.[10] That particular mystery has never been solved, but pales in comparison to the massive changes brought about by the eventual case against the Shuberts.

***

Regardless of who blew the whistle on the Shuberts, it is more likely that the *Paramount* litigation was the test case, and the Shubert investigation was the natural offshoot of the government's victory in the movie case. The antitrust investigation of the Shuberts appears to have begun in earnest in 1946 when lawyers from the Antitrust Division visited Lee to talk about the Shubert theater empire and the UBO.[11]

The investigation targeted the many sprawling corporations, entities, and entities comprising the Shubert Organization. Like the movie industry, the Shuberts had a dominant share of all levels of the theater industry: production, booking, and presentation on Broadway and on the road. Plays and musicals were produced in house, or purchased from independent producers, distributed (booked in theater parlance), and presented at theaters around North American either owned, managed, or contracted on an exclusive basis by the Shuberts.

Entire seasons of plays were offered to theaters, akin to the bundles of films licensed together by the movie studios. The legal issues included accusations of self-preferencing for Shubert productions and exclusion, coercion, and discrimination aimed at independent producers, bookers, and presenters. The fact that, at one time the Shuberts were the upstarts and the victims of the same type of conduct by the Syndicate, was now a mere vestige of the past.

***

The Shuberts also had Congress to worry about. Emmanuel Celler was a long time Congressman from New York City (but not the district covering Broadway), who was first elected in 1923. He served an astonishing fifty years in Congress. In 1950, he was at the height of his powers and was intensely interested in the evils of monopoly. Celler chaired the House Judiciary Antitrust Subcommittee and could investigate anything and anybody of concern. He relished both highlighting the harms monopolies inflicted on society and the resulting publicity for his crusade.

In February 1950, Celler announced that the subcommittee would investigate the monopolies that dominated the U.S. economy, including the Shubert theater holdings.[12] He railed against a host of industries, including both the motion picture studios and the Shuberts, to anyone who would listen including an hour-long appearance on *Meet the Press.* The Shuberts and their legal team devoured the printed transcript of the show, as if it were a play script, to look for clues as to what might come next from his subcommittee.

Even before the Justice Department acted on their long running investigation of the theater industry, Celler denounced the Shubert "stranglehold" on theater and told the world that President Truman himself had blessed his investigations. He told the press:

> "[The Shuberts] control over 60% of the theaters in New York and 90% throughout the country. They dominate the League [now known as the Broadway League], and arrange for the allocation of tickets to their own pet brokers, using kickbacks of all kinds."[13]

He also alleged that the Shuberts were tax cheats and that the people in the know were afraid to testify. He seemed more interested in the charges of ticket scalping, kickbacks, and the failure to pay income taxes, than the antitrust issues already under investigation by the DOJ.

Celler ultimately held antitrust hearings on the steel and liquor industries but never got around to the promised hearings on the Shubert monopoly. He later spearheaded the passage of the landmark 1950 Celler-Kefauver anti-merger legislation that is still in effect today. By this time though, the Justice Department had brought their own case.

***

Gerry Shoenfeld played a key role for the Shuberts in the antitrust litigation with the government long before he became the co-head of the organization with fellow lawyer Bernie Jacobs in the 1970s. Shoenfeld was born on the upper west side of Manhattan in a middle-class Jewish family where his father was a furrier. He graduated second in his class at NYU Law School in 1949 at a time when the leading Wall Street law firm did not hire Jewish attorneys. A family friend suggested that he speak with Milton Weir, a partner at the time in the firm Klein & Weir, whose biggest client was the Shubert Organization.

William Klein was the attorney travelling with Sam Shubert to Pittsburgh on the evening of the fatal accident in 1905. Klein had survived the crash of the passenger train with the Army freight train carrying its load of dynamite and had tried to save Sam after the crash and explosion. While J.J. Shubert and Lee quarreled about many things and rarely spoke, they gratefully rewarded Klein and his firm with their legal business over the next fifty years. Although the now elderly Klein was out of the office for several months in 1949 recovering from a serious illness, his partner Weir interviewed Shoenfeld and offered him a job at the salary of $40 a week.

Shoenfeld started at Klein & Weir in July 1949. Seven months later, in February 1950, the Justice Department brought its civil antitrust case to break up the Shubert Organization. No one at the firm had any experience in antitrust litigation. Gerry Shoenfeld, as the junior associate, was assigned to respond to the Government's complaint, and quickly became the point person navigating the existential threat to their biggest client. At this stage of his career, Shoenfeld had never met either Lee or J.J. in person.

Shoenfeld began to research antitrust law and figure out a strategy. For months he worked alone, before eventually bringing in the venerable Wall Street firm of Cravath Swaine & Moore to assist with the litigation. Later the firm also engaged a former senior staff member of the Antitrust Division to join the team. Despite his youth and inexperience, Shoenfeld was the architect of the Shubert defense for the next ten years, with Cravath often executing Shoenfeld's strategy, rather than directing it.

The Government accused the Shubert defendants of monopolizing the theatre business. The complaint named as defendants Lee Shubert, J.J. Shubert, Marcus Heiman, United Booking Office, Inc., Select Theatres Corporation, and the L.A.B. Amusement Corporation. The Shuberts controlled Select Theatres. Marcus Heimen was a fifty percent owner of the UBO and separately controlled L.A.B. Amusement, which was later dissolved before the end of the litigation.

The complaint focused on what was left in the Shubert empire -- producing legitimate theatrical attractions, booking legitimate theatrical shows in theaters throughout the United States, and owning and operating forty theaters in eight states. The complaint alleged that the key individuals and corporations comprising the Shubert Organization violated the antitrust laws through a conspiracy to:

compel other producers to book their legitimate attractions exclusively through the defendants, (b) to exclude others from booking legitimate attractions, (c) to prevent competition in the presentation of legitimate attractions, (d) to discriminate in favor of their own productions with respect to booking and presentation, and (e) to combine their power in booking and presentation in order to maintain and strengthen their domination in each of these fields.[14]

The Government sought to force the divestiture of the booking operation and the sale of key theaters in New York City and the road. In short, it sought a type of corporate death penalty for the Shuberts, akin to what the Justice Department achieved against the movie studios.

***

The Shuberts fought back first in the press, and then in court. Lee issued a bland statement carefully parsed by the legal team that announced:

[W]hen afforded the opportunity, we shall be able to demonstrate beyond all doubt that we have never engaged in anything that could possibly be construed as a violation of the anti-trust laws. Quite on the contrary, we shall be able to prove that we have operated with an efficiency that deserves the encouragement, rather than the criticism, of a government department.[15]

Later on in the statement, he struck a more exasperated tone of surprise that the government could find anything wrong with the conduct of the Shuberts:

It is incomprehensible that any part of the legitimate theatre which has made such an admirable uphill struggle for survival for many years past should be subjected to anti-trust litigation. Our company has sought to fill, capably and fairly, its particular role in the activities of this basic branch of the amusement world upon which so many, stagehands, musicians and others depend for their livelihood.[16]

Their long-time in-house lawyer, Milton Weir, added in his own statement:

Upon conferring with Mr. J.J. Shubert, I find that these charges are utterly unfounded and the public may be assured that they will be completely

> refuted. To classify the stage today as "big business" must come as a surprise to any one with even a slight knowledge of the theatre. All to[o] regrettably, it has become "little business", with numerous theatres that once housed legitimate productions being increasingly used now for radio, television and other media of entertainment.
>
> It is in fact not conceivable that what remains of the legitimate stage should be included in even the most sweeping "monopoly hunt."[17]

The Shuberts rallied their friends in the industry to support their cause. Billy Rose, the legendary impresario and columnist, weighed in with a column in more than 1,200 papers across the country about everything positive the Shuberts had done for show business.[18] The critic George Jean Nathan wrote a column for the *New York Journal-American* sarcastically titled "Let's Forget Russia and Fight the Shuberts."[19]

***

In civil cases in federal court, defendants have a short period of time after the filing of the case to either 1) answer the complaint by admitting or denying the allegations or 2) file a motion to dismiss arguing why (even if the facts were true) the allegations do not violate the law.

Either path requires reviewing a vast amount of facts, records, and law to determine what really happened, and whether there were any good-faith grounds to deny the factual or legal basis for the complaint. It also required understanding nearly a half century of the American theater and vaudeville industries.

The defendants filed a general denial contesting everything in the government's complaint, alleged that the government had waited too long in filing their case, and alleged their favorite legal theory, dating back to 1907, that the antitrust laws did not apply to the theater business. [20]

Simultaneously, the defendants entered in contentious negotiations with the government to see if they could reach an agreement to settle the case in a way that the Shubert organization could live with. Much had changed since the Shuberts had defeated the Syndicate, outlived the Vaudeville Combine, and survived the Great Depression.

The Shubert Organization of the 1950s was a quiet monopoly that was profitable but took few risks. It had mostly stopped producing new plays, musicals, or revues by 1949. It was content to make steady profits as a landlord and through booking fees. It still made investments in the new productions of others, but was no longer the all-encompassing octopus, the fearsome vertically integrated monopolist, of past years.

The Shuberts still owned and operated many theaters. They owned seventeen of the thirty-two Broadway theaters, seven of the nine Broadway houses in Chicago, all the Broadway theaters in Boston, and dozens of theaters in other cities across the United States. And they still had the UBO which they had acquired back in 1932 from the wreckage of the Syndicate and the collapse of vaudeville.

Within a month of the filing of the complaint, the head of the Antitrust Division talked about the possibility of a settlement backed up by the not so subtle threat that the government won ninety percent of the cases it brought. Lee and J.J. put on a good face and publicly stated that they weren't worried about the antitrust case.

The Shuberts received mostly favorable coverage from the press. The press noted the irony of attacking the Shuberts, who had broken the stranglehold of the Syndicate. Others hailed the Shuberts as the saviors of Broadway (from the Depression and the effects of the movies) and denied they were a predatory abuser of the public or the industry.

More sophisticated observers noted that, in several markets like Chicago, rival theaters had failed, converted to showing movies, or sold out to the movie industry (before the *Paramount* decree) leaving the Shuberts in a powerful position, but not of their own making. Less helpful theater managers and producers often spoke off the record, or provided documents, to the government, but were reluctant to speak out or publicly cooperate with the government for fear of retribution.

There were additional pending and threatened private antitrust cases. A plaintiff injured by illegal conduct by the Shuberts could sue for triple damages, plus attorney fees and costs. A 1949 antitrust case brought by a Chicago theater manager alleged that the Shuberts conspired to prevent him from booking successful attractions. That particular case ultimately settled for $40,000 but there would be dozens more if the Justice Department won their more significant case at trial.

The Shuberts stuck to their business-as-usual line and even acquired a one-third interest in the Music Box Theater in New York City from the estate of Irving Berlin. Artistically, they continued to focus on the long running tours of musicals and operettas on the road that were their perennial money makers.

***

Shoenfeld and the Cravath firm led the negotiations with the Justice Department. The real client was Lee Shubert, who would make the final call whether there would be a settlement or a trial. J.J. had minimal involvement at this stage, which was probably just as well for delicate negotiations of this sort. Meanwhile everything else in the case was slow walked by the defendants. The defendant filed the bare minimum of pleadings with the court, held off on motions to dismiss the case, and provided some documents, but not the usual array of pretrial discovery and depositions.

The government's playbook was a replay of the strategy from the *Paramount* case – pushing hard to get the Shuberts to agree to sell key parts of their operations to restore competition in the theater industry. The Shuberts and their lawyers studied everything about the prior movie industry case, trying to figure out whether they could win their case or negotiate an acceptable settlement.

The negotiations with the government began in earnest in the spring of 1951. Each conversation and letter was a detailed granular dispute about the definition of what was legitimate theater, what other industries competed with legitimate theater, and which theaters the Shuberts would have to sell to satisfy the government. In late 1951, the head of the Antitrust Division wrote to Milton Weir that any settlement must include "divestitures of substantial number of theaters." The lawyers for the defendants responded cautiously that their "clients were willing to agree to some extent to divestitures."

The lawyers for the Shuberts were increasingly concerned the United Booking Office "is the organization that was most liable."[21] While the lawyers for the Shuberts were arguing that the death of touring Broadway meant that the company wasn't the behemoth the government contended, Lee was touting the vitality of the road and the health of the company on a summer 1951 radio show on WINS in New York. While an awkward situation, the lawyers weren't wrong.

The situation on the road was in fact quite dire. Theaters were going dark, being used for other purposes, or just being sold and demolished for the value of the empty land. Some of the theaters that remained were only open five to ten weeks a year.

The negotiations intensified in 1952 into detailed discussions of which theaters in key markets like Chicago, Philadelphia, and Boston would be sold, and what changes the UBO would make so there would be no favoritism between Shubert and non-Shubert shows in terms of fees, service, and bookings.

By the end of 1952, the Shubert legal team reported to Lee that the Department of Justice had finally accepted everything necessary for a settlement, but that new senior staff in charge of the investigation insisted on additional theaters being sold, and that the UBO must also be spun off. The parties also continued to negotiate about whether there would be an arbitration mechanism created to resolve disputes over whether the Shuberts complied with the terms of any consent decree.

In February 1953 the Department of Justice persuaded the judge to set a trial date even as settlement talks continued. The Shuberts continued to provide information on a piecemeal basis when requested by the Justice Department to verify their position on settlement terms. By the summer of 1953, the case seemed on track for trial the following year, with both sides filing pre-trial briefs and meeting for a pretrial conference in Washington, D.C. in October of that year.

Avoiding a trial meant somehow finding a way to dismiss the government's entire case without having to complete lengthy and expensive discovery or the prospect of a potentially disastrous trial. Shoenfeld devised a plot twist worthy of a Broadway melodrama. He crafted a motion to dismiss that reflected his intelligence but revealed his lack of experience in antitrust matters. It raised several creative, but ultimately unsuccessful, theories why the case should be dismissed.

The Shuberts' main (and only real) defense focused on the ancient, but key, issue of whether the legitimate theater business was interstate trade or commerce, making it subject to the antitrust laws. Arguing that theater was in effect a luxury and an art, but not trade or commerce, may have worked in 1907, but by the 1950s this was an increasingly untenable proposition.

The Supreme Court had held that Major League Baseball was not interstate commerce in both 1923 and 1953.[22] The problem was that at the same time, the Court had held that touring vaudeville could be interstate commerce and that the making and distribution of motion pictures was most certainly interstate commerce in nature, decades before the *Paramount* decision of 1948. Other industries such as insurance, news gathering, real estate brokerage, and the practice of medicine had also been classified as interstate commerce and subject to the federal antitrust laws. The trend in the Supreme Court was decidedly against the Shuberts. Baseball's unique status looked more and more an anomaly.

Lee did not live long enough to see the unexpected (albeit temporary) victory of this theory in the district court. Lee Shubert died on Christmas day 1953 of complications from a stroke at the age of 78.[1] His funeral was held on December 28, 1953 at Temple Emanu-el, one of the leading and wealthiest congregations in New York City, but one that Lee had never joined and attended only on rare occasions. It was the same synagogue where Charles Frohman's elaborate funeral had been held in 1915.

Lee's funeral lasted a mere forty minutes and was attended by fifteen hundred mourners, including a who's who of the American theater and entertainment industry. Despite their decades of conflict, J.J. was so overcome with emotion that he could not attend the funeral. He instead attended the internment in the Brooklyn cemetery that immediately followed the service.

At the funeral, Lee was eulogized by Dr. Nathan Perilman, the head rabbi of Temple Emanu-el, in remarks that were reprinted in *Variety*. Dr. Perilman noted that: "Writers will delight in the story of his success and the theme will always be how the destroyer of giants achieved the status of a giant."[23] He conceded that Lee was not a demonstrative man, but could be a good friend

---

[2]His age is subject to some dispute given the many conflicting dates that exist for his birth and some conflicts as to the actual date of his death.

who "enjoying doing for others" quietly and without regard to race, religion, or condition of life.

The co-director of the Theater Guild, who worked with Lee on the national tours of Guild productions reminisced in the *New York Times* the following week that Lee could be a generous man, but also a tough adversary when crossed. He praised Lee for making theater more accessible to producers, actors, and the public across America and contrasted (perhaps through overly rosy glasses) the Syndicate's policy of profits through scarcity with the Shubert's policy of expansion. He quoted Lee as saying: "I'll tell you one of the secrets of our success. Because we own a number of theatres, the profits we earn on one theatre go to pay the losses on the others, so we can keep them all open."[24]

Lee's passing and the contents of his will (wildly speculated about in the press and the industry after his death) had dramatic consequences for the future of the Shubert Organization and the antitrust case that would shape that future. J.J. Shubert, himself aging and in poor health, was now in charge. However, Lee's final slight to J.J. came in his final will and trust, dropping J.J. as his executor, and installing Lee's nephew Milton as heir apparent to the Shubert throne. Moreover, Lee's will bequeathed his shares of the business and other substantial assets to a new charitable foundation. This led to decades of litigation and required special approval from the IRS to allow the new non-for-profit foundation to operate the very much for profit theaters that would remain in the Shubert orbit.[25]

***

J.J. was now the sole surviving brother of the founders of the theater empire. The younger brother had been relegated to upstate New York while Sam and Lee invaded New York City and shunted aside after Sam's death. The brother who had run, at most, half of the business for decades, was now in charge. He wasn't just in charge of a messy and fraught business, he oversaw a group of companies whose very existence was being challenged by the United States Department of Justice.

While still in mourning, J.J. received unexpected good news on the legal front. A mere five days after Lee's death, and two days after the funeral, Chief Judge Knox dismissed the case in its entirety, delighting J.J. and the defense team.[26]

Judge Knox ruled there were no grounds to distinguish the *Shubert* case from the Supreme Court's holdings that professional baseball was not interstate commerce. He further held that the presentation of Broadway and touring legitimate theater was inherently a local performance, like baseball, and did not constitute interstate commerce. Therefore, the antitrust laws did not apply.

The case was dismissed, but not over. The government appealed directly to the Supreme Court. In light of the Supreme Court's *Paramount* decision, the Shubert defense relied on the increasingly fragile argument that the antitrust laws applied to most of the modern national economy, but not to the theater industry. By 1954, Shoenfeld and the law firm had relocated to Lee Shubert's former apartment and operated effectively as the in-house legal department for the Shubert Organization.

In 1955, the Supreme Court surprised almost no one and unanimously held that live theater, like the movies and most other industries, was interstate commerce, and enjoyed no special immunity from the antitrust laws.[27] Baseball was left alone as the only modern form of live entertainment or sports deemed not subject to the antitrust laws and the Shubert case was sent back to the district court for trial.

Although the Supreme Court's opinion technically did not deal with whether the Shubert Organization violated the antitrust laws, the handwriting was on the wall. But J.J. was still not ready to settle. He told his lawyers, "How could they expect us to try and do business under a decree of this kind?" and "I am too old to try and learn a business of Mr. Marcus' [DOJ trial counsel] making. Therefore I want you to go to trial."[28]

The government's hand was strong in light of the Supreme Court's *Shubert* and *Paramount* decisions. The *Paramount* case had already ruled that the type of vertically integrated entertainment business that the movie studios used engaged in raised serious antitrust problems and that a single slice of the entertainment industry like the movies (or the theater) could be the proper focus of the case. Worse yet, the movie cases approved the divestiture of the businesses as the proper remedy for these antitrust violations which were very similar to how the Shuberts operated. The outcome was obvious to everyone, except for J.J.

14

The End of the Road

The government restarted negotiations with J.J. and agreed that any promises made by Lee were not binding on the Shubert organization. However, the Department of Justice insisted on a larger number of immediate theater sales, and additional forced sales if the defendant failed to meet certain deadlines.

The parties met in Washington, D.C. in the fall of 1955 to resume negotiations on the terms of a settlement while J.J. continued to fume to his lawyers back in New York that the case was "only an effort to put us out of business." J.J. used every occasion to throw his late brother Lee under the bus, writing that they "never saw eye to eye" and "were not on speaking terms for the past two decades."

According to J.J., everything was Lee's fault. J.J. claimed that he was "only interested in producing plays and looking after certain real estate properties" while Lee "took care of all the theaters in New York and also the booking of the theatres through the United Booking Office."[1]

J.J. claimed he never understood the booking office and that it was all Lee's domain. This claim is undercut by earlier correspondence from J.J. to his son John that "to try and destroy the booking office, would destroy our whole theatrical system of operation."[2]

J.J. alternated between truculence and self-pitying. In September 1955, he told his lawyer that there had never been any boycott or blacklist of shows that played in a non-Shubert house. He ended on a strangely ambiguous note: "What happened in the past, is past. My policy is entirely different, if there was any difference, from the late Mr. Lee Shubert."[3] He later complained to his lawyers "how could they expect us to try and do business under a decree of this kind?"[4]

Despite his bluster, it was increasingly evident that J.J. no longer had the stomach to fight. He was increasingly aware of the likely outcome and the mounting legal bills in continuing the fight. In addition, the lawyers were not eager to have the still volatile J.J. called as a witness by the government.

Depending on the day, J.J. wanted to go to trial, reach a consent decree, or sell the entire business. All this came at a time when the Shubert Organization was rarely producing new shows and was increasingly comfortable in the lucrative, but less exciting, business of being a landlord and theater owner.[5]

J.J. began to prepare for the inevitable. He admitted to his outside counsel at the Cravath firm that the "antitrust case was something that I could never quite understand."[6] He disposed of the once legendary UBO by September of 1955 and soon offered eight theaters for sale.

Even such a pared down version of the Shubert operation might not have survived a government victory at trial. The antitrust laws allow anyone injured by the unlawful acts of the defendant to sue for *triple* damages *plus* attorneys' fees and costs. Both Lee and J.J. knew this quite well, having sued, and been sued, under the antitrust laws many times before.

A government victory in an antitrust case brings with it an additional problem. Once a defendant has been found liable, it is presumed liable for that same conduct in any later cases. The Shuberts were likely to be hit with triple damages in any subsequent cases filed by victims of that same conduct. This potentially included most producers and presenters in theaters anywhere in North America.

All the new plaintiffs had to do is produce a copy of the judgment in the government case, and show they were in fact harmed by the same conduct and provide the court with a reasonable estimate of the damages it suffered. *Business Week* in 1950 dubbed these kind of cases "Easy Pickings."[7] J.J. continued to complain to his lawyers, and anyone else who would listen, that he was the victim of a government witch hunt by lawyers who never understood the theater business and who failed to appreciate the many real contributions the Shubert brothers made to the theater industry and the country.

J.J. and the rest of the defendants eventually agreed to the government's demands and signed a settlement in the form of a binding consent decree, committing them to dispose of their interest in more than a dozen theaters and bar their participation in the booking and ticketing sides of the business. The consent decree was signed by both sides and accepted on February 17, 1956 by the same judge who had initially dismissed the case. Other than accepting the jurisdiction of the court, the defendants did not admit that they had broken the law. Although the Shubert Organization was past its prime, the price was still high.

The consent decree included a requirement that the defendants dispose of their interest in numerous theaters located throughout the country within two years and that all transfers must be to buyers using the theaters for legitimate theatrical purposes. While the consent decree required the sale of the National Theatre, located in New York City, it was not perceived as a major loss because it was located out-of-the-way on Fortieth Street. The terms of the decree required the defendants to sell the New York St. James Theatre within two years and, if it was not disposed of within that time, the defendants were required to lease the St. James Theatre or the Imperial Theatre.

In May 1956, the Shubert defendants received a $2,100,000 bid for the St. James Theatre (the former Erlanger Theatre), satisfying that part of the settlement. The defendants also were required to sell the National Theatre within one year and two of the following theaters within two years: the Adelphi, Ambassador, Belasco, Elliott, Longacre, or Ritz. The Shubert Organization was also prohibited from acquiring more theaters in the future without government and court approval.

The consent decree required more forced sales across the country. The defendants had two years to sell the Colonial or the Shubert and the Wilbur Theatre in Boston. In Chicago, they were required to sell the Blackstone or Great Northern plus the Erlanger or Shubert theaters. In Cincinnati, either the Cox or Shubert Theatre had to go. In Detroit, the decree required the sale of either the Cass or Shubert-Lafayette theaters. In Philadelphia, the Locust or Walnut theaters plus the Shubert must be sold. If the defendants were unable to sell their interest in any theater within the required period, they would have to apply to the court for an extension or risk being held in contempt of court.

The Shubert defendants also were required to divest their interests in the UBO, which had already taken place. Booking had been key to the power of the Keith-Albee circuit, the Syndicate cartel, and eventually the Shubert monopoly by controlling the ability of producers to book a successful tour in North America and presenters to having a full schedule throughout the year. A central part of the case was the allegations that if a producer used a non-Shubert house in New York, the producer would have trouble finding theaters for a road trip. The Shubert defendants could not own, control, or have any financial interest in any ticket agency doing business in any city where the defendants operated a theater.

***

The divestitures still left the Shuberts a powerful theater owner in New York and the other cities where they retained theaters. But it also created a new three firm oligopoly that controlled most of the theaters in New York.

William McKnight, the heir to the Minnesota Mining and Manufacturing Company fortune (the company now known as 3M), created a new firm to purchase the St. James Theater on Broadway and Shubert theaters in Boston and Philadelphia. The new theater venture was called Jujamcyn Theaters after the abbreviation of the names of his children. McKnight ultimately paid for the theaters in cash. J.J., in hindsight, foolishly turned down an offer of 3M stock, which went on to triple in value over the next three years. McKnight later acquired four additional Broadway theaters. Jujamcyn was acquired by the Ambassador Theater Group (ATG) in 2023, bringing ATG's Broadway holdings to seven theaters.

The largest indirect beneficiary of the Shubert breakup was the Nederlander Organization. The Nederlanders had been in the live entertainment business since 1912 when David Tobias (known as D.T.) Nederlander began operating the original Detroit Opera House along with the Shubert Brothers. As they grew, the Nederlanders remained partners and clients of the Shubert, but also competitors on the road.

Over time, the Nederlanders came to own or operate multiple theaters in the Detroit area and took advantage of the government's forced divestiture of the Shuberts assets to expand from their original regional base. They entered the Broadway theater business by purchasing the Palace (once the pinnacle of big time vaudeville) from RKO in 1965. They quickly expanded in New York and on the road. They bid on Shubert properties subject to the consent decree but never offered enough to satisfy J.J. who thought they were trying to buy on the cheap.

The Nederlanders now own or operate nine Broadway theaters in NYC, all three of the large commercial theaters in downtown Chicago, as well as more than a dozen theaters, performing arts centers, and outdoor amphitheaters around the country.[8] The Nederlanders no longer own or operate theaters in the Detroit area, having sold their interests in 2021 to the English Ambassador Theater Group (ATG), which entered the US commercial theater business by buying out Jujamcyn.

Today these three firms own approximately seventy-five percent of the Broadway theaters. The Shubert Organization (through their foundation), the Nederlanders, and the Ambassador Theater Group (after buying the former Jujamcyn theaters) own thirty-three of the forty-one Broadway theaters. The importance of this high collective market share is enhanced by the fact that most of the remaining Broadway are used by Disney or various nonprofit theaters for their own productions. For most producers, leasing a Broadway theater means doing business with one of the big three.

***

J.J. dumped The UBO before the consent decree was even signed. The once mighty UBO was spun off to the non-profit League of Broadway Theaters (now The Broadway League) in a move that struck most observers as odd. Few trade associations, and none in the entertainment business, operated a business of this sort. This mismatched and under-resourced booking office, now with no connection to a producing or presenting entity, received a paltry $75 a week per show, and ceased to be much, if any, of a competitive bottleneck for producers or presenters. Most of the tours it booked were based on a simple revenue sharing formula between the producer and the presenting theater. The League shut down its booking office in the 1980s to focus on a more traditional industry association role of promoting Broadway as well as representing theater owners in labor and lobbying matters.[9]

Selling the required theaters on Broadway and on the road proved to be a lengthy and cumbersome process. J.J.'s son, John Shubert, organized the logistics of advertising and selling the theaters covered by the consent decree.

Under the terms of the settlement, most of the theaters had to be sold or leased as ongoing theatrical concerns, rather than for demolition or conversion for other business purposes. The idea was that competition could only be restored in the major cities if new theater owners could be introduced into the market. The government opposed to the Shuberts pocketing the cash with the new owners demolishing the theaters for parking lots or office buildings. This worst-case scenario might actually increase the Shuberts' power in some markets if the sale decreased the number of viable options for live theaters in those cities.

The divestiture process was arduous work but was welcomed by John. In 1960 he told an interviewer: "The consent decree has made my life easier. In fact, we kept selling theaters, even beyond the terms of the decree."[10]

Real estate brokers were hired in every city to work with prospective buyers. Ads ran for months in *Variety* and major newspapers in the cities covered by the consent decree. The consent decree also required that the Shuberts provide the DOJ with copies of the advertising, make periodic progress reports on the sale of each theater, and submit any correspondence with buyers and brokers to verify compliance.

Since the consent decree required court approval for each sale, but did not specify a price, negotiations were contentious. Any buyer, deadline extensions, or changes to the consent decree had to be approved by the Court. But not even the Justice Department and the federal courts could force a buyer to buy a piece of property they did not want.

Several of the theaters that had to be sold were in dire need of repair and sat empty most—if not all—of the year, hardly an enticing opportunity to most prospective theater buyers. Although the Shuberts were under the gun of the consent decree, they generally set the highest justifiable price for each theater they were forced to sell and refused to lower the offering price. Most of the interested buyers were looking for fire sale bargains.

For example, the Shuberts were particularly suspicious of the initial bids from the Nederlanders, who seemed to be offering bargain basement prices. For example, the Blackstone Theatre in Chicago was being offered for $400,000, the Nederlander's bid was only $182,000. Neither side would budge and the theater remained on the market in the 1960s at the same offering price.

The Cass Theater in Detroit presented a different sort of problem. J.J. told the government that he was only a part-owner of the theater and could not sell without the agreement of his co-owner, the local presenting partner. Lee and J.J. had built the Cass in 1926 with a local partner, E.D. Stair, an occasional producer, real estate developer, and the owner of the Detroit Free Press. J.J. contended (not unreasonably) that the theater could not be sold without the co-owner's permission, consent decree or no consent decree.

In addition, the Cass was in decline, as was downtown Detroit in this era. In 1958, the Cass presented shows for only seven weeks and sat dark the rest of the year. When J.J. reached an impasse with Stair's heirs, he petitioned the federal court for an exception to the decree, arguing that it was commercially impossible to comply. The court was unimpressed. It denied the request holding the defendant had not clearly shown a "grievous wrong evoked by new and unforeseen conditions."[11]

Eventually the Shuberts sold its interest in the Cass Theater back to Stair's son, who held on for several more years until the Cass was converted into a movie theater. By the 1970s, the Cass was showing pornographic films and closed in March 1971. It briefly reopened to show international films, then closed again for good in 1975, and was demolished for a parking lot.[12]

***

By 1958, the Shubert Organization disposed of their interest in ten theaters but sought a modification to the consent decree for two remaining properties. The problem was that the Shubert defendants still owned both the Blackstone and Great Northern Theatre in Chicago and the Cox and Shubert Theatre in Cincinnati after the deadlines established in the original consent decree had passed.

In Chicago, they eventually sold the Erlanger Theatre to an independent theater presenter. The Harris and Selwyn Theaters were sold to Michael Todd, the Oscar winning movie and theater producer who was Elizabeth Taylor's third husband.[13] Bowing to the commercial realities, the government and the court eventually allowed the Shuberts to keep the Blackstone Theatre.

There were no takers for the Great Northern, the final required sale. The Shuberts were saved by a more unusual buyer – the federal government itself.

After years of fruitless advertising, occasional showings, and unsuccessful negotiations, the Shuberts finally caught a break. In the early 1960s, the federal government used its powers of eminent domain under the United States Constitution to take over and demolish the theater to build a new federal courthouse.

This welcome, but unforeseen, development relieved the Shuberts of having to find a buyer for the ageing, and no longer commercially viable theater. It also guaranteed them the eventual payment of the fair market price, even if that was little more than the value of the real estate, minus the cost of demolition.

Selling the Cincinnati theaters took even longer and presented the greatest hurdles. The Shuberts had to dispose of one of two adjacent theaters, the Cox and the Shubert. At least one of the theaters had to remain an ongoing theatrical venture under the terms of the decree.

Neither building was particularly attractive as an ongoing theater. Years of advertising yielded no firm offers that satisfied the Shuberts or the conditions of the consent decree. One proposed lease for the attractive Shubert theater was approved by the government, but the new operator ultimately pulled out of the deal.

Eventually, the court waived the requirement that one of the theaters be used as an ongoing legitimate theater. The process took so long that there was still no sale in sight when J.J. died in 1963. The government finally released the Shuberts of the obligation to sell in March of 1964. The Shubert, and the adjoining Cox theater were eventually demolished for a parking lot. The Shubert monopoly in Cincinnati ended with a whimper, but so did the ability to see Broadway theater in downtown Cincinnati for years to come.

The Shubert Organization also faced a private treble damage antitrust case from a competing theater operator in Philadelphia.[14] This new antitrust case alleged that the Shuberts had prevented him from booking first class theater attractions. Although the settlement with the Justice Department technically was not an admission of guilt, it nonetheless provided an easy roadmap of what to allege in this later case. A confidential, but substantial, settlement ensued after several years of pretrial wrangling.

***

Decades later, the Shubert Organization successfully filed a motion seeking permission to manage the National Theatre in Washington, DC for a five-year period. This time, the Antitrust Division did not oppose the application. The government advised the court that granting the application would foster, rather than restrain, competition.

The government argued that if the Shuberts attempted to use the right to manage the National Theater to gain a competitive advantage, the provisions of the original 1956 consent decree would provide an adequate remedy. The court determined that the consent decree was still in force and that the Shubert organization had shown that its proposed management of the theater contributed to increased competition in the nation's capital.

The consent decree was again modified in 1981 to eliminate the prohibition on the Shuberts operating a theatrical ticket agency. The Shubert organization began a "group sales" division, which sold tickets to shows appearing in Shubert theaters and in theaters operated by Shubert's competitors.

The Shubert Foundation became the sole owner of the remaining Shubert theaters following the final settlement of the estate of Lee Shubert. It was so unusual for a non-profit foundation to own and operate a for-profit business theater chain that a special letter ruling was needed from the IRS to allow the Foundation to remain in the theater business.

Finally, the consent decree simply expired. This left the commercial arm of the Shubert Foundation (the entity owning the theater under the terms of Lee's will) free to compete in the theater business as it sees fit, without antitrust constraint or court supervision. The Shubert Organization had been subject to government investigation or court supervision to some degree for more than thirty years. In comparison, ATT, the former telephone monopoly, was subject to its court supervised antitrust consent decree for a mere twelve years after its agreed-upon breakup in 1984.

The Shubert antitrust litigation represented the end of an era. For the first time in nearly seventy years no single company or organization controlled the ownership, booking, or presentation of legitimate theater in New York City or on the road. The cartels and monopolies that had characterized vaudeville and the legitimate theater since the late 1800s were now a thing of the past.

What followed was a golden age of theater, both artistically and competitively. Perhaps the two developments were linked as the critics of the Syndicate and the Shuberts had always contended. The age of true theatrical monopoly was over, but the problem of the abuse of corporate power in live entertainment is still very much with us today.

Act V

The Mergers

15

The New Bottlenecks of Broadway

Competition issues continue to affect today's theater industry. Competition, or the lack of it, affects what it means to produce a play or musical, own a theater, book a production in New York or on tour, or present legitimate theater on Broadway and the road.

Producing theater remains an alluring business despite its many risks. Most of the currently active commercial producers on Broadway came of age in the 1980s and 1990s. They replaced a legendary generation of showmen such as David Merrick, Cy Feuer, and Hal Prince who took the financial risks to produce what we now think of as the golden age of musicals in the 1960s and 1970s.

Most Broadway producers are individuals, or small partnerships, who create a producing office to make the artistic, management, and financial decisions to bring a promising script to the stage. They typically raise money from investors on a show-by-show basis.[1] Only the Disney Theatrical Productions self-finances Broadway and touring productions as part of a large corporate structure.

Broadway investors can be friends or family of the producers, wealthy angel investors interested in shepherding great art to the stage, or affluent individuals seeking to diversify their investments in a fun and high-profile way. Bundlers also gather smaller investors together to pool substantial sums for a new production or a revival of an old favorite. Substantial investors may receive a producer or associate producer credit but rarely make any of the artistic decisions for the show.

Every show needs a theater, and Broadway theaters are a scarce commodity. Only forty-one theaters qualify as Broadway theaters, in the sense of being eligible for a Tony award for best musical or play.[2] The Shubert Foundation currently owns seventeen theaters, the Nederlanders own or operate nine, and the Ambassador Theatre Group from the UK owns seven theaters, five of which it acquired from Jujamcyn in 2023. The remainder include three theaters owned or managed by non-profits theater companies that present a subscription season of limited engagements, several individually owned theaters, and one leased for ninety-nine years by Disney.

In 1995, Disney leased and renovated the New Amsterdam Theatre on 42nd Street from the City of New York, which owns the then-dilapidated landmark theater built in 1903. The New Amsterdam was the headquarters of Klaw and Erlanger and in later years the UBO before it was sold to the Shuberts. It operated as a Syndicate house for its first three decades and was the home of the perennial money maker, the *Ziegfeld Follies*. Disney premiered the smash hit *The Lion King* at the renovated New Amsterdam and has used it as the home of several of its productions including *Aladdin* and *Mary Poppins*.[3]

New productions must vie for the limited number of available Broadway theaters. Familiar competition issues remain, with industry observers concerned about different aspects of self-preferencing. Larger theater owners acting as both producers and landlords have the incentive to favor their own productions over those of competing producers. When Broadway theater owners also own or manage theaters on the road, issues of self-preferencing and tying remain a concern. Many fear that renting a Broadway theater may be conditioned explicitly, or implicitly, on the use of that company's theater in another city. From a producer's perspective, the price of the rent is always too high and comes with too many strings attached.

***

One of the many changes from the old days is the lack of a single booking monopoly that determined the fate of a tour and the chance to turn a profit. Today, there is no single United Booking Office serving as the linchpin of a theatrical cartel or monopoly. Booking remains a critical and lucrative part of the industry but is dispersed among several competing external and internal booking agencies.

The dissolution of the Shubert-owned UBO created a power vacuum. Initially, the vacuum was filled by two unlikely groups: The League of New York Theatres and Producers (League) and the Legitimate Independent Theatres of North America (LITNA). LITNA opened its own booking activities, while the League incorporated the Independent Booking Office (IBO) in 1956 as a central booking office and successor to the UBO for touring shows.

The IBO began operations the following year. A great deal of conflict between the two groups ensued, but the IBO proved to be the more successful booking agency. The two groups consolidated under the IBO name. This merger ultimately helped to better maintain the flow of shows to theaters throughout the United States and Canada in the post-Shubert monopoly era.

For the next twenty years, the IBO continued its booking operations with the purpose of improving conditions for touring road shows. As the market changed in the 1980s, the IBO gradually ceased its booking operations and transformed into a computerized national clearinghouse for performing arts touring information.

This new clearinghouse system did not last very long. The IBO quickly dissolved due to increasing costs and a declining need for its services as new independent booking agents entered the market. The IBO's assets were transferred to the League to form a professional resource center to assist producers and presenters on Broadway and on the road.

The booking industry quickly evolved to become more competitive. It was no longer the major bottleneck to competition the Syndicate and the Shuberts had exploited. One of the first new entrants was an independent booking agent named Irving Siders who previously was a talent manager. Others soon followed. One new booking agency was a familiar name – the William Morris Endeavor agency bearing the name of the legendary vaudeville talent agent-that booked theatrical tours through the 2011-12 season. A later entry was Alan Wasser Associates that booked the musicals of Cameron Mackintosh (*Les Misérables*) and Andrew Lloyd Webber (*Cats, The Phantom of the Opera*). Over time, other booking firms entered the field such as Bond Theatrical, The

Booking Group, Broadway Booking Office, NAMCO, Columbia Artists Management Inc. (CAMI), The Road Company, Avid Touring, and On the Road.

New booking agencies continued to form when key employees left existing firms to form their own agencies, often taking clients with them. Several of the booking agencies had close ties or ownership links with leading producers, giving them a natural pipeline for new plays and musicals, as in the days of Charles Frohman and the Syndicate. A handful of booking agencies failed, were sold, or merged into existing firms. Standing apart from the fray is Disney, which created an in-house booking department, handling the booking of the touring productions of Disney theatrical hits such as *The Lion King*, *Beauty and the Beast*, *Frozen*, and many others.

In any given year, there typically are three or four leading booking agencies that book tours for most of the shows on the road across North America. Booking fees can still be hefty and range from weekly flat fees running into the thousands of dollars and/or an agreed percentage of profits. But the bad old days where booking operated as the choke point to monopolize the presentation of live theater on the road are long gone and unlikely to return.

***

The theater industry was devastated by the COVID pandemic. Broadway went dark on March 12, 2020, and remained closed until September of 2021. Broadway theater returned, led by three of the big hit musicals from before the pandemic – *Hamilton*, *Wicked*, and *The Lion King* which simultaneously reopened on September 14, 2021. They were quickly joined by *The Book of Mormon*. Interestingly, all were produced by different organizations.

Other shows never opened at all because of the pandemic where finances were inadequate to hold on for the two years of public health closures. Some pre-pandemic productions never reopened where sales were insufficient to justify reopening. Other shows reopened but closed relatively quickly because audiences hadn't returned in sufficient number. One show, *Harry Potter and the Cursed Child*, used the pandemic to retool from a two-part, five-plus-hour production into a shorter three-hour, one-part production and was able to increase ticket sales post-COVID.

By April 2022, twenty-three shows were back on Broadway. A revival of *The Music Man*, starring Hugh Jackman and Sutton Foster, set a post-pandemic Broadway box office record with $3.5 million in a single week and had lines around the block for the limited day of sale tickets. But it was a long slow economic recovery with Broadway box office receipts not exceeding pre-COVID levels until spring 2025.[4]

After a record nearly 15,000 performances over thirty-five years, *The Phantom of the Opera* closed on Broadway on April 16, 2023. *Phantom* continues to play around the world and began yet another tour in November 2025.[5] *Phantom* was an unusually successful example of a blockbuster musical of the 1980s that is no longer a viable economic model. It was an immensely expensive visual spectacle that no producer would mount today. The producers of *Spiderman: Turn off the Dark* found out the hard way in 2011 with a reported $75 million budget. The show closed in 2014 never recouping this record-setting initial outlay.

Even a more modest musical today typically involves a still hefty twenty to twenty-five million dollar budget. Such shows normally would not break even until two years or more of near sellouts because of the high costs of mounting and running a Broadway show. Even the most successful shows are vulnerable to external events, such as competition from streaming services, changing audience tastes, weather, the economy, and more unforeseen events like COVID or terrorism. The enormous success of a *Lion King*, *Wicked*, *Hamilton*, *Les Misérables*, or *Phantom* disguises the fact that eighty percent or more of shows each season lose all, or nearly all, of their initial investment, regardless of their artistic merit.

***

Live commercial theater has become increasingly dependent on adaptations from existing intellectual property as well as the revival of past hits and beloved classics. Most producers are thrilled to work on a quality theatrical version of a well-known property with a potentially built-in audience. For example, Disney adapts its movies for the Broadway stage followed by highly successful tours.

The story of *The Wonderful Wizard of Oz* and its many adaptations is an example of the reliance of modern Broadway on existing brands and intellectual property. The Oz saga began as the 1900 children's book co-written by L. Frank Baum, a former actor, theater producer, and playwright. The book became a huge bestseller and followed by thirteen sequels.

Baum and his co-author adapted the original book into a musical called *The Wizard of Oz* that premiered on Broadway in 1902 for more than 300 nights, and then toured on and off until 1911. Baum even contemplated a theme park based on the Oz series that never came to fruition.

Long after Baum's death, MGM Studios released the hit technicolor movie musical version of *The Wizard of Oz* in 1939, featuring an outstanding cast, and making a star out of Judy Garland in the role of Dorothy. This adaptation of the first Oz book was a huge hit in a year that has been described as the finest in the history of Hollywood, featuring such classics as *Gone with the Wind, Wuthering Heights, Of Mice and Men, Dark Victory, Ninotchka, Goodbye, Mr. Chips*, and *Mr. Smith Goes to Washington.*

Oz returned to Broadway in 1974 with a musical adaptation called *The Wiz*, starring an all African American cast. *The Wiz* ran for four years on Broadway and toured North America for years. *The Wiz* also was revived on Broadway in 1984 and 2024.

The success of *The Wiz* on stage led to a 1978 hit film of the same name with an all-star cast including Michael Jackson, Lena Horne, Richard Pryor, and Diana Ross. Both the stage musical and the movie musical also spawned successful cast albums.

In 1995, a new author, Gregory McGuire, created a new darker, more adult themed alternate history of the story of *The Wizard of Oz* called *Wicked: The Life and Times of the Wicked Witch of the West. Wicked* tells a complex story set before Dorothy arrives in Oz. It focuses on the friendship between Glinda and Elphaba, and how Elphaba was branded as "wicked" by a power mad Wizard seeking to control his land and people by creating scapegoats and enemies for them to hate.

This brilliant, but dense, novel was a huge hit which led to almost inevitably to the 2003 hit musical *Wicked*, which began its pre-Broadway run at the Curran Theatre in San Francisco. Overall, *Wicked* won three Tony awards and continues to play on Broadway and in London today. It remains a staple of Broadway series across North America and around the world more than twenty years later. It has been seen on stage by more than 63 million people.

The most recent installment is a two-part movie musical version of *Wicked*, totaling more than double the length of the Broadway musical it is based upon. Part I was released in late November 2024, grossing $358 million worldwide in its first ten days in theaters, followed by even the equally successful *Wicked: For Good* in November 2025. The two parts together quickly became the highest grossing movie musical of all-time exceeding $1 billion in total box office revenues.

The movies have helped, rather than hurt, ticket sales of the Broadway and touring version of the show. *Wicked* (the movie) has introduced a whole new generation of fans to the show who may never have had the chance to see the musical on stage and created new demand for the show in New York and on the road.

While only a select few musicals can match the success of *Wicked*, many of the other recent and upcoming Broadway productions are also adaptations of movies, books, recordings, popular culture, or revivals. Some are original works. Some are stunning works of art, regardless of their source material. But all raise the same questions of how the business of Broadway and the quest for profits shape what we see on the stage in New York, Chicago, Des Moines, and throughout North America.

***

Why would producers and their investors risk so much on Broadway where there are few winners and even fewer runaway smashes? Besides commitment to high art and confidence in one's artistic and commercial instincts, producers have found ways to limit their risks. One way to reduce risk is to open the production for an out-of-town run prior to opening on Broadway, a tried-and-true technique dating back to the 19th century productions of Charles Frohman.

The real answer lies on the road. A high-quality Broadway musical or drama can have a very profitable tour that offset the losses on Broadway, as long as the show receives decent reviews and can be booked in enough theaters for enough weeks to generate substantial profits. In general, the tour production is separately capitalized and reconfigured so the sets, props, costumes, and other equipment can travel on trucks (rather than the railroads of yore) and be easily loaded in and out of the theaters across North America.

The road offers two enticements that make most tours less risky and more predictably profitable than a Broadway production. First, most cities outside of New York have long since switched to a subscription model, where subscribers buy a season long Best of Broadway series of six or more shows for any given year, offering a mix of musicals and dramas, including new shows on their first tours and returning favorites.[6] In addition, road theaters are often larger than their Broadway counterparts.

The more successful presenters build a subscription base for the whole season. This enhances the chance that the engagement will sell enough additional tickets to cover the weekly guarantee owed to the producer and generate additional profits that are split between the presenter and the producer. Each city also typically offers additional shows "off" subscription to fill holes in their schedule where the producers (rather than the presenting theater) bear all, or most, of the financial risk.

There are approximately seventy cities in North America that can fill their theater for a week or more for a tour of a Broadway show. Each presenter typically offers the producer a guaranteed amount per week (often hundreds of thousands of dollars) plus a percentage of profits after local expenses. If the producer creates an artistically appealing show with an operating budget significantly less than the guarantee (and with the prospect of some additional share of profits), they can recoup their total investment in many cases in months, rather than years.

Higher profits, with greater risk, can also be obtained through what is called a "four-wall" arrangement. In a four-wall the producer foregoes a guarantee, rents the theater, and retains the revenues after reimbursing the presenter for certain agreed upon costs. "Terms" deals fall somewhere in the middle where the producer and the presenting venue split all the revenues on a sliding scale at an agreed upon percentage.

Unlike the old days, the national tour ideally consists mostly of longer engagements, until the demand for week and multi-week engagements has been exhausted. The national tour of the largest markets can be a highly profitable multi-year prospect, compared to a hit Broadway production which might have barely broken even in the same time period.

Modern tours typically continue playing the kind of smaller and mid-sized markets that once helped connect the stops in larger cities and shorten the jumps in the old days. In rare cases, a second touring company begins while the first tour is still making the rounds of the largest markets.

Unlike the first national tour, the route of later touring companies of most successful Broadway shows normally consists of one night and split week engagements in smaller markets. Some of these later tours may also be a less expensive, or even a non-equity, version of the original tour. Other than the ticket prices, and the use of trucks instead of railroads, these types of lengthy and profitable tours would have made sense to both the Syndicate and Shuberts.

Occasionally there are blockbuster hits with multiple touring companies crossing North America for years, if not decades. But today, this means at most two to four touring companies, and not the fourteen separate touring companies Charles Frohman used for his 19th century hit *Hazel Kirke*.

At some point, the producer will also begin licensing local productions of the musical or drama. Some Broadway productions never tour for a variety of reasons. Instead, these shows live on in licensed local productions on the season subscriptions at the larger residential non-profit theaters across North America in award-winning theaters like the Goodman and Steppenwolf Theatres in Chicago, Berkeley Repertory, La Jolla Playhouse, and the Guthrie in Minneapolis. Later on, there will be local productions by smaller theater companies, amateur groups, and schools for many years to come, all of which generate royalties for the producers and their investors.

In a few cases, producers will simply skip Broadway and make their money on the road. For a revival of a beloved show this offers the predictability and profitability of a tour without the larger investment and risk of a Broadway production. If all goes well, the production can always be remounted on Broadway or play Broadway on a short-term basis as part of a tour. If the timing of a limited Broadway run can be arranged to fill a hole in the tour, there can be fewer dark nights and greater revenues.

All of these scenarios depend on being able to book the show on the road for long enough to make a profit. In 2019, the last full year of theater before the pandemic, tours generated $1.633 billion in ticket revenues compared to $1.758 billion on Broadway.[7] The most successful shows also have productions in the England and other international markets and the occasional tour outside of North America.

***

The most serious competition issues in legitimate theater today now relate to the presenter side of the business, the actual theaters in markets across North America which present the shows and are the most predictable flow of profits for a producer. One company, Broadway Across America (BAA), owns or operates over forty theaters in major and mid-sized markets in the United States, Canada, and Mexico. It is difficult for a Broadway shows to mount a successful North American tour without booking some BAA cities.

In addition to BAA there are two groups of presenters. The other is the Independent Presenters Network (IPN), a consortium sharing best practices of forty presenters, theaters, and presenting arts centers.[8] The IPN includes both the Nederlander organization and the Ambassador Theatre Group. Either BAA or IPN can sustain a national tour, but ideally the most successful tours include both.

BAA was created through a lengthy series of mergers and acquisitions that largely flew under the antitrust radar. BAA originally gathered information about Broadway shows for Clear Channel Communications, a major radio, media, and live entertainment conglomerate. BAA became a powerful theatrical presenting company by acquiring Pace Theatrical Group, a well-respected presenter of touring Broadway. BAA's continued acquisition and management of local venues and Best of Broadway Series fueled its continued rise to the top.

In 2005, Clear Channel's live entertainment unit renamed itself Live Nation, making BAA part of the concert giant Live Nation for a brief time. In January 2008, Live Nation sold BAA to Key Brand Entertainment, which continues to own it today.

Key Brand Entertainment is now known as the John Gore Organization, named after its founder John Gore. If Clear Channel's operation of the major theaters in key cities across North America raised some antitrust concerns, then the continued growth of BAA in its new form should raise similar concerns. BAA now controls more than forty-five regional markets on the road and has at least 475,000 subscribers, making it an essential facility for most successful tours.[9]

Touring productions rely on BAA for all aspects of a given show, ranging from receiving capital for the Broadway run from the company's investment subsidiary to booking BAA venues for their tours, a practice akin to those of the Syndicate and Shuberts in the days when they dominated live theater.

The John Gore Organization continues to grow through acquisitions and expansion into related theater businesses. After acquiring BAA, the John Gore Organization also acquired Broadway.com; Group Sales Box Office, the Broadway Channel; and BroadwayBox.com, a marketer of discount show tickets. The company also has a film and television division that expanded in 2025 by acquiring English horror studio Tyburn Films.

Although there are many theaters across the country that are not part of BAA, it can be difficult for shows desiring to create a successful tour without doing business with BAA. Despite these concerns, there only one publicly known antitrust investigations or litigation against the John Gore Organization or BAA. In 2026, the Justice Department investigated, but declined to prosecute BAA for an agreement with "Company A", widely understood to be ATG, for agreeing not compete with each other in dozens of cities of the road. History suggests that if BAA continues to grow it may well eventually face the same broader antitrust challenges that the Syndicate and Shuberts confronted.

***

The enormous number of non-commercial theaters throughout the country face an even more fraught market. COVID, and the economic shutdown that followed, had devastating consequences for hundreds of smaller theaters that closed for good. As subscriptions, public support, grants, and donations have declined, theaters have cut productions and staff. Single ticket sales have also fallen and more alarmingly become less predictable last minute impulse purchases. This creates a smaller and less stable revenue stream. To make matters worse, corporate, foundation, and government giving has also declined. Donors have shifted funding toward other causes. Federal funding for the arts has been slashed by the second Trump Administration. State and local funding for the art remains precarious.

The relationship between commercial and non-commercial theaters has also shifted, providing a new possible lifeline to regional theaters across the United States, but carrying with it the potential to change the nature and content of the plays and musicals that make it to the stage. There is a long tradition of Broadway shows premiering at non-profit theaters before transferring to the Broadway stage and eventually embarking on a national tour. Both *Rent* and *Hamilton,* began in non-profit New York theaters before going to Broadway. Other shows like *The Outsiders, Six, Waitress*, and *August Osage County* premiered in non-profit theaters outside of New York.

Numerous plays and musicals over the years have started at theaters like the La Jolla Playhouse near San Diego, and the Goodman and Steppenwolf theaters in Chicago. In addition, Broadway producers search the country for exciting and successful new work that could be brought to the Broadway stage.

What is new is the increasingly popular practice of commercial Broadway producers providing direct funding (usually called enhancement money) to a non-profit theater to produce an early version of a project with significant commercial potential. The use of enhancement money goes back to the 1970s, when commercial producers partnered with the non-profit Arena Stage in Washington, D.C. to produce an early version of *The Great White Hope*, later a hit on Broadway and on tour. But the practice has become more routine, and the enhancement money can often to be the difference between a balanced budget and a money losing season.

Under this model, the local production is larger, fancier, and more fully formed than any local non-profit theater could afford on its own. The commercial producer can better evaluate the commercial and artistic potential of the new show without having to raise the full funds (or take the full risk) for an out-of-town tryout of a fully capitalized Broadway show. If the enhanced local non-profit production generates good ticket sales and good reviews, then the producers have a leg up on raising the funds and mounting a production for Broadway.

Shows like *Six: The Musical*, *The Notebook*, and the 2024 revival of *The Who's Tommy* made the leap to Broadway with varying degrees of success. Some local productions with enhancement deals never make it to Broadway for financial or artistic reasons.

Such productions can be a win-win for everyone concerned. The local theater gets a well-produced crowd pleaser to add to its season with increased ticket sales, publicity, and the chance to receive royalties if the show succeeds to Broadway and on tour. At the same time, the risk to the non-profit theaters is that such shows become a continuing economic necessity, change the mix and content of the plays and musicals for the resident theater, and begin to eat at the foundation of their non-profit mission and artistic vision. Today's theater landscape may not feature the cartels and monopoly problems of old, but competition (and the lack thereof) is still an important feature of how and what theater is made in the United States.

Broadway and touring Broadway are more competitive today compared to in the days of the Syndicate and the pre-break up Shubert Organization. It is still not an ideal situation. The remaining problems are real, but are dwarfed by the continuing antitrust problems that plague the live concert industry and the continuing dominance of Live Nation and Ticketmaster.

16

Pearl Jam, Taylor Swift, and Live Nation

If it were not for the band Pearl Jam, I never would have given much thought to the role of antitrust in current live entertainment. In 1994, I was a junior faculty member at a law school in New York City when I received an invitation to appear on CNN's show *Inside Business* to discuss Pearl Jam's antitrust dispute with Ticketmaster. I immediately said yes and began to prepare for a thirty-minute taped interview with the CNN anchor and representatives from both sides.

Pearl Jam was at the peak of its popularity as alternative rockers, perhaps second in popularity and influence only to Nirvana. Despite their success, they felt they could not tour the country without doing business with Ticketmaster, which dominated the market for primary ticketing of live events.

Ticketmaster had grown through a seemingly endless series of acquisitions of traditional and electronic ticketing competitors. Ticketmaster used exclusive contracts with its customers (the venues) and offered its clients large rebates that made it difficult for bands or concert promoters to book a successful national tour without using Ticketmaster for the ticket sales of the shows.[1]

Ticketmaster was already notorious for charging high fees for the ticketing services it provided to most of the big rock stadiums and amphitheaters, and the exclusive ticketing rights it demanded from the venues who were their customers. Ticketmaster typically charged 20-30% of the ticket price as a service charge, which it shared with the venues. It also charged additional "convenience" fees. Together the additional fees often totaled a substantial percentage of the ticket's original face value and were widely denounced as a form of junk fees that unfairly and deceptively took advantage of music fans.

As Rolling Stone magazine noted at the time:

> In Chicago, for example, a band can't play the Rosemont Horizon, the United Center, Soldier Field, the Arie Crown Theater or the New World Music Theater – the major venues in the city – unless they agree to have Ticketmaster sell and distribute tickets for shows at those venues. What's more, many venues have stopped staffing their own box offices for concerts since no service fees are generated at those sites.[2]

Pearl Jam responded with a two-prong strategy similar to the independents of the theater world battling the Syndicate and the Shuberts. The band first tried to cobble together a national tour using independent venues, even if it meant playing smaller and less lucrative sites. They also tried to work with smaller ticketing services to sell tickets for under $20 a show with a service fee limited to 10% of the ticket price that was clearly disclosed to concert buyers.

They took the more unusual step of responding to inquiries from the United States Justice Department Antitrust Division and enthusiastically cooperating with a civil antitrust investigation already underway. Although most people thought Pearl Jam had complained to the Justice Department, the Department was already in the early stages of digging into Ticketmaster's business practices. By the mid-1990s, Ticketmaster commanded a 70-90% national market share for primary ticketing services and faced only limited competition from smaller regional competitors.

Pearl Jam vocally complained to fans and the press about Ticketmaster's monopolistic behavior and poorly disclosed price gouging. Members of the band testified in Congress along with representatives from fellow rockers Aerosmith and R.E.M. Almost unheard of for a rock band of thirty-somethings, they also hired Sullivan & Cromwell, a premier Wall Street law firm whose antitrust practice dates back to the 1870s when the firm helped Standard Oil organize as the nation's first industrial trust.

In June 1994, CNN sent a car service to pick me up at my apartment and take me to the CNN studios near Penn Station on the west side of Manhattan. After a quick trip to the hair and makeup chair, I was ushered to the studio to meet the host. I was seated between the lawyer from Sullivan & Cromwell representing Pearl Jam and the lawyer from Cravath, Swaine & Moore representing Ticketmaster (the same firm that had represented the Shuberts during their antitrust case in the 1950s).

For nearly a half hour, the host probed the lawyers, who vigorously disputed almost every point in contention, alternating between the Pearl Jam and Ticketmaster lawyers. After nearly each exchange, she would then turn to me and say words to the effect of "Well Professor Waller, you are the expert. What do you think?"

I patiently explained the basics of antitrust law and cautioned that the case would probably turn on facts that were not in the public record. When pressed, the most aggressive thing I was willing to say in my first substantial television appearance was that if the facts presented by Pearl Jam were true, then I could see why the Justice Department would want to take a serious look at the matter. When the taping concluded, the same black car took me back to my apartment and I set my then state-of-the-art VCR for that coming Sunday evening when the show would air.

As luck would have it, I was able to see the show when it first aired, but under unusual circumstances. On Sunday morning, I traveled from New York to Los Angeles to join my wife for the opening night of the Broadway tour of *The Who's Tommy* at the Universal Amphitheater (then a Ticketmaster client). Because this was a work event for her, we stayed in a hotel that was a short walk to the Amphitheater. There, I watched the Pearl Jam *Inside Business* episode in the late afternoon L.A. time while getting dressed for the show.

When I returned to New York, there was a series of increasingly urgent voice mails and email messages asking me to call the dean of my law school. When I reached the dean, I learned that the President of Ticketmaster was an alum of our law school and had bombarded her with a series of phone calls and voicemails about my performance on the show. He demanded that I be fired and vowed never to donate to the law school again. She reassured me that I was not being fired, and that this was hardly the first time he had complained or threatened not to support the law school.

The Pearl Jam no-Ticketmaster tour ultimately fizzled because the band struggled to schedule a viable national tour without Ticketmaster venues and its ticketing platform. Unlike Sarah Bernhardt or Minnie Maddern Fiske of the past, rock bands don't have the option of performing in churches, tents, or the side of a hill.

Pearl Jam eventually returned to the Ticketmaster fold, suggesting that resistance was futile against the power of a national monopoly. If a prosperous well-known articulate group of performers with a passionate national following could not make a difference, the lessons were clear for newer or lesser-known acts. Even worse, the Antitrust Division of the Justice Department ultimately declined to take any action.

Eddie Vedder, Pearl Jam's lead singer, echoed the weary sentiments of the independents from the early 20th century who tried, and failed, to buck the powers that be of their day. Vedder told the press: "The way I feel about it is we got to see up close how things work in this country, we got to be crushed by a huge corporate giant right up close."[3] This is a familiar story from the vaudeville era, the days of the Syndicate, the Shubert era, and a host of modern high-tech industries where the dominant firm or firms control how competitors gain access to customers.

Only a couple of bands succeeded where Pearl Jam failed in its dealing with Ticketmaster. The most successful exception was the Grateful Dead which handled ticketing in-house (even in Ticketmaster venues) to satisfy the needs of its adoring fans.[4]

The lesser-known jam band, The String Cheese Incident, used publicity and their own antitrust litigation to achieve a settlement with Ticketmaster, allowing them to handle a portion of their own ticketing for tours.[5] The band's bassist said at the time: "It costs us money to sell the tickets. But we are going to eat that cost this summer in order to make a better deal for our fans and let them know how much we appreciate them."[6]

***

Ticketmaster was not always been a powerhouse in primary ticketing, although it sometimes feels that way. It began like so many powerful firms as an upstart, a fringe firm taking on an earlier market leader. Ticketmaster began its policy of exclusive, full inventory contracts providing rebates to venues more as a survival technique, rather than a power move to exclude competition.

It grew by acquiring in 1991 its rival Ticketron, which at one time was the dominant ticketing firm. By the early 1990s, Ticketron was on the edge of bankruptcy and probably would have collapsed without the acquisition. Ticketmaster continued to grow with a series of acquisitions of smaller promoters around the country. None of these transactions by themselves were significant enough to warrant serious antitrust concerns.

As the president of Ticketmaster described:

> "We didn't revolutionize the rock concert business. We helped monetize it. We had all the data, so we knew what people would pay to hear certain artists and bands. If Broadway charged $100 to see a show from seats in the orchestra, why was that more valuable than Elton John or David Bowie singing? If a sports team charged $100 to sit in the front row, why couldn't you take the first twenty rows and make them special?"[7]

The next phase in Ticketmaster's growth led it to diversify from ticketing into other portions of the live music space so it could profit from music management, sponsorships, and secondary ticketing. While the Justice Department ultimately took no action in the Pearl Jam-Ticketmaster disputes of the 1990s, it could not ignore the 2010 merger between Ticketmaster and Live Nation.

This transaction combined the largest primary ticketing service with the largest vertically integrated live music firm with operations not only in ticketing services, but also in talent management, concert promotion, and venue ownership and management. Over time, Live Nation expanded into owning much of the merchandise, food, beverages, and services sold in its venues.[8] The merger raised important antitrust issues in terms of potential harm to competitors, performers, and suppliers.

To the surprise of many in the industry, the Ticketmaster/Live Nation transaction ultimately was challenged, but settled, by the Antitrust Division, seventeen state Attorneys General, and separately by Canada's Competition Bureau. The consent decree in the United States permitted the merger but required both structural and behavioral changes.[9]

To address the horizontal overlap in the primary ticketing services market, the merged Ticketmaster/Live Nation had to divest one ticketing service to a buyer acceptable to the Justice Department and license its primary ticketing platform with an option to purchase to AEG, the largest remaining competitor in the primary ticketing industry.

Allowing the merger and the ambiguous terms of the consent decree was controversial. Musicians, talent managers, concert promoters, venues, and competing ticketing services feared they would be shut out from mounting meaningful national tours unless they did business with Ticketmaster/Live Nation.

To address these concerns, the consent decree contained numerous provisions in addition to the required divestitures. The consent decree approving the merger contained "anti-bundling" provisions that prevented the merged entity from requiring ticketing clients to use the merged companies' other services. There also were anti-retaliation provisions, which prohibited the new merged entity from retaliating against any venue owner who chooses to use a competing ticketing or promotional company. No one in the concert business, except for the merging parties, was happy with this settlement.

My next opportunity to discuss the antitrust issues of Ticketmaster and Live Nation came shortly after the merger. I spoke at an annual conference sponsored by the Broadway League, the trade organization that had briefly operated the United Booking Office after it was spun off by the Shuberts. Hardly the headliner, I was scheduled mid-morning, sandwiched between more sizzling panels and speakers including stars, producers, and playwrights.

I tried to make my talk as accessible as possible, and hoped I hit the sweet spot of informative, but not dull. I was relieved when an Emmy and Tony nominated actress stopped me as I left the stage and said that she finally understood what all the fuss about Ticketmaster and antitrust meant.

Complaints mounted over the next ten years against Live Nation's behavior and whether it was complying with the many conditions of the settlement that had permitted the merger. In late 2019, the Justice Department went back to court to strengthen and extend the consent decree for another five and a half years. It argued that Live Nation had repeatedly violated the original settlement approving the merger. The Court strengthened the earlier settlement to include additional provisions:

1) prohibiting Live Nation from withholding or threatening to withhold concerts from a venue if the venue chooses a ticketer other than Ticketmaster;
2) appointing an independent monitor to investigate and report on Live Nation's compliance with the Final Judgment;
3) requiring Live Nation to appoint an internal antitrust compliance officer and conduct regular internal training to ensure its employees fully comply with the Final Judgment;
4) requiring Live Nation to provide notice to current or potential ticketing customers of the clarified and extended terms of the Final Judgment; and
5) subjecting Live Nation to an automatic penalty of $1,000,000 for each violation of the Final Judgment.[10]

Live Nation's only real argument was that it believed that the original agreement had only barred it from conditioning all, and not just some, of the company's services in dealing with independent firms. The company agreed to the changes only to see most live entertainment shut down as the COVID pandemic swept through the United States almost immediately in the following year.

***

The competitive concerns of a combined Ticketmaster/Live Nation continue to play out across the theater world and all of live entertainment post-pandemic. The concert and music worlds were rocked in late 2022 as tickets for Taylor Swift's new tour went on sale exclusively through Ticketmaster. Ticket prices were high, service fees were an enormous additional expense, and worst of all, thousands of fans were shut out of the web-based ticketing platform which either crashed or involved enormous wait times. Taylor Swift spoke out to her many fans: "It's truly amazing that 2.4 million people got tickets, but it really pisses me off that a lot of them feel like they went through several bear attacks to get them."[11]

The Swifties, the army of Taylor Swift fans, reacted with fury and turned to the antitrust laws as a potential remedy for their grievances. Taylor Swift told her fans: "It's really difficult for me to trust an outside entity with these relationships and loyalties, and excruciating for me to just watch mistakes happen with no recourse."[12] Social media was flooded with calls for the breakup of Ticketmaster and Live Nation.[13] Fans even brought a triple damage class action lawsuit accusing Ticketmaster and Live Nation of racketeering and collusion with their business partners.[14]

The Justice Department quickly confirmed a renewed investigation of the company and all of its practices. The Senate held high profile hearings in January of 2023 with Senators trying to top each other with quotes and puns based on Taylor Swift lyrics as they excoriated Live Nation witnesses.[15] Senator Richard Blumenthal of Connecticut suggested that "Ticketmaster ought to look in the mirror and say, '*I'm the problem. It's me.*'"[16] Senator Amy Klobuchar of Minnesota, the author of a recent book on antitrust, ad-libbed, "You can't have too much consolidation — something that unfortunately for this country, as an ode to Taylor Swift, I will say, we know *all too well*."[17]

Country star Zach Bryan released a live album reflecting these frustrations called "All My Homies Hate Ticketmaster."[18] Antitrust became a kitchen table issue for music fans and the general public more than any time in the recent past.

Fans of the English band Oasis erupted with similar ire for the mishandling of the on-sale for the band's surprise reunion tour in 2024. Fans waited for hours on the Ticketmaster site, only to find that prices had increased, if they were lucky enough to buy tickets at all. This also stimulated antitrust scrutiny in both the United States and the Competition and Markets Authority of the United Kingdom.[19]

In spring 2024, the United States Justice Department finally had enough. The Department brought a new antitrust case challenging the earlier merger (which it had allowed with conditions) as a form of monopolization, and sought to force a breakup of the company.[20] The complaint accused Ticketmaster/Live Nation of colluding with one of its few remaining rivals, retaliating against potential entrants, threatening and retaliating against venues that work with rivals, locking out competition with exclusive contracts, restricting artists' access to venues, acquiring competitors, and harming competition.

Michael Carrier, a leading antitrust professor, described the case to PBS: "The DOJ showed how Live Nation really has its tentacles in each element of the supply chain, which means that it has a lot more control than it is letting on. And, in terms of justifications, there is really very little that (Live Nation) can offer in terms of how they're helping the consumer."[21]

The Trump administration continued to press this important antitrust case brought by the Biden administration and three dozen state Attorneys General. The Trump FTC also has brought a separate case charging that Ticketmaster's fees and opaque disclosures for resale of tickets on the secondary market are unfair and deceptive.

It appeared that the time was past where Live Nation could merely promise to behave and not continue to abuse its dominance. The case offered the possibility of the first great antitrust divestiture in live entertainment since the Shubert breakup almost seventy years ago.

The legal world was stunned when the Trump administration fired the top leadership of the Antitrust Division in early 2026 and entered into a settlement with Live Nation during the first week of the trial. That proposed settlement offered additional changes to Live Nation's behavior and required minor divestitures but left the basic structure of the company intact.

Allegations abound that the settlement was the result of lobbying of the White House and the leadership of the Justice Department over the objections of the staff of the Antitrust Division. More than thirty of the State antitrust enforcers refused to go along with the settlement and continued the trial.

On April 15, 2026, the states won. A jury found that Live Nation had abused its monopoly power and overcharged concert goers. As this book goes to press the final result of the Live Nation case remains unresolved.

The judge must still decide what the full remedy will be in addition to damages. It would be a rare case where a court orders the divestiture of a dominant firm where the federal government has chosen to settle for less. We can only hope that the judge understands the lessons of history and law. That decision is months away and any appeal will further prolong the case.

Thirty years of monopoly is enough. The story of the Combine, the Syndicate, and the Shuberts has taught us that we can do better.

These are the same issues that have plagued live entertainment since the Gilded Age. Too often, the law has been too slow, or the enforcers too disinterested, to confront effectively the many competition problems in the vaudeville and live theater industries. Going forward, the real issue remains whether the law is up to the task of controlling the abuse of corporate power over what we see on the concert stage, whom we pay, and how much.

Epilogue

Picture a world where one of the plans for world domination of live entertainment had come to fruition. Had they succeeded, the Combine, the Syndicate, the Shuberts, or some combination of all the above, would have controlled the production, booking, and presentation of vaudeville, legitimate theater, and related art forms in North America, Great Britain, continental Europe, and beyond.

Of course, they did not succeed. But it was a close call. An economic downturn foiled the most developed plans in the early 20th century to expand the Syndicate or the Combine abroad. Afterwards, the lords of vaudeville and theater mostly stuck to their slice of the North American live entertainment. The Syndicate and the Shuberts fought, colluded, and attempted to merge until the Syndicate aged out of the business. The Syndicate and the Shuberts tried to monopolize big time vaudeville but failed almost comically. The Shuberts tried it again a decade later, this time alone, and failed even more spectacularly. The barons of big time vaudeville threatened to invade live theater but never followed through on their boasts. Everyone talked about global domination but eventually stuck to their own corner of the U.S. live entertainment market.

By the time the Shuberts reigned supreme, their real rivals were the Great Depression and the unstoppable rise of the motion picture industry. They survived, and even prospered at times, but it was again a close call. Either the ravages of the Depression or the impact of the new technologies of radio and movies (and eventually television and cable) could have destroyed live theater as we know it. The streaming wars of today pose such an existential threat.

Live entertainment has survived multiple economic downturns, technological change, wartime emergencies, pandemics, and more, because it provides a visceral connection between the audience and the performers.

Commercial and nonprofit theater can still fill venues, both large and small, from Broadway to the edgiest black box theater far from an urban downtown. Live music fills rooms from a small club or bar to the largest stadiums and arenas.

Theater is an expansive medium ranging from the corniest musical comedy or revue to the darkest and most experimental dramas. The commercial end of the theater world depends on attracting a mass audience. It must be large enough to fill a Broadway theater, and eventually theaters on the road, so the producers (and their investors) make enough to pay the actors, the creative team, the crew, the bookers, the theater owners, and hopefully earn a profit. There is a vast and beautiful world of noncommercial theater. But to understand the business end requires following both the money and the art over the lifetime of a show from its initial creative spark to its final performance, if it makes it that far.

Commercial theater, and its competition for our attention and dollars, remains a combination of business, artistic, and legal forces. The technology has changed, the performances have changed, and the players have changed. But human nature, and the urge for power and a break from the rigors of artistic and business competition have not changed.

Now picture a different world where robust enforcement of the antitrust laws produced a more workably competitive market for live entertainment. In this world, the Courts worked out earlier that theater (and vaudeville) were indeed interstate trade and commerce, and the normal rules applied as in the rest of the economy of the late 19th and early 20th centuries. Cartel agreements between actual and potential competitors were attacked as criminal and civil violations of the antitrust laws. All monopolies and attempts to monopolize live entertainment markets were stopped by the government and the courts and not just the later stages of the Shubert monopoly of the legitimate theater.

In such a world no one producer, booker, or presenter would have dictated what was seen on the stage. New competitors, and presumably new ideas and ways of doing business and art, would have a chance to flourish without being forced to do business through the dominant vaudeville circuits, the Syndicate, or the Shuberts. Many productions would have failed financially or artistically in any market. Commercial theater would have still favored the most lucrative ventures with the widest audience appeal. But competition, rather than collusion or monopoly, holds forth the promise of lower prices, higher quality, and more innovation that would have benefitted audiences, performers, and society.

The art we see is the product of the power of those who create it. The story of the Syndicate, the Vaudeville Combine, the Shuberts, and the current dominant players in live entertainment show us how the forces of market competition and competition law can shape, but never eliminate, the worst impulses of those in power and help preserve the very nature of the live entertainment that we crave.

Appendix A The American Theatrical Syndicate Agreement 1896 as published in The Dramatic Mirror 1898

This Agreement, in triplicate, made and entered into this [date blank] day of [date blank]. eighteen hundred and ninety-six, between AL. Hayman and Charles Frohman, hereinafter designated as parties of the first part: Samuel F. Nirdlinger and J. Fred Zimmerman, trading as Nixon and Zimmerman, hereinafter designated as parties of the second part, and Marc. Klaw and Abraham L. Erlanger., hereinafter designated as parties of the third part.

WITNESSETH:

WHEREAS, The said several parties hereto of the first, second and third parties respectively are interested in or own or hold leases of various theaters and places of amusement in the United States, or are in receipt of sundry proceeds from divers theatres for services rendered to such theatres; and

WHEREAS, The theatrical business as at present conducted has resulted in great loss from indiscriminate bookings, in consequence of which similar attractions of the first class repeatedly oppose each other in the same point and thereby injure the other; and

WHEREAS, From the geographical location of the theaters and places of amusement unless tours are arranged in as nearly a direct line as possible needless expense results from railroad fares and hauling theatrical paraphernalia and properties, large companies with equipments being now too often moved forward and backward for the causes mentioned; and

WHEREAS, Under the present system, the losses already sustained by managers and owners of theatres and of companies from such indiscriminate bookings, as well as from railroad "jumps," so-called, have been incalculable: and

WHEREAS, To guard against, the repetition of losses of a like character, not only to the parties hereto, but to all parties in the theatrical business, who either control companies or own theatres, it is necessary that the defects in the particulars mentioned should be remedied;

Now, THEREFORE for the benefit and protection of the parties hereto, and of the premises and of the sum of one dollar by each party to the other in hand paid, the receipt whereof is hereby acknowledged, and of the mutual promises and covenants hereinafter contained, it is agreed as follows:

FIRST: This agreement shall commence on the 31st day of August, 1896, and continue in full force and effect for the period of five years from said last named date.

SECOND: That during the continuance of this agreement, all of the following named theatres and places of amusement, to wit, Columbia and Hooley's Theatres, Chicago: Colombia and Montauk Theatres, Brooklyn: Museum, Boston: California and Baldwin Theatres, San Francisco: New Century Theater, St. Louis: Taylor Grand Opera House, Denver: Walnut Street Theatre, Philadelphia: Coates' Opera House, Kansas City: Euclid Avenue Opera House, Cleveland: Alvin Theatre, Pittsburg: New Creighton Theatre, Omaha: Talma Theatre, Providence: New Southern and Grand Opera House, Columbus: Valentine Theatre, Toledo; Lyceum Theatre, Cleveland and Davidson's Theatre, Milwaukee, all of which are controlled by the parties of the first part or in which there are interested or from which they are in receipt of income for services rendered; also the Broad Street Theatre, Chestnut Street Theatre and Chestnut Opera House, Philadelphia; Academy of Music, Baltimore: Lyceum Theatre, Baltimore: Lafayette Square Opera House and Columbia Theatre, Washington, D.D., and Park Theatre, Philadelphia, all of which are controlled by the parties of the second part or in which they are interested or from which they are in receipt of income from services rendered; and also the New Masonic Theatre, Nashville; Grand Opera House, Memphis; Staub's Theatre, Knoxville; St. Charles Theatre and Academy of Music, New Orleans; Walnut Street Theatre, Philadelphia: Coates' Opera House, Kansas City; Euclid Avenue Opera House, Cleveland; Alvin Theatre, Pittsburg; New Creighton Theatre, Omaha; Talma Theatre, Providence: New Southern and Grand Opera House, Columbus; Valentine Theatre, Toledo; Lyceum Theatre, Cleveland, and Davidson's Theatre, Milwaukee, all of which are controlled by the parties of the third part or in which they are interested or from which they are in receipt income or services rendered; and all other theatres or place of amusement which may be hereafter (during the continuance of this agreement) acquired by either of the parties of the first, second, or third parts hereto, shall be booked with attractions in conjunction with each other; that is to say, no attraction shall be booked in any of the said theatres or places of amusement (or in any which may be hereafter acquired as aforesaid) which will insist on playing an opposition theatre or place of amusement in any of the cities above named (any which may hereafter come under this agreement) unless the party hereto having the theatre or place of amusement in said competitive point shall give his or their consent In writing to permit said attraction to play in the opposition theatre or place of amusement.

THIRD: The parties hereto mutually covenant and agree that so far as the attractions owned by them respectively are concerned (or in which they may hereafter, during the continuance of this agreement, become interested) they will play the same in theaters or places of amusement hereinabove mentioned (or hereinafter to be included), or they will remain out of the cities in which said theatres or places of amusement are respectively located. It is hereby understood and agreed that the respective parties hereto can only play any of their attractions in any opposition theatre or place of amusement if they obtain the written consent of the party hereto having a theatre or a place of amusement in said competitive point.

FOURTH: The parties hereto in consideration aforesaid, also hereby respectively covenant and agree to and with each other to pool the net profits and other income derived from the theatres or places of amusement specifically mentioned in this article, and none other, and to divide the same in the manner hereinafter specified. To the end aforesaid the parties of the first part contribute to the pool the net profits or other income derived from the following theatres or places of amusement, to wit: Century Theatre, St. Louis, Tahor Grand Opera House; Denver: Walnut Street Theatre, Philadelphia: Coates' Opera House, Kansas City; Euclid Avenue Opera House, Cleveland; Alvin Theatre, Pittsburg; New Creighton Theatre, Omaha: Talma Theatre, Providence, New Southern Theatre and the Grand Opera House, Columbus: Valentine Theatre, Toledo: Lyceum Theatre, Cleveland; and Davidson's Theatre, Milwaukee. The parties of the second part contribute to the pool of the net profits or other income derived from the following theatres or places of amusement, to wit; Lyceum Theatre, Baltimore, Lafayette Square Opera House and Columbia Theatre, Washington D.C. Park Theatre, Philadelphia. And the third parties contribute to the said pool the net profits or other income derived from the following theatres or places of amusement, to wit: Walnut Street Theatre, Philadelphia: Coates' Opera House, Kansas City: Euclid Avenue Opera House and Lyceum Theatre, Cleaveland: Alvin Theatre, Pittsburg; New Creighton Theatre, Omaha; Talma Theatre Providence; New Southern Theatre and the Grand Opera House, Columbus: Valentine Theatre, Toledo and Davidson's Theatre, Milwaukee. That the net profits or other income accruing or derived from the said above specified parts or shares of which the parties of the first part shall receive on equal part or share thereof; the parties of the second part a like share, and the parties of the third part a like share; settlements to be made on the first day of July in each year, during the continuance of this agreement.

FIFTH: No theatre or place of amusement shall be admitted under this agreement without the written consent of all parties hereto.

SIXTH: As regards all other theatres and places of amusement mentioned in Article Fourth hereof and included in said pool, each of the parties hereto bind themselves that they will respectively keep just and true books of account in respect to each of said theatres in which there shall be entered all the receipts from each of the said theaters and places of amusement mentioned, as well as all expenses of every kind and nature which may be incurred in their management, and true vouchers of all and every such expense shall be kept, which books and vouchers shall at all times be accessible to either and all the parties hereto.

SEVENTH: If, during the term of this agreement, any of the theatres or places of amusement herein mentioned (or any hereafter coming under this agreement) shall pass out of the control or interest of the parties now controlling the same respectively, from any cause whatever not the act, negligence or default either directly, indirectly or collusively, of said such party or parties or if said control and interest shall be lost by destruction of said theatres and places of amusement by fire or other casualty, such party or parties, so losing such control and interest therein shall not be held accountable or responsible for such loss, but this agreement shall continue to operate upon the remaining theatres and places of amusement herein mentioned.

EIGHTH: It is agreed that Messrs. Klaw and Erlanger, the parties of the third part, shall have charge of all the bookings of the theatres specified in Article Second above, and the Messrs, Hayman and Frohman, the parties of the first part shall have charge of the finances and of the profits and other income arising from the theatres mentioned in Article Fourth above; and that Messrs. Nixon and Zimmermann, the parties of the second part, shall be traveling representatives under this agreement. That all and any expense incurred by either of the parties hereto in respect to the duties imposed upon either of them hereunder shall be paid out the fund to be held by the parties of the first part upon the production of proper statements and vouchers, whenever possible, showing each expenditures; each party to advance the necessary expense which may be incurred by them until the first parties shall become possessed of funds; all such expenses to be included in the general expense account.

Ninth: Finally, it is expressly understood and agreed by all of the parties hereto, that nothing contained herein shall be construed to disturb or change the control which the respective parties hereto now have in the theatres and places of amusement specifically mentioned and described in Article Second hereof, excepting so far as the arrangement herein provided for the bookings may be concerned.

IN WINTESS WHEREOF the said parties hereto and to triplicate hereof, have hereunto set their respective hands and seals the day and year first above written.

Signed and Delivered
in the Presence of Alfred Rhemshom.

AL. HAYMAN AND CHAS. FROHMAN
NIXON AND ZIMMERMAN
KLAW AND ERLANGER

Appendix B
United States v. Shubert, 348 US 222 (1955) (footnotes omitted)

MR. CHIEF JUSTICE WARREN delivered the opinion of the Court.

This is a civil antitrust action brought by the Government in the United States District Court for the Southern District of New York. Named as defendants are Lee Shubert, Jacob J. Shubert, Marcus Heiman, and three corporations controlled by them. The defendants are principally engaged in the business of producing legitimate theatrical attractions, booking legitimate attractions in theaters throughout the United States, and operating approximately 40 theaters in eight states for the presentation of legitimate attractions. The Government's complaint charges that the defendants, in the course of this business, have violated §§ 1 and 2 of the Sherman Act. On the defendants' motion, after this Court's decision in *Toolson v. New York Yankees,* 346 U. S. 356; the District Court, 120 F. Supp. 15, dismissed the Government's complaint on the authority of the *Toolson* decision, and *Federal Baseball Club of Baltimore v. National League of Professional Baseball Clubs,* 259 U. S. 200. The case is here on direct appeal under the Expediting Act, 15 U.S.C. § 29.

The Government's complaint, which is summarized in an appendix to this opinion, describes the interstate phases of the defendants' theatrical business in considerable detail. It concludes that the business of producing, booking, and presenting legitimate attractions requires "a constant, continuous stream of trade and commerce between the States of the United States, consisting of the assemblage of personnel and property for rehearsals, the transportation of said personnel and property to various cities throughout the United States, the making and performing of contracts under which attractions are routed and presented in various States of the United States, and the transmission of applications, letters, memoranda, communications, commitments, contracts, money, checks, drafts and other media of exchange across State lines."

The complaint alleges that the defendants have restrained this trade and commerce, and have monopolized certain phases of it, through a conspiracy (a) to compel other producers to book their legitimate attractions exclusively through the defendants, (b) to exclude others from booking legitimate attractions, (c) to prevent competition in the presentation of legitimate attractions, (d) to discriminate in favor of their own productions with respect to booking and presentation, and (e) to combine their power in booking and presentation in order to maintain and strengthen their domination in each of these fields. The main relief sought by the Government is the divorcement of the booking and presentation branches of the business.

The allegations of the complaint, on a motion to dismiss, must, of course, be taken as true. And the defendants do not deny that the allegations state a cause of action if their business is subject to the Sherman Act. The question presented is thus a narrow one: whether the business of producing, booking, and presenting legitimate attractions on a multistate basis constitutes "trade or commerce" that is "among the several States" within the meaning of those terms in the Sherman Act.

Both terms have been interpreted broadly in the decisions of this Court. "[T]rade or commerce" has been held to include the production, distribution, and exhibition of motion pictures, *United States v. Paramount Pictures,* 334 U. S. 131; *Schine Chain Theaters v. United States,* 334 U. S. 110; *United States v. Griffith,* 334 U. S. 100; *United States v. Crescent Amusement Co.,* 323 U. S. 173; *Interstate Circuit v. United States,* 306 U. S. 208; *Binderup v. Pathe Exchange,* 263 U. S. 291; real estate brokerage, *United States v. National Association of Real Estate Boards,* 339 U. S. 485; the gathering and distribution of news, *Associated Press v. United States,* 326 U. S. 1; medical services to members of a health cooperative, *American Medical Association v. United States,* 317 U. S. 519; and insurance underwriting, *United States v. South-Eastern Underwriters Association,* 322 U. S. 533. A similarly liberal construction has been given the requirement of §§ 1 and 2 that the "trade or commerce" be "among the several States." Thus, in the *South-Eastern Underwriters* case, the requirement was satisfied by a "continuous and indivisible stream of intercourse among the states" involving the transmission of large sums of money and communications by mail, telephone, and telegraph. *Cf. Electric Bond & Share Co. v. Securities and Exchange Commission,* 303 U. S. 419, 303 U. S. 432-433; *North American Co. v. Securities and Exchange Commission,* 327 U. S. 686, 327 U. S. 694-695. In the *Associated Press* case, the requirement was satisfied by the interstate dissemination of news. *See also Lorain Journal Co. v. United States,* 342 U.S. 143. And, in the motion picture cases, the requirement was satisfied by the interstate transportation of films, *Binderup v. Pathe Exchange, supra,* even though the actual "showing of motion pictures is, of course, a local affair." *United States v. Crescent Amusement Co., supra,* at 323 U. S. 183. *See also Hart v. B. F. Keith Vaudeville Exchange,* 262 U. S. 271.

These decisions, apart from *Federal Base Ball* and *Toolson,* make it clear beyond question that the allegations of the Government's complaint bring the defendants within the scope of the Sherman Act, even though the actual performance of a legitimate stage attraction "is, of course, a local affair." The defendants contend, however, that *Federal Base Ball* and *Toolson* have already established their immunity under the Act. While conceding, as they must, that the motion picture industry is subject to the antitrust laws, they insist that all other businesses built around the performance of local exhibitions are exempt. We believe that *Federal Base Ball* and *Toolson* afford no basis for such a conclusion.

In *Federal Base Ball,* the Court, speaking through Mr. Justice Holmes, was dealing with the business of baseball, and nothing else. The Court considered the nature of the game, its history and league organization, the necessity of arranging games between cities in different states, and the resulting travel across state lines. The travel, the Court concluded, was "a mere incident, not the essential thing." On that basis, the Court held that "the restrictions by contract that prevented the plaintiff from getting players to break their bargains and the other conduct charged against the defendants were not an interference with commerce among the States." 259 U.S. at 259 U. S. 209.

At the very next Term, in *Hart v. B. F. Keith Vaudeville Exchange,* 262 U. S. 271, the Court was directly concerned with the effect of the *Federal Base Ball* decision on the status of the theatrical business under the Sherman Act. The complaint in the *Hart* case, much like the complaint here under review, alleged a conspiracy to control the booking and presentation of vaudeville acts in theaters throughout the country. The district court, like the district court in the instant case, dismissed the complaint on the authority of *Federal Base Ball.* This Court, again speaking through Mr. Justice Holmes, unanimously reversed. The Court took note of the plaintiff's argument "that in the transportation of vaudeville acts the apparatus sometimes is more important than the performers," and concluded that the complaint, at least to that extent, sufficiently alleged a violation of the Act to permit the case to go to trial. The Court distinguished *Federal Base Ball* on the ground that "what in general is incidental in some instances may rise to a magnitude that requires it to be considered independently." The Court thus established, contrary to the defendants' argument here, that *Federal Base Ball* did not automatically immunize the theatrical business from the antitrust laws.

In *Toolson,* where the issue was the same as in *Federal Base Ball,* the Court was confronted with a unique combination of circumstances. For over 30 years, there had stood a decision of this Court specifically fixing the status of the baseball business under the antitrust laws, and, more particularly, the validity of the so-called "reserve clause." During this period, in reliance on the *Federal Base Ball* precedent, the baseball business had grown and developed. *Compare Helvering v. Hallock,* 309 U. S. 106, 309 U. S. 110. And Congress, although it had actively considered the ruling, had not seen fit to reject it by amendatory legislation. Against this background, the Court in *Toolson* was asked to overrule *Federal Base Ball* on the ground that it was out of step with subsequent decisions reflecting present day concepts of interstate commerce. The Court, in view of the circumstances of the case, declined to do so. But neither did the Court necessarily reaffirm all that was said in *Federal Base Ball.* Instead, "[w]ithout reexamination of the underlying issues," the Court adhered to *Federal Base Ball* "so far as that decision determines that Congress had no intention of including the business of baseball within the scope of the federal antitrust laws." In short, *Toolson* was a narrow application of the rule of *stare decisis.*

The defendants would have us convert this narrow application of the rule into a sweeping grant of immunity to every business based on the live presentation of local exhibitions, regardless of how extensive its interstate phases may be. We cannot do so. If the *Toolson* holding is to be expanded -- or contracted -- the appropriate remedy lies with Congress. *See United States v. South-Eastern Underwriters Association,* 322 U. S. 533, 322 U. S. 561.

Moreover, none of the considerations which led to the decision in *Toolson* is present here. This Court has never held that the theatrical business is not subject to the Sherman Act. On the contrary, less than a year after the *Federal Base Ball* decision, the Court in the *Hart* case put the theatrical business on notice that *Federal Base Ball* could not be relied upon as a basis for exemption from the antitrust laws. The rule of *stare decisis* undoubtedly embodies a policy of basic importance, but the rule cannot help the defendants here. If it is to be applied, *Hart* and the motion picture cases -- not *Federal Base Ball* and *Toolson* -- are the controlling decisions.

We are not yet called upon to determine whether the defendants have, in fact, violated the Sherman Act, or, if they have, what relief would be appropriate. We hold only that the allegations of the complaint state a cause of action, and that the Government is entitled to an opportunity to prove those allegations. The judgment of the court below is *Reversed.*

MR. JUSTICE BURTON, retaining the views expressed in his dissent in the *Toolson* case, 346 U. S. 356, 346 U. S. 357, joins the opinion and judgment of the Court in this case. MR. JUSTICE REED joins in this concurrence.

MR. JUSTICE MINTON agrees with the judgment in this case because, as it comes here on the pleadings, it is controlled by the *Hart* case. Whether the Government can prove its case now to the satisfaction of present courts, which the plaintiff could not do in the *Hart* case, 12 F.2d 341, remains to be seen.

Notes

Introduction

1 Michael Riedel. *Razzle Dazzle: The Battle for Broadway*. New York: Simon & Schuster, 2016.

2 Billy Rose Theatre Division, The New York Public Library. "The black crook: an original magical and spectacular drama in four acts" New York Public Library Digital Collections. Accessed September 15, 2025. https://digitalcollections.nypl.org/items/ee6f0c70-0031-0130-6bda-58d385a7bc34.

3 Willa Cather. "Amusements." *Nebraska State Journal*, April 3, 1894, 5. Available online: https://cather.unl.edu/writings/journalism/j00010.

4 21 Cong. Rec. S2457 (daily ed. Mar. 21, 1890) (statement of Sen. John Sherman).

1 Live Entertainment Becomes a National Business

1 Alfred Bernheim was an economist who was hired by Actors Equity in the 1920s to research and write a series of articles eventually collected in a book that described the business history of the theater industry in the United States and the economics of how plays and musicals were developed, presented on Broadway, and then toured across the country. *See* Alfred L. Bernheim, *The Business of the Theatre: An Economic History of the American Theatre, 1750-1932*. 1932. Reprinted. New York: B. Blom, 1964, 20.

2 Isaac F. Marcosson and Daniel Frohman, *Charles Frohman: Manager and Man*, with an appreciation by James M. Barrie. 1916. Reprint. New York: Jefferson Publishing, 2015, 33.

3 Bernheim, *The Business of the Theatre*, 40.

4 *Annie Get Your Gun*, music and lyrics by Irving Berlin, dir. Joshua Logan, Imperial Theatre, New York, NY, May 16, 1946.

5 Sarah Lyall, "Fact and Fiction Hobnob in 'The Gilded Age'." *New York Times*, February 22, 2022, 2.

6 Trav S.D., *No Applause – Just Throw Money*. New York: Faber & Faber 2005, 273-95.

7 Robert W. Snyder, "Vaudeville and the Transformation of Popular Culture" in *Inventing Times Square: Commerce and Culture at the Crossroads of the World*, edited by William R. Taylor. New York: Russell Sage Foundation, 1991, 133.

8 Charles W. Stein, *American Vaudeville as Seen by its Contemporaries*. New York: Alfred A. Knopf, 1984, xi.

2 The Entertainment Barons of the Gilded Age

1 Douglas Gilbert. *American Vaudeville, Its Life & Times*. 1940. Reprinted, New Dover edn. New York: Dover Publications, 1963, 205.

2 B.F. Keith. "The Vogue of the Vaudeville." *National Magazine*, November 1898, 146.

3 Before 1906, vaudeville bookings were done through the Association of Vaudeville Managers of the United States (AVM). The AVM was controlled by Keith, Albee, Meyerfeld, and Beck. In 1919, the UBO officially changed its name to the B.F. Keith Vaudeville Exchange. Outside the industry most continued to refer to it as the UBO until the death of vaudeville in the late 1920s.

4 Stewart F. Lane. *It Happened at the Palace: A History of New York's Iconic Broadway Theater*. Broad Book Press 2024; Arthur F Wertheim. *Vaudeville Wars: How the Keith-Albee and Orpheum Circuits Controlled the Big- Time and its Performers*. New York: Palgrave Macmillan, 2006, 199-207.

5 Wertheim, Arthur F. *Vaudeville Wars* at 29, 60.

6 Alfred L. Bernheim. *The Business of the Theatre: An Economic History of the American Theatre, 1750-1932*. 1932. Reprinted. New York: B. Blom, 1964, 30.

7 Nat C. Goodwin. *Nat Goodwin's Book*. 1914. Boston: Richard G. Badger, 1914, 99-100.

8 Bernheim, *The Business of Theatre*, 36.

3 The Rise of the Syndicate

1 The text of the Syndicate Agreement is reprinted in Appendix A.

2 Cecile A. Rukgaber. "The Theatrical Syndicate and its Effects Upon the American Theatre.", MA thesis, University of Wyoming, 1955, 27.

3 Alfred L. Bernheim, *The Business of the Theatre: An Economic History of the American Theatre*, 1750-1932. 1932. Reprinted. New York: B. Blom, 1964, 42.

4 Walter Prichard Eaton. "The Theatre: The Rise and Fall of the Theatrical Syndicate." *The American Magazine*, October 1910, 832-42, 838.

5 Lee Shubert. "Mr. Lee: As Set Down by Ed Sullivan." Unpublished manuscript, c. 1950, typescript. 35.

6 Bernheim, *The Business of the Theatre*, 43.

7 Isaac F. Marcosson and Daniel Frohman. *Charles Frohman: Manager and Man*, with an appreciation by James M. Barrie. 1916. Reprint. New York: Jefferson, 2015, 5-6; Frohman, Daniel. *Daniel Frohman Presents: An Autobiography*. New York: Claude Kendall & Willoughby Sharp, 1935, 8-11.

8 Marcossan & Frohman, *Charles Frohman*, 5.

9 *Ibid* at 7.

10 *Ibid* at 12-17.

11 *Ibid* at 20-23.

12 *Ibid* at 25.

13 Charles Frohman continued to be haunted by play piracy and the weakness of copyright protection of his productions throughout his career. In 1912, the United States Supreme Court issued the landmark ruling holding that Frohman held the exclusive rights to present an English play that he had licensed for the US market and sustained an injunction prohibiting a competing unauthorized production of the same work. *Ferris v. Frohman*, 223 U.S. 424 (1912). This landmark case continues to be taught in copyright law courses to this day.

14 Frohman, *Daniel Frohman Presents*, 30-37.

15 Eaton, "The Theatre," 832; Bernheim, *The Business of the Theatre*, 48.

16 Monroe Lippman. "The History of the Theatrical Syndicate: Its Effect Upon the Theatre in America." PhD diss., University of Michigan, 1937, 51.

17 It is possible that the British syndicate that inspired the Americans related to the British music hall industry, their rough equivalent of vaudeville. *See* Andrew Crowhurst. Big Men and Big Business: The Transition from "Caterers' to 'Magnates in British Music-Hall Entrepreneurship, 1850-1914", *Nineteenth Century Theater*, 1997, 33; M. B. Leavitt. Fifty Years in Theatrical Management, *Fifty Years in Theatrical Management*. New York: Broadways Publishing Co., 1912, 211-14.

18 Lippman, "The History of the Theatrical Syndicate", 275; Charles Frohman, "New Phases of Theatre Management." *Harper's Weekly*, December 31, 1904, 2022-24, 2022.

19 The Editors. "The Great Theatrical Syndicate: How a Group of Speculators Have Gained Despotic Control of the Amusements of the American People—The Results,

Good and Bad. Part I—The Dictators Rise from Obscurity." *Leslie's Monthly Magazine* 53, no. 6, October 1904, 581-02, 590.

20 See Appendix A.

21 David Belasco. "The Theatrical Syndicate. One Side." *The Cosmopolitan*, December 1904, 193-98, 194.

22 Nat C. Goodwin, *Nat Goodwin's Book*. Boston: Richard G. Badger, 1914, 107-08.

23 Jerry Stagg. *The Brothers Shubert*. New York: Random House, 1968, 37.

24 Eaton, "The Theatre", 838.

25 Belasco. "The Theatrical Syndicate", 194.

26 Jack Poggi. *Theater in America: The Impact of Economic Forces 1870-1967*. Ithaca, New York: Cornell University Press, 1968, 257.

27 Stagg, *The Brothers Shubert*, 38.

28 Wisconsin Center for Film and Theater Research, Teischman Oral History, tape 7.

29 Broadway: The American Musical, episode 1.

4 Trustbusting and its Loopholes

1 Richard M. Steuer. "The Simplicity of Antitrust Law." *University of Pennsylvania Journal of Business Law* 14, no. 2 (Winter 2012), 543.

2 15 U.S.C. §§ 1-4, 15a (1890).

3 15 U.S.C. § 15 (1914).

4 *Standard Oil Co. of New Jersey v. United States*, 221 U.S. 1 (1911); *United States v. American Tobacco Co.*, 221 U.S. 106 (1911).

5 James Chace. *1912: Wilson, Roosevelt, Taft & Debs – The Election that Changed the Country*. New York: Simon & Schuster, 2004.

6 15 U.S.C. §§ 12-27 (1914).

7 15 U.S.C. § 45 (1914).

8 *United States v. E. C. Knight Co.*, 156 U.S. 1 (1895).

9 *People v. Klaw*, 55 Misc. 72, 90–91, 106 N.Y.S. 341 (Gen. Sess. 1907).

10 Alfred L. Bernheim. *The Business of the Theatre: An Economic History of the American Theatre, 1750-1932*. 1932. Reprinted. New York: B. Blom, 1964, 59 (citing "Syndicate No Trust." *The Billboard*, June 29, 1907, 28).

11 *H.B. Marienelli, Ltd. v. United Booking Offs. of Am.*, 227 F. 165, 170 (S.D.N.Y. 1914).

12 *Metropolitan Opera Co. v. Hammerstein*, 162 A.D. 691, 695-96, 147 N.Y.S. 532, 534-35 (App. Div. 1914).

13 Fed. Trade Comm'n. Ann. Rep. (1919), Complaint No. 128, 51.

14 For more details on Advanced Vaudeville see chapter 8.

15 "Theatre Trust May Face Federal Suit." *New York Times*, August 15, 1908, 7.

16 *Ibid.*

17 *Fed. Baseball Club v. Nat'l League*, 259 U.S. 200, 209 (1922). For more on the peculiar baseball exemption from antitrust see Spencer Weber Waller, Neil B. Cohen, and Paul Finkelman. *Baseball and the American Legal Mind*. New York: Garland Pub. 1995.

18 *Hart v. B.F. Keith Vaudeville Exch.*, 262 U.S. 271 (1923).

19 *Ibid.* at 273.

20 *Hart v. B.F. Keith Vaudeville Exch.*, 12 F.2d 341, 344 (2d Cir. 1926).

5 The Price of Independence

1 Vincent Landro. "Media Mania: The Demonizing of the Theatrical Syndicate." *The Journal of American Drama and Theatre* 13, no. 2 (Spring 2001), 42.

2 David Belasco. "The Theatrical Syndicate. One Side." *The Cosmopolitan*, December 1904, 201.

3 Isaac F. Marcosson and Daniel Frohman. *Charles Frohman: Manager and Man*, with an appreciation by James M. Barrie. 1916. Reprint. New York: Jefferson, 2015, 69.

4 The Syndicate agreement is reprinted in its entirety in Appendix 1.

5 "Great Actors and the Theatre Trust." *The World*, November 22, 1897, 6.

6 Monroe Lippman. "The History of the Theatrical Syndicate: Its Effect Upon the Theatre in America." PhD diss., University Michigan, 1937, 57-60.

7 "Belasco Scores the Trust." *New York Times*, September 18, 1904, 7.

8 *Ibid.*

9 David Belasco. "A Card from David Belasco." *New York Times*, October 11, 1904, 8.

10 Celcile A. Rukgaber. "The Theatrical Syndicate and its Effects Upon the American Theatre." MA thesis, University of Wyoming, 1955, 58.

11 Arthur Hornblow. *A History of the Theatre in America*. Philadelphia: J.B. Lippincott Co., 1919, 320.

12 Craig Timberlake. *The Life & Work of David Belasco: The Bishop of Broadway*. New York: Library Publishers, 1954, 244-76.

13 "Actors' Alliance Scores The Trust." *Buffalo Evening News*, December 13, 1897, 1.

14 Norman Hapgood. "The Theatrical Syndicate." *The International Monthly,* January 1900, 105.

15 Norman Hapgood. *The Stage in America: 1897-1900*. New York: The MacMillan Company, 1901, 17 (quoting William Dean Howells).

16 *Ibid*. (quoting Thomas Bailey Aldrich).

17 *Ibid*. at 18 (quoting Richard Mansfield).

18 Hapgood. "The Theatrical Syndicate",108.

19 Lippman. "The History of the Theatrical Syndicate", 65-66.

20 William Winter, "The Department Store Theatre", New York Dramatic Mirror, June 17, 1905, 10 (https://archive.org/details/per_new-york-dramatic-mirror_the-new-york-dramatic-mirror_1905-06-17_53_1382/page/10/mode/2up); Castigated By the Press", The New York Dramatic Mirror, May 20, 1905, 15 (reprinting article from the New York Evening Post). (https://archive.org/details/per_new-york-dramatic-mirror_the-new-york-dramatic-mirror_1905-05-20_53_1378/page/n13/mode/2up).

21 Anthony P. Hatch. *Tinder Box: The Iroquois Theatre Disaster*, 1903. Chicago: Academy Chicago Publishers, 2003, 26-27.

22 Timberlake. *The Life & Work of David Belasco*, 263.

23 Marc Klaw. "The Theatrical Syndicate. The Other Side." *The Cosmopolitan*, December 1904, 201.

24 Charles Frohman. "New Phases of Theatre Management." *Harper's Weekly*, December 31, 1904, 2022.

25 Monroe Lippman. "The Effect of the Theatrical Syndicate on Theatrical Arts in America." *Quarterly Journal of Speech* 26, no. 2 (April 1940), 280.

26 Landro. "Media Mania", 47.

27 Rukgaber. "The Theatrical Syndicate", 65.

28 Lippman. "The History of the Theatrical Syndicate", 71-72.

6 The Shubert Challenge

1 A different biographer has David coming by himself in 1881 and then sending for the family a year later. Jerry Stagg. *The Brothers Shubert*. New York: Random House, 1968, 5.

2 Stagg. *The Brothers Shubert*, 9. Lee Shubert's late in life memoirs recalled it was an earlier production of *Uncle Tom's Cabin*, another touring stalwart of the era. Lee's memoirs also differ on his age at the time and the age difference between him and Sam. Lee Shubert. "Mr. Lee: As Set Down by Ed Sullivan." Unpublished manuscript, c. 1950, typescript, 3; Maryann Chach, ed. "Lee Shubert's Reminiscences." *The Passing Show: Newsletter of the Shubert Archive* 13/14, no. 2/1 (Fall 1990/Spring 1991), 8-9.

3 Stagg. *The Brothers Shubert*, 9.

4 Foster Hirsch tells two different versions of this key moment, but both include Sam beginning the highly lucrative process of using outside investors to finance Shubert productions. Foster Hirsh. *The Boys from Syracuse: The Shuberts' Theatrical Empire*. Lanham: Cooper Square Press, 1998, 17-18.

5 Shubert. "Mr. Lee", 8.

6 Michael Riedel. *Razzle Dazzle: The Battle for Broadway*. New York: Simon & Schuster, 2016, 24.

7 New York Public Library, Bill Rose Theater Collection, Klaw & Erlanger Scrapbook v. 323.

8 Shubert. "Mr. Lee", 28, 30.

9 Stagg. *The Brothers Shubert*, 38-39.

10 *Ibid.* at 43-44.

11 Isaac F. Marcosson and Daniel Frohman. *Charles Frohman: Manager and Man*. 1916. Reprint. New York: Jefferson, 2015, 70.

12 Riedel. *Razzle Dazzle*, 26.

13 Monroe Lippman. "The History of the Theatrical Syndicate: Its Effect Upon the Theatre in America." PhD diss., University of Michigan, 1937, 116. Texas and Missouri later passed antitrust legislation designed in part to force the Syndicate to open their theaters to all attractions.

14 John Tenney. "In the Trenches: The Syndicate-Shubert Theatrical War." *The Passing Show: Newsletter of the Shubert Archive* 21, no. 2 (Fall-Winter 1998), 4; Jack Poggi. *Theater in America: The Impact of Economic Forces 1870-1967*. Ithaca, New York: Cornell University Press, 1968, 16.

15 The theater later became a television studio in the 1950s, again a movie theater for a time, and eventually was demolished for a parking lot in 1961.

16 "Iroquois Theater Opened with 'Mr. Blue Beard'." The Chicago Tribune, November 24, 1903, 3.

17 Scott G. Knowles. *The Disaster Experts: Mastering Risk in Modern America*. Philadelphia: University of Pennsylvania Press, 2011, 68.

18 "Iroquois Theater Opened with "Mr. Blue Beard", 3.

19 Anthony P. Hatch. *Tinder Box: The Iroquois Theatre Disaster 1903*. Academy Chicago Publishers, 2003. 121.

20 Brooks McNamara, *The Shuberts of Broadway: A History Drawn from the Collection of the Shubert Archive*. New York: Oxford University Press, 1900, 27-29.

21 *Ibid.* at 31.

22 Shubert. "Mr. Lee", 44.

23 Stagg. *The Brothers Shubert*, 70.

7 War, Peace, and Dirty Tricks

1 Brooks McNamara. *The Shuberts of Broadway: A History Drawn from the Collection of the Shubert Archive*. New York: Oxford University Press, 1990, 40.

2 J.J.'s son John estimated that the Shuberts owned more than seventy theaters by 1910. *See* McNamara, *The Shuberts of Broadway*, 35.

3 Alfred L Bernheim., *The Business of the Theatre: An Economic History of the American Theatre, 1750-1932*. 1932. Reprinted. New York: B. Blom, 1964, 67.

4 Jerry Stagg. *The Brothers Shubert*. New York: Random House, 1968, 107, 168.

5 *Ibid.* at 273–74.

6 The leading vaudeville circuits also used initial public offerings of stock to finance their expansion. *See* "Keith Vaudeville Will Offer Stock." *The New York Times*, March 17, 1926, 34.

7 Bernstein, Richard. *Only in America: Al Jolson and the Jazz Singer*. New York: Knopf Doubleday Publishing Group, 2024, 55.

8 Leonard W. Conolly. *Bernard Shaw on the American Stage: A Chronicle of Premiers and Notable Revivals*. London: Palgrave Macmillan, 2022, 138.

9 S.M. Weller. "Competition has Given Authors, Acts, Managers Opportunities They Never Could Have Had Under Monopolistic Conditions –the Young Playwright Now Gets Hearing – The Actor Can Select His Own Part and Name his Own Salary – Both Can Look Managers in the Eye and Tell Them Where to Go." *New York Review*. July 10, 1910, 1.

10 Maryann Chach. "Behind the Scenes of The New York Review." *The Passing Show: Newsletter of the Shubert Archive* 12, no. 2 (Fall 1989): 2–14.

11 Foster Hirsch. *The Boys from Syracuse: The Shubert's Theatrical Empire*. Lanham: Cooper Square Press, 1998, 77.

12 *Ibid.*

13 *Ibid.*

14 McNamara, *The Shuberts of Broadway*, 66.

15 *Ibid.* at 67.

16 *Ibid.* at 68.

17 Bennett, H. Whitman. "'C.F. 'Now Stands for 'Complete Failure.'" *New York Review*, July 23, 1910.

18 M.B. Leavitt. *Fifty Years in Theatrical Management: 1859-1909*. New York: Broadway Publishing Co., 1912, 614.

19 John Tenney. "In the Trenches: The Syndicate-Shubert Theatrical War." *The Passing Show: Newsletter of the Shubert Archive* 21, no. 2 (Fall-Winter 1998): 13.

20 *Ibid.*

21 Hirsch, *The Boys from Syracuse*, 77.

22 "Attacked Chicago In Will. A. Toxen Worm Left-Small Bequests to Charity, Residue to Niece." *The New York Times*, January 16, 1992, 5.

23 Stagg, *The Brothers Shubert*, 114–15.

8 The First Vaudeville War and Dreams of Global Domination

1 Douglas Gilbert. *American Vaudeville, Its Life & Times*. 1940. Reprinted, New Dover edn. New York: Dover Publications, 1963, 198.

2 Jerry Stagg. *The Brothers Shubert*. New York: Random House, 1968, 29.

3 Marian Spitzer. "The Business of Vaudeville." *The Saturday Evening Post*, May 24, 1924, 18-19; 125; 129-30; 133, 19.

4 Arthur F. Wertheim. *Vaudeville Wars: How the Keith-Albee and Orpheum Circuits Controlled the Big Time and its Performers*. New York: Palgrave Macmillan, 2006, 132.

5 Unknown author. "New Syndicate Afoot in Theatrical World. Will Be on Vast Scale, with $30,000,000 Capital." *The New York Times* 55, No. 17629, May 1, 1906, 9.

6 A.L Erlanger. *Letter to George Lederer.* February 28, 1907, Klaw & Erlanger Collection, Billy Rose Theatre Division, New York Public Library, New York.

7 Marlis Schweitzer. "A Failed Attempt at World Domination: 'Advanced Vaudeville,' Financial Panic, and the Dream of a World Trust." *Theatre History Studies* 32, no. 1 (2012): 53-79, 23.

8 Jack Poggi. *Theater in America: The Impact of Economic Forces 1870-1967*. Ithaca, New York: Cornell University Press, 1968, 18.

9 Unknown author. "Fight Starts Monday. Klaw & Erlanger Fire Their First Vaudeville Bill Against the United Booking Offices." *Variety* 6, No. 6, April 20, 1907, 2.

10 Craig Timberlake. *The Life & Work of David Belasco: The Bishop of Broadway*. New York: Library Publishers, 1954, 283.

11 Wertheim. *Vaudeville Wars*, 135.

12 Unknown Author. "Managers Desert Morris. Follow Into the United Booking Offices, Leaving the Morris Office Bare Excepting Two Houses Keith Does Not Want—From $125,000 to Nothing Within a Year." *Variety* 5, No. 11, February 23, 1907, 2.

13 Monroe Lippman. "The History of the Theatrical Syndicate: Its Effect Upon the Theatre in America." PhD diss., University of Michigan, 1937, 123.

14 Brooks McNamara. *The Shuberts of Broadway: A History Drawn from the Collection of the Shubert Archive*. New York: Oxford University Press, 1990, 42.

15 Unknown Author. "Klaw & Erlanger Enter Vaudeville Successfully. Reports From All Over the 'Advanced Vaudeville' Circuit Give Favorable Expression to the Entertainment Offered by the Vaudeville Opposition." *Variety* 7, No. 13, September 7, 1907, 2.

16 Unknown author. "Will Buy Theatres Here and Abroad. A.L. Erlanger Tells the Plans of His New $100,000,000 Syndicate." *The New York Times* 56, No. 18072, July 13, 1907, 7.

17 Wertheim. *Vaudeville Wars*, 140.

18 Lee Shubert. "Mr. Lee: As Set Down by Ed Sullivan." Unpublished Manuscript, c. 1950, typescript, 59.

19 Unknown Author. "Warring Managers Meet in Vain Peace Conference—A.L. Erlanger, Martin Beck and Marc Klaw Closeted in the St. Regis Hotel Without Avail." *Variety* 8, No. 5, October 12, 1907, 2.

20 Unknown Author. "'Chipping In' for Second 'Settlement' Assessment: $125,000 in Certified Checks Will Be Turned Over to Klaw & Erlanger by the United Booking Offices on February 3rd." *Variety* 9, No. 6, January 18, 1908, 1.

21 Shubert. "Mr. Lee", 62.

22 Unknown author. "Gigantic Theatrical Corporation Proposed. Klaw & Erlanger Planning to Form a $100,000,000 Company to Build and Operate Theatres. Control of European Vaudeville Houses Aimed At." *Variety* 7, No. 6, July 20, 1907, 2.; Unknown author. "A World Theatre Now?." *The New York Dramatic Mirror* 58, No. 1492, July 27, 1907, 4.

23 *Ferris v. Frohman*, 223 U.S. 424 (1912).

24 Unknown author. "Levy Mayer on Merger. Klaw & Erlanger Lawyer Arrives at Plymouth and Explains." *The New York Times* 56, No. 18078, July 24, 1907, 3.

25 Schweitzer. "A Failed Attempt at World Domination", 66.

26 *Ibid.* at 66-67.

27 Unknown author. "England Discusses American Invasion by Oscar Stoll." *Variety*, Vol. XVIII No 4. April 2, 1910.

28 W.L. Hicks. "Breezes From the Windy City." *The Conjurers' Monthly Magazine*, February 1908, 184.

29 Unknown author. "Morris Advertising for Vaudeville Theatres. Advertisements Asking for Houses Placed in Pittsburg, Cincinnati, Baltimore and Washington Papers." *Variety* 9, No. 1, December 14, 1907, 1; Wertheim. *Vaudeville Wars*, 143-44.

30 For more on the remarkable career of Marcus Loew see Chapter 12.

31 Frank Rose. *The Agency: William Morris and the Hidden History of Show Business.* New York: Harper Business, 1995, 42-51.

32 Unknown author. "Morris Opposition in Vaudeville Opens To-Day." *Variety* 40, No. 13, September 5, 1908, 7.

33 Unknown author. "Theatre Managers Draw Lines Tighter. Object of a Meeting Yesterday Interpreted to Keep Some Theatres Closed." *The New York Times* 57, No. 18458, August 7, 1908, 1.

34 McNamara. *The Shuberts of Broadway*, 49.

35 Shubert. "Mr. Lee", 65.

36 Francis Wilson. *Francis Wilson's Life of Himself.* Boston and New York: Houghton Mifflin, 1924, 167.

37 Unknown author. "Too Many Theatres Bring Truce in War. 'Syndicate' and Shuberts and Allies Agree to Eliminate Ruinous Competition." *The New York Times* 62, No. 20111, February 15, 1913, 15.

38 Shubert. "Mr. Lee", 65.

39 Unknown author. "Theatrical Men Form New Nation-Wide Association." *New Jersey Telegraph*, May 31, 1914.

40 N.J. Telegraph, Jan. 15, 1915.

41 Stagg. *The Brothers Shubert,* 136-37.

9 Labor and Monopoly

1 The International Alliance of Theatrical Stage Employees. "IATSE Through the Years: A Proud History of Progress." Edited by James B. Wood. *The Official Bulletin: 125 Years of IATSE*, no. 660 (Q2 2018), 7. https://iatse.net/the-official-bulletin-2018-q2-no-660/.

2 Foster Hirsch. *The Boys from Syracuse: The Shuberts' Theatrical Empire*. New York: Cooper Square Press 2000, 111.

3 William Mailly. "Plays and Players." *The Worker*, November 23, 1907, 2.

4 Hirsch, *The Boys from Syracuse*, 112.

5 John Kenrick. *Musical Theatre: A History*. 2nd ed. London: Bloomsbury Publishing Plc, 2017, 113.

6 IATSE Local 18032. "History of ATPAM." ATPAM. Accessed July 7, 2025. https://www.atpam.com/history.

7 *Shubert Theatre Corp. v. Richman*, No. 16847 (N.Y. Sup. Ct. filed Apr. 29, 1927).

8 Jerry Stagg. *The Brothers Shubert*. New York: Random House, 1968, 250.

9 Brent Salter and Catherine L. Fisk. "The Fragility of Labor Relations in the American Theatre." *Ohio State Law Journal* 83, no. 2 (2022), 240.

10 *See Ring v. Spina*, 148 F.2d 647, 649 (2d Cir. 1945).

11 Arthur Franklin Wertheim, *Vaudeville Wars: Hoe the Keith-Albee and Orpheum Circuits Controlled the Big-Time and its Performers*. New York: Palgrave MacMillian, 2006, 175.

12 Walter J. Kingsley. "The Reconstruction of Vaudeville", *National Magazine*, May 1919, 173.

13 E.F. Albee. "Twenty Years of Vaudeville." *Theatre Magazine*, May 1920, 450.

14 Wertheim, *Vaudeville Wars*, 233.

15 National Recovery Administration. "Proposed Code of Fair Competition for the Legitimate Full Length Dramatic and Musical Theatrical Industry as Approved on August 16, 1933 by President Roosevelt." National Recovery Administration, August 16, 1933, iv.

16 *A.L.A. Schechter Poultry Corp. v. United States*, 295 U.S. 495 (1935); *Panama Ref. Co. v. Ryan*, 293 U.S. 388 (1935).

10 Empire

1 Lee Shubert. "Mr. Lee: As Set Down by Ed Sullivan." Unpublished Manuscript, c. 1950, typescript, 228-30.

2 John Kenrick. *Musical Theatre: A History*. 2nd ed. London: Bloomsbury Publishing Plc, 2017, 120-23. The Shuberts eventually licensed the *Ziegfeld Follies* from Ziegfeld's widow after his death in 1932 and produced revues under that name for more than another decade.

3 *Ibid.* at 123.

4 "Theatrical Merger Reported." *Wall Street Journal,* October 22, 1918, 6.

5 Shuberts in Combine of Playhouses." Los Angeles Times, June 9, 1923, 2.

6 Arthur F. Wertheim. *Vaudeville Wars: How the Keith-Albee and Orpheum Circuits Controlled the Big Time and its Performers.* New York: Palgrave Macmillan, 2006, 243.

7 Jerry Stagg. *The Brothers Shubert.* New York: Random House, 1968, 185.

8 "Mr. Lee", 167-68.

9 Shubert Archives, Lee Shubert to Arthur Klein Dec 13, 1921, General Corr., Box 2401 Folder 326B.

10 Stagg. *The Brothers Shubert,* 190.

11 *Ibid.* at 191.

12 "Mr. Lee", 144.

13 Shubert Archives, Corporation Series, B.F. Keith Box 32. 8/21/21 and 8/24/21.

14 Jack Poggi, *Theater in America: The Impact of Economic Forces 1870-1967.* Ithaca, New York: Cornell University Press, 1968, 22-23.

15 Brooks McNamara. *The Shuberts of Broadway: A History Drawn from the Collection of the Shubert Archive.* New York: Oxford University Press, 1990, 136.

16 Stagg. *The Brothers Shubert,* 221.

17 McNamara. *The Shuberts of Broadway,* xxiv.

18 *Ibid.* at 145.

19 *Ibid.* at xxvi.

20 Mary C. Henderson. *Theater in America: 200 Years of Plays, Players, and Productions.* New York: Harry N. Abrams, 1986, 29.

21 Poggi. *Theater in America,* 21.

22 Stagg. *The Brothers Shubert,* 217.

23 *Ibid.* at 222.

24 "Mr. Lee", 267.

25 *Ibid.* at 164.

26 Foster Hirsch. *The Boys from Syracuse: The Shuberts' Theatrical Empire.* Lanham: Cooper Square Press, 1998, 144.

27 A.J. Liebling. "The Boys from Syracuse--I." *The New Yorker,* November 10, 1939, 28; Gerald Schoenfeld. *Mr. Broadway: The Inside Story of the Shuberts, the Shows, and the Stars.* New York: Applause Books, 2012, 12.

28 Stagg. *The Brothers Shubert*, 128.

29 Alfred L. Bernheim. *The Business of the Theatre: An Economic History of the American Theatre, 1750-1932*. 1932. Reprinted. New York: B. Blom, 1964, 77.

30 *Ibid.* at 79; McNamara. *The Shuberts of Broadway*, 136.

31 Bernheim, *The Business of the Theatre*, 81.

32 A glimpse of this world is depicted in Herman Wouk's *Marjorie Morningstar*. New York: Doubleday, 1955.

33 Bernheim, *The Business of the Theatre*, 106-110.

11 Survival

1 Brooks McNamara. *The Shuberts of Broadway: A History Drawn from the Collection of the Shubert Archive*. New York: Oxford University Press, 1990, 144, 163.

2 Draft Memorandum of Agreement, Shubert Archives, Shubert Organization Business Records; Corporation Series; Erlanger, A.L. 1921-33; Box 19, Folder 1.

3 Unknown author. "United Booking in Effect August 1." New York Time, July 25, 1932.

4 Stewart F. Lane. *It Happened at the Palace: A History of New York's Iconic Broadway Theater.* Edwardsville, IL: Broad Book Press, 2024, 78-80.

5 John Kendrick. *Musical Theatre: A History*. 2nd ed. London: Bloomsbury Publishing Plc, 2017, 192.

6 Library of Congress. *Federal Theatre Project, 1935 to 1939*. https://www.loc.gov/collections/federal-theatre-project-1935-to-1939/.

7 *Ibid.* at 41.

8 James Shapiro. *The Playbook: A Story of Theater, Democracy, and the Making of a Culture War.* New York: Penguin Press, 2024, 85-105.

9 *Ibid.* at 103.

10 *Ibid.* at xvi.

11 *Ibid.* at 93.

12 *Ibid.* at 253.

13 McNamara. *The Shuberts of Broadway*, 75.

14 Arthur F. Wertheim. *Vaudeville Wars: How the Keith-Albee and Orpheum Circuits Controlled the Big Time and its Performers*. New York: Palgrave Macmillan, 2006, 259-61.

15 *Ibid.* at 266-68.

16 Kevin Lewis. "A World across from Broadway: The Shuberts and the Movies." *Film History* 1, no. 1 (1987), 40.

17 McNamara. *The Shuberts of Broadway*, 80.

18 Frank Rose. *The Agency: William Morris and the Hidden History of Show Business.* New York: Harper Business, 1995, 32.

19 Marcus Loew. "The Motion Picture and Vaudeville." In *The Story of the Films,* pp. 285-300, Joseph P. Kennedy, ed., Chicago & New York: A.W. Shaw Company, 1927, 287.

20 Frank Caso. "Marcus Loew, 1870-1927." *Immigrant Entrepreneurship*, September 22, 2011. https://www.immigrantentrepreneurship.org/entries/marcus-loew/.

21 *United States v. Paramount Pictures, Inc.*, 334 U.S. 131 (1948).

22 Today, MGM is a subsidiary of Amazon whose library of films stream on Amazon Prime or for rent on other streaming platforms.

23 *Fed. Trade Comm'n v. Paramount Famous-Lasky Corp.*, 57 F.2d 152 (2d Cir. 1932).

24 Caso. "Marcus Loew, 1870-1927."

25 *United States v. Paramount Pictures, Inc.*, 334 U.S. 131 (1948); *United States v. Loew's Inc.*, 371 U.S. 38 (1962).

26 Tino Balio. 'Marcus Loew and the Founding of Metro-Goldwyn-Mayer (1905-1924)'. In *MGM*, pp. 11-28. New York: Routledge, 2018, 28.

27 Jerry Stagg. *The Brothers Shubert.* New York: Random House, 1968, 258.

12 The Quiet Life

1 John R. Hicks. "Annual Survey of Economic Theory: The Theory of Monopoly." *Econometrica* 3, No. 1 (Jan. 1935), 8.

2 Brooks McNamara. *The Shuberts of Broadway: A History Drawn from the Collection of the Shubert Archive*. New York: Oxford University Press, 1990, 72.

3 Foster Hirsch. *The Boys from Syracuse: The Shuberts' Theatrical Empire*. Lanham: Cooper Square Press, 1998, 186.

4 McNamara. *The Shuberts of Broadway*, 188-91.

5 *Ibid.* at 200.

6 Hirsch. *The Boys from Syracuse*, 190.

7 McNamara. *The Shuberts of Broadway*, 203.

8 Jerry Stagg. *The Brothers Shubert*. New York: Random House, 1968, 29.

9 Frank Rich. "How Broadway Became Broadway." *Vulture* (New York Magazine), April 8, 2025. https://www.vulture.com/article/how-broadway-became-broadway-history-frank-rich-column.html.

10 *Ibid.*

11 The last play JJ actively produced was in rehearsal at the time of Lee's death in late 1953. A young Christopher Plummer starred in *The Starcross Story* which openRd on January 13, 1954, and closed the next day. The last show produced by any member of the Shubert family was John's 1961 comedy called *Julia, Jake and Uncle Joe* starring Claudia Cardinale. It also closed after one performance.

12 Stagg. *The Brothers Shubert*, 351-52.

13 Kerry Segrave. *Ticket Scalping: An American History, 1850-2005*. Jefferson: McFarland & Co., Inc. Publishers, 2007, 10-12.

14 Unknown Author. "Managers Call Scalpers Pests. Say They Make It Impossible to be Fair with the Theatregoers." *The New York Times* 57, No. 18499, September 17, 1908, 7.

15 Segrave. *Ticket Scalping*, 30.

16 Unknown Author. "Ticket Scalpers Accuse Managers. Say They Are Secretly Duping the Public by Having Their Own Ticket Speculators." *The New York Times* 57, No. 18497, September 15, 1908, 18.

17 Segrave. *Ticket Scalping*, 13.

18 Unknown Author. "Ticket Speculation Ordinance Passes. If Signed by the Mayor All Trading in Theatre Tickets Will Be Illegal." *The New York Times* 58, No. 18575, December 2, 1908, 1.

19 *Ibid.* at 59.

20 By the 1960s the numbers of house seats reported hit 100 for some shows. William Goldman. *The Season: A Candid Look at Broadway*. New York: Harcourt, Brace, & World, 1969, 342-43.

21 Unknown Author. "President Spurs Anti-Trust Study. Urges Celler to 'Go Ahead Full Steam'—U.S. Steel and Newsprint to Be Studied." *The New York Times* 99, No. 33620, February 10, 1950, 37.

22 Stagg. *The Brothers Shubert*, 355-56.

23 Unknown Author. "Top Shubert Aide Seized in Inquiry. Ticket Man Got $70,000 in 'Ice' in '63, Hogan Says." *The New York Times* 113, No. 38834, May 21, 1964, 1.

24 Michael Riedel. *Razzle Dazzle: The Battle for Broadway*. New York: Simon & Schuster, 2016, 47; Gerald Schoenfeld. *Mr. Broadway: The Inside Story of the Shuberts, the Shows, and the Stars*. New York: Applause Books, 2012, 85-86.

25 Stagg. *The Brothers Shubert*, 251.

26 Hirsch. *The Boys from Syracuse*, 235-36.

27 Ed Sullivan Correspondence, Box 1251 undated, Shubert Archives.

28 Lee Shubert. "Mr. Lee: As Set Down by Ed Sullivan." Unpublished Manuscript, c. 1950, typescript, viii.

29 *Ibid.* at 48.

30 *Ibid.* at 313.

13 Justice

1 *See* Spencer Weber Waller. *Thurman Arnold: A Biography*. New York: New York University Press, 2005.

2 *Interstate Circuit, Inc. v. United States*, 306 U.S. 208 (1939).

3 *FTC v. Motion Picture Advert. Serv. Co.*, 344 U.S. 392 (1953); *United States v. Griffith*, 334 U.S. 100 (1948); *Schine Chain Theatres, Inc. v. United States*, 334 U.S. 110 (1948); *Bigelow v. RKO Radio Pictures, Inc.*, 327 U.S. 251 (1946); *United States v. Crescent Amusement Co.*, 323 U.S. 173 (1944). The one exception was *Theatre Enters., Inc. v. Paramount Film Distrib. Corp.*, 346 U.S. 537 (1954) where the Supreme Court held that the jury's verdict in favor of the defendant was legally permissible.

4 *United States v. Paramount Pictures*, 66 F. Supp. 323 (S.D.N.Y. 1946).

5 *United States v. Paramount Pictures, Inc.*, 334 U.S. 131 (1948).

6 *United States v. Paramount Pictures, Inc.*, Equity No. 87-273, Consent Decree at 1-2 (S.D.N.Y. Mar. 3, 1949) (Paramount Defs.).

7 *United States v. Paramount Pictures, Inc.*, 2020 U.S. Dist. WL 4573069/LEXIS 141427 1, 2 (S.D.N.Y. Aug. 7, 2020).

8 Unknown Author. "Serlin Threatens Monopoly Action Against the UBO." *Variety* 141, No. 13, March 5, 1941, 49.

9 Gerald Schoenfeld. *Mr. Broadway: The Inside Story of the Shuberts, the Shows, and the Stars*. New York: Applause Books, 2012, 49.

10 Danton Walker, "Broadway Beat." *New York Daily News*, April 5, 1950.

11 Jerry Stagg. *The Brothers Shubert*, 357.

12 N.Y. Daily News, February 10, 1950, p. 64.

13 Foster Hirsch. *The Boys from Syracuse: The Shuberts' Theatrical Empire*. Lanham: Cooper Square Press, 1998, 217.

14 *United States v. Shubert,* 11 F.R.D. 528, 531 (S.D.N.Y. 1951).

15 Lee Shubert. *Statement in Response to Government Suit*, n.d., Shubert Archive, Lyceum Theatre, New York, NY.

16 *Ibid.*

17 Milton R. Weir (Klein & Weir, counsel for the Shubert brothers). *Statement on the Government's Monopoly Complaint*, n.d., Shubert Archive, Lyceum Theatre, New York, NY.

18 Milton Shubert. *Letter to Lee Shubert, John Shubert, and Milton Weir*, March 2, 1950.

19 George Jean Nathan. "Let's Forget Russia and Fight the Shuberts." *New York Journal-American*, March 20, 1950.

20 Unknown Author. "Shuberts File Denial to Suit. Claim Producing or Booking Plays Not Within Scope of Anti-Trust Act." *Theatre News Weekly*, June 2, 1950.

21 *Klein File Memo*, July 30, 1951, Shubert Archive, Lyceum Theatre, New York, NY.

22 *Federal Baseball Club v. National League*, 259 U.S. 200 (1922); *Toolson v. New York Yankees, Inc.*, 346 U.S. 356 (1953).

23 Rev Dr. Nathan A. Perilman. "Mr. Lee." *Variety* 193, No. 4, December 30, 1953, 58.

24 Lawrence Langer. "Memories of 'Mr. Lee'. Career of Recently Deceased Showman Reviewed by a Theatre Associate." *The New York Times* 103, No. 35043, January 3, 1954, sec. 2, X1, X3.

25 That foundation still exists today. It operates the remaining Shubert theaters, a substantial philanthropic program, and maintains the Shubert Archives.

26 *United States v. Shubert*, 120 F. Supp. 15 (S.D.N.Y. 1953).

27 *United States v. Shubert*, 348 U.S. 222 (1955).

28 J.J. Shubert to Mr. Lund, Box 4, USA v. Shubert, S704, 2d Folder, November 8, 1955, Shubert Archives.

14 The End of the Road

1 J.J. Schubert to Alfred McCormick, September 6, 1955. USA v. Shubert, Box 4 S704, Drafts Corres. Misc. Shubert Archives.

2 J.J. to John Shubert, March. 25, 1953. *Ibid.*

3 J.J. to Alfred Lund, September 8, 1955. *Ibid.*

4 J.J. to Alfred Lund, October 15, 1955, *Ibid.*

5 The Shuberts did not again produce any production until the hit musical *Pippin* in 1972, where their net investment was a mere $10,000. Gerald Schoenfeld. *Mr. Broadway: The Inside Story of the Shuberts, the Shows, and the Stars.* New York: Applause Books, 2012, 121.

6 J.J. to Alfred McCormack, September 6, 1955. USA v. Shubert, Box 4 S704, Drafts Corres. Misc. Shubert Archives.

7 "Triple Damages—It's Murder." *Business Week* 59, April 22, 1950, 60.

8 The Nederlander Organization, "About Us", https://nederlander.com/about-us.

9 The Broadway League. https://www.broadwayleague.com/home/947.

10 Foster Hirsch. *The Boys from Syracuse: The Shuberts' Theatrical Empire*. Lanham: Cooper Square Press, 1998, 238.

11 *United States v. Shubert*, 163 F. Supp. 123, 124 (S.D.N.Y. 1958).

12 Dan Austin. "Cass Theatre." *Historic Detroit*, https://historicdetroit.org/buildings/cass-theatre.

13 These two Chicago theaters were eventually converted into movie theaters. They later sat empty for many years once single screen downtown movie theaters were no longer viable. Eventually these theaters were purchased, combined, and restored to become the home of the Goodman Theatre, the only large non-profit theater located in downtown Chicago. Goodman Theatre. "Our History." https://www.goodmantheatre.org/about/our-history/.

14 *Goldlawr, Inc. v. Shubert* 268 F. Supp. 965 (E.D. Pa. 1967).

15 The New Bottlenecks of Broadway

1 Different aspects of the role of the modern producer are explored in Peter Boygo, *Broadway General Manager: Demystifying the Most Important and Least Understood Role in Show Business* and Jack Viertel, *The Secret Life of the American Musical: How Broadway Shows are Built.*

2 Tony Awards Administration Committee, Tony Awards: Rules & Regulations (2023-2024), Exhibit A. https://www.tonyawards.com/documents/18/2023-2024_Tony_Rules_and_Regulations.pdf.

3 "New Amsterdam Theatre | History." https://newamsterdamtheatre.com/history.php.

4 Michael Paulsen. "Broadway Surpasses Prepandemic Peak." New York Times. May 15, 2025 C1-2.

5 "The Phantom of the Opera." https://www.thephantomoftheopera.com/.

6 "The Fabulous Fox Theatre's 2023-2024 Spectacular Broadway Series Is Simply the Best!" https://www.fabulousfox.com/news/detail/the-fabulous-fox-theatres-2023-2024-spectacular-broadway-series-is-simply-the-best.

7 The Broadway League. *Broadway Season Statistics: 2009-10 through 2023-24*. n.d. https://www.broadwayleague.com/static/user/admin/media/statistics_broadway_2009-10_2023-24.pdf.

8 "Independent Presenters Network Resumes its Biennial Meeting in London." Press release, Blumenthal Arts, November 14, 2022. https://www.blumenthalarts.org/news/detail/independent-presenters-network-resumes-its-biennial-meeting-in-london.

9 The John Gore Organization. "Brands." https://www.johngore.com/brands/baa/.

16 Pearl Jam, Taylor Swift, and Live Nation

1 Dean Budnick & Josh Baron. *Ticket Masters: The Rise of the Concert Industry and How the Public Got Scalped*. Toronto: ECW Press, 2011, 55-90.

2 Eric Boehlert. "Pearl Jam: Taking on Ticketmaster." *Rolling Stone*, December 28, 1995. https://www.rollingstone.com/music/music-news/pearl-jam-taking-on-ticketmaster-67440/.

3 Niall Doherty. "Eddie Vedder on Pearl Jam's Battle with Ticketmaster." *Louder Sound*, May 5, 2024. https://www.loudersound.com/features/eddie-vedder-looks-back-on-pearl-jams-war-with-ticketmaster.

4 Dennis McNally. *A Long Strange Trip: The Inside History of the Grateful Dead*. New York: Crown Publishing Group, 2007, 547-48.

5 "Ticket Masters – Part 3: The Ticketmaster's Challenge: The Grateful Dead, Pearl Jam and String Cheese Incident." Music Business Research, September 20, 2011. https://musicbusinessresearch.wordpress.com/2011/09/20/ticket-masters-part-3-the-ticketmaster%E2%80%99s-challenge-the-grateful-dead-pearl-jam-and-string-cheese-incident/

6 Ben Sisario. "A Band Battles Ticketmaster on Sales Fees." *New York Times*, May 15, 2012. https://www.nytimes.com/2012/05/16/arts/music/string-cheese-incident-takes-on-ticketmaster.html.

7 Mark Myers, *Rock Concert: An Oral History as Told by the Artists, Backstage Insiders, and Fans Who were There*. New York: Grove Press, 2021, 283.

8 Amrita Khalid. "It's not just tickets and fees: How Live Nation quietly takes your money at ever possible opportunity." *Sherwood News*, December 5, 2024. https://sherwood.news/business/its-not-just-tickets-and-fees-how-live-nation-quietly-takes-your-money-at/.

9 Christine A. Varney. "The TicketMaster/Live Nation Merger Review And Consent Decree In Perspective." *U.S. Department of Justice* (Austin, Texas, March 18, 2010). https://www.justice.gov/atr/speech/ticketmasterlive-nation-merger-review-and-consent-decree-perspective.

10 "Court Enters Judgment That Significantly Modifies and Extends Consent Decree With Live Nation/Ticketmaster", Press Release, U.S. Department of Justice, January 28, 2020, https://www.justice.gov/opa/pr/court-enters-judgment-significantly-modifies-and-extends-consent-decree-live.

11 Chris Williams & EJ Panaligan. "Taylor Swift Says Ticketmaster Fiasco 'Pisses Me Off': 'It's Excruciating for Me to Just Watch Mistakes Happen'." *Variety*, November 18, 2022. https://variety.com/2022/music/news/taylor-swift-addresses-eras-tour-ticketmaster-fiasco-1235436036/.

12 *Ibid.*

13 Virginie Berger. "How Taylor Swift's Ticketing Fiasco Fuels DOJ's Live Nation Antitrust Lawsuit." *Forbes*, June 14, 2024. https://www.forbes.com/sites/virginieberger/2024/06/14/how-taylor-swifts-ticketing-fiasco-fuels-dojs-live-nation-antitrust-lawsuit/.

14 "Lawsuit Accuses Ticketmaster and Live Nation of 'Racketeering Activity'." *PYMNTS*, November 18, 2024. https://www.pymnts.com/legal/2024/lawsuit-accuses-ticketmaster-and-live-nation-of-racketeering-activity/.

15 Ben Sisario & Matt Stevens. "Ticketmaster Cast as a Powerful 'Monopoly' at Senate Hearing." *New York Times*, January 24, 2023. https://www.nytimes.com/2023/01/24/arts/music/ticketmaster-taylor-swift-senate-hearing.html.

16 María Luisa Paúl & Daniel Wu. "They quoted Taylor Swift in a Senate hearing — but who's the top Swiftie?" *Washington Post*, January 27, 2023. https://www.washingtonpost.com/nation/2023/01/27/senators-taylor-swift-lyrics-ticketmaster-hearing/.

17 *Ibid.*

18 Zach Bryan. *All My Homies Hate Ticketmaster (Live from Red Rocks)*. Belting Bronco Records. Released December 25, 2022.

19 "CMA launches investigation into Ticketmaster over Oasis concert sales." Press release, Competition and Markets Authority, September 5, 2024. https://www.gov.uk/government/news/cma-launches-investigation-into-ticketmaster-over-oasis-concert-sales. Ticketmaster agreed to change its practices going forward. "CMA secures changes from Ticketmaster following Oasis tickets investigation." Press release, Competition and Markets Authority, September 25, 2025. https://www.gov.uk/government/news/cma-secures-changes-from-ticketmaster-following-oasis-tickets-investigation.

20 "Justice Department Sues Live Nation-Ticketmaster for Monopolizing Markets Across the Live Concert Industry." Press Release, U.S. Department of Justice, May 23, 2024. https://www.justice.gov/opa/pr/justice-department-sues-live-nation-ticketmaster-monopolizing-markets-across-live-concert.

21 Associated Press. "Justice Department Sues Ticketmaster Owner, Asks Court to Break Up Company's Monopoly on Live Events." *WTTW News*, May 23, 2024. https://news.wttw.com/2024/05/23/justice-department-sues-ticketmaster-owner-asks-court-break-company-s-monopoly-live.

22 "FTC Sues Live Nation and Ticketmaster for Engaging in Illegal Ticket Resale Tactics and Deceiving Artists and Consumers about Price and Ticket Limits." Press Release, United States Federal Trade Commission, September 18, 2025. https://www.ftc.gov/news-events/news/press-releases/2025/09/ftc-sues-live-nation-ticketmaster-engaging-illegal-ticket-resale-tactics-deceiving-artists-consumers.

Bibliography

Books

Balio, Tino. 'Marcus Loew and the Founding of Metro-Goldwyn-Mayer (1905-1924)'. In *MGM*, pp. 11-28. New York: Routledge, 2018.
Bernheim, Alfred L., *The Business of the Theatre: An Economic History of the American Theatre, 1750-1932*. 1932. Reprinted. New York: B. Blom, 1964.
Bernstein, Richard. *Only in America: Al Jolson and the Jazz Singer*. New York: Knopf Doubleday Publishing Group, 2024.
Binns, Archie. *Mrs. Fisk, and the American Theatre*. New York: Crown Publishers, 1955.
Bogyo, Peter. *Broadway General Manager: Demystifying the Most Important and Least Understood Role in Show Business*. New York: Allworth Press, 2017.
Bordman, Gerald M., and Richard Norton. *American Musical Theater: A Chronicle*. 4th edn. Oxford: Oxford University Press, 2010.
Brocket, Oscar G., and Franklin J. Hildy. *History of the Theatre*. 10th edn. Boston: Pearson, 2008.
Budnick, Dean, and Josh Baron. *Ticket Masters: The Rise of the Concert Industry and How the Public Got Scalped*. Toronto: ECW Press, 2011.
Chace, James. *1912: Wilson, Roosevelt, Taft & Debs — The Election that Changed the Country*. New York: Simon & Schuster, 2005.
Christiansen, Richard. *A Theater of Our Own: A History and a Memoir of 1,001 Nights in Chicago,* foreword by Brian Dennehy. Evanston: Northwestern University Press, 2004.
Connolly, Leonard W. *Bernard Shaw on the American Stage: A Chronicle of Premieres and Notable Revivals*. London: Palgrave Macmillan, 2022.
Curtis, James. *Buster Keaton: A Filmmaker's Life*. New York: Alfred A. Knopf, 2022.
Frohman, Daniel. *Daniel Frohman Presents: An Autobiography*. New York: Claude Kendall & Willoughby Sharp, 1935.
Gilbert, Douglas. *American Vaudeville, Its Life & Times*. 1940. Reprinted, New Dover edn. New York: Dover Publications, 1963.
Goldman, William. *The Season: A Candid Look at Broadway*. New York: Harcourt, Brace & World, 1969.
Grange, William. *The Business of American Theatre*. New York: Routledge, 2021.
Hagy, Jim. *The Instant Illusionist and the Cleveland Bunch: Dreams of a Vaudeville Life*. Glenview: Reginald Scot Books, 2023.
Hatch, Anthony P. *Tinder Box: The Iroquois Theatre Disaster, 1903*. Chicago: Academy Chicago Publishers, 2003.

Henderson, Mary C. *Theater in America: 200 Years of Plays, Players, and Productions*. New York: Harry N. Abrams, 1986.

Hirsch, Foster. *The Boys from Syracuse: The Shuberts' Theatrical Empire*. Lanham: Cooper Square Press, 1998.

Hornblow, Arthur. *A History of the Theatre in America*. Philadelphia: J.B. Lippincott Co., 1919.

Jones, Chris. *Rise Up ! Broadway and American Society from Angels in America to Hamilton*. London: Methuen Drama, 2019.

Kantor, Michael, and Lawrence Maslon. *Broadway: The American Musical*. New York: Bulfinch Press, 2004.

Kenrick, John. *Musical Theatre: A History*. 2nd edn. London; New York: Bloomsbury Metheuen Drama, 2017.

Knowles, Scott G. *The Disaster Experts: Mastering Risk in Modern America*. Philadelphia: University of Pennsylvania Press, 2011.

Lane, Stewart F. *It Happened at the Palace: A History of New York's Iconic Broadway Theater*. Edwardsville, IL.: Broad Book Press 2024.

Letwin, William. *Law and Economic Policy in America: The Evolution of the Sherman Antitrust Act*. New York: Random House, 1965.

Marcosson, Isaac F., and Daniel Frohman. *Charles Frohman: Manager and Man*, with an appreciation by James M. Barrie. 1916. Reprint. New York: Jefferson, 2015.

Marx, Harpo. *Harpo Speaks!* New York: Bernard Geis Associates, 1961.

Masters, Edgar L. *Levy Mayer and the New Industrial Era: A Biography*. New Haven: Yale University Press, 1927.

McNamara, Brooks. *The Shuberts of Broadway: A History Drawn from the Collection of the Shubert Archive*. New York: Oxford University Press, 1990.

Morris, Lloyd. *Curtain Time: The Story of the American Theatre*. New York: Penguin Random House, 1953.

Poggi, Jack. *Theater in America: The Impact of Economic Forces 1870-1967*. Ithaca, New York: Cornell University Press, 1968.

S.Z. Poli's Theatrical Enterprises. circa 1908. Reprinted. Elmhurst: Theatre Historical Society of America, 1978.

Riedel, Michael. *Razzle Dazzle: The Battle for Broadway*. New York: Simon & Schuster, 2016.

Riley, Judy. *66 Success Facts — Marcus Loew: Everything You Need to Know*. Queensland: Emereo Publishing, 2014.

Rose, Frank. *The Agency: William Morris and the Hidden History of Show Business*. New York: Harper Business, 1995.

Schoenfeld, Gerald. *Mr. Broadway: The Inside Story of the Schuberts, the Shows, and the Stars*. New York: Applause Books, 2012.

Schweitzer, Marlis. *Transatlantic Broadway: The Infrastructural Politics of Global Performance*. London: Palgrave Macmillan, 2015.

SD, Trav. *No Applause--Just Throw Money: The Book That Made Vaudeville Famous*. New York: Faber and Faber, 2005.

Segrave, Kerry. *Ticket Scalping: An American History, 1850-2005*. Jefferson: McFarland & Co., Inc., Publishers, 2007.

Seller, Jeffery. *Theater Kid: A Broadway Memoir*. New York: Simon & Schuster, 2025.

Senelick, Laurence, David F. Chesire and Ulrich Schneider. *British Music Hall, 1840-1923: A Bibliography and Guide to Sources, with a Supplement on European Music Hall*. Hamden: Archon Books, 1981.

Shapiro, James. *The Playbook: A Story of Theater, Democracy, and the Making of a Culture War*. New York: Penguin Press, 2024.

Stagg, Jerry. *The Brothers Shubert*. New York: Random House, 1968.

Stein, Charles W. *American Vaudeville as Seen by its Contemporaries*. New York: Alfred A. Knopf, 1984.

Taylor, William R. *Inventing Times Square: Commerce and Culture at the Crossroads of the World*. New York: Russell Sage Foundation, 1991.

Thorelli, Hans B. *The Federal Antitrust Policy*. Baltimore: Johns Hopkins Press, 1954.

Timberlake, Craig. *The Life & Work of David Belasco: The Bishop of Broadway*. New York: Library Publishers, 1954.

Waller, Spencer W. *Thurman Arnold: A Biography*. New York: New York University Press, 2005.

Vinci, J., ed. *Reconstructing the Garrick: Adler & Sullivan's Lost Masterpiece*. With contributions by Tim Samuelson, Eric Nordstrom and Chris Ware. Chicago: Alphawood Exhibitions, 2021.

Wertheim, Arthur F. *Vaudeville Wars: How the Keith-Albee and Orpheum Circuits Controlled the Big-Time and its Performers*. New York: Palgrave Macmillan, 2006.

Wharton, John F. *Life Among the Playwrights: Being Mostly the Story of the Playwrights' Producing Company*. New York: Quadrangle/The New York Times Book Co., 1974.

Wilson, Edwin, and Alvin Goldfarb. *Living Theatre: A History of Theatre*. 7th edn. New York: W.W. Norton & Company, 2017.

Articles

Belasco, David. "Art for Business' Sake: Some Conditions of American Dramatic Production." *The Cosmopolitan*, December 1905, 231-39.

Belasco, David. "The Theatrical Syndicate. One Side." *The Cosmopolitan*, December 1904, 193-98.

Crowhurst, Andrew. "Big Men and Big Business: The Transition from 'Caterers' to 'Magnates' in British Music-Hall Entrepreneurship, 1850-1914", *Nineteenth Century Theatre* 25, no. 1 (Summer 1997): 33-59.

Davis, Hartley. "The Business Side of Vaudeville." *Everybody's Magazine*, July-December 1907, 527-37.

Douglas, W.A.S. "The Passing of Vaudeville." *The American Mercury*, October 1927, 188-94.

Eaton, Walter Prichard. "The Theatre: The Rise and Fall of the Theatrical Syndicate." *The American Magazine*, October 1910, 832-42.

Frohman, Charles. "New Phases of Theatre Management." *Harper's Weekly, December* 31, 1904, 2022-24.

Gopnick, Adam. "What made Buster Keaton's Comedy so Modern" (Jan. 31, 2022): https://www.newyorker.com/magazine/2022/01/31/what-made-buster-keatons-comedy-so-modern-biography-james-curtis-dana-stevens.
Keith, B.F. "The Vogue of the Vaudeville." *National Magazine*, November 1898, 146-53.
Klaw, Marc. "The Theatrical Syndicate. The Other Side." *The Cosmopolitan*, December 1904, 199-201.
Klaw, Marc. "The Theatrical Syndicate from the Inside – The Story of Its Growth and Profits." *The Saturday Evening Post*, April 1909, 3-4.
Landro, Vincent. "Media Mania: The Demonizing of the Theatrical Syndicate." *The Journal of American Drama and Theatre* 13, no. 2 (Spring 2001): 23-50.
Liebling, A.J. "The Boys From Syracuse--I." *The New Yorker*, November 10, 1939, 26-30.
Liebling, A.J. "The Boys From Syracuse--II." *The New Yorker*, November 25, 1939, 23-27.
Liebling, A.J. "The Boys From Syracuse--III." *The New Yorker*, December 2, 1939, 33-37.
Lippman, Monroe. "The Effect of the Theatrical Syndicate on Theatrical Arts in America." *Quarterly Journal of Speech* 26, no. 2 (April 1940): 275-82.
Mayer, Frank D. "Levy Mayer." *The Law School Record* 8, no. 2 (Summer 1959).
[W. Golden] Mortimer. "Magicians' Vaudeville Contracts." *Mahatma* (January 1902) 569.
Orbach, Barak. "The *Paramount* Decrees: Lessons for the Future." *The Antitrust Source* 19, no. 5 (April 2020): 1-16.
Salter, Brent, and Catherine L. Fisk. "The Fragility of Labor Relations in the American Theatre." *Ohio State Law Journal* 83, no. 2 (2022): 217-82.
Schwartz, Jonathan A. "Bringing Balance to the Antitrust Force: Revising the *Paramount* Decrees for the Modern Motion Picture Market." *UCLA Entertainment Law Review* 27, no. 1 (2020): 45-110.
Schweitzer, Marlis. "A Failed Attempt at World Domination: 'Advanced Vaudeville,' Financial Panic, and the Dream of a World Trust." *Theatre History Studies* 32, no. 1 (2012): 53-79.
Slowik, Michael. "Documents of Performance: Keith-Albee Managers' Reports." *Nineteenth Century Theatre and Film* 39, no. 2 (November 2012): 93–103.
Spitzer, Marian. "The Business of Vaudeville." *The Saturday Evening Post*, May 24, 1924, 18-19.
Steuer, Richard M. "The Simplicity of Antitrust Law." *University of Pennsylvania Journal of Business Law* 14, no. 2 (Winter 2012): 543-57.
Tenney, John. "In the Trenches: The Syndicate-Shubert Theatrical War." *The Passing Show: Newsletter of the Shubert Archive* 21, no. 2 (Fall-Winter 1998): 2-18.
Woodward, Frederic C. and Frank O. Smith. "The Iroquois Theater Cases–A Flagrant Instance of the Law's Delays." *Illinois Law Review* 1, no. 7 (February 1907): 429-436.

Other Periodicals

Artist Era (1895-1896).
Houdini, Harry and Harry Houdini Collection. *Conjurers' Monthly Magazine*. New York: Conjurers' Magazine Pub. Co., (1906-08), https://www.loc.gov/item/08004682/.

The Conjurors' Magazine (Gibson/Dart 1945-1949).
Crest Magician, The (1907-1908).
Dyer's News Letter (1899).
Eagle Magician, The (1915-1935).
Felsman's Magical Review (1919 - c. 1924).
Genii, The Conjurors' Magazine (1936- present).
Gibiciere (2005 - present).
Hugard's Magic Monthly (1943-1965).
125 Years of IATSE, The Official ITASE Bulletin, Number 660, Second Quarter 2018.
Jinx, The (1934-1941).
Linking Ring, The (1922 - present).
Magazine of Magic, The 1914-1921).
Magic (Stan Allen, editor 1991-2016).
Magic Wand, The (1910-1957).
Magic Circular, The (London, 1906 - present).
Magic World, The (1917-1924).
Mahatma (1895-1906).
M-U-M (1911-1927, 1951 - present).
National Magazine (1917).
New Tops, The (1961-1983).
Osirian, The (1925).
The Passing Show, Newsletter of the Shubert Archives (1987 - present).
Seven Circles, The (1931-1934).
Sphinx, The (1902-1953).
Thayer's Magical Bulletin (1914-1925).
Tops (1936-1957).
Billboard Digital Archives.
New York Dramatic Mirror Digital Archives.
New York Herald.
New York Times Digital Archives.
Variety Magazine Digital Archives.
The World.

Podcasts

Bowery Boys, The Shuberts: The Brothers Who Built Broadway, Episode 372, September 24, 2021.
Bowery Boys, When Longacre Square Became Times Square: Before the Bright Lights of Broadway, Episode 440, August 30, 2024.
Freakonomics Radio, How is Live Theater Still Alive, Episode 629, April 11, 2025.
Freakonomics Radio, On Broadway, Nobody Knows Nothing, Episode 630, April 18, 2025.
Freakonomics Radio, Will 3 Summers of Lincoln Make it to Broadway?, Episode 631, April 25, 2025.

Cases and Government Reports

Fed. Trade Comm'n. Ann. Rep. (1918-20).

Binderup v. Pathé Exch., 263 U.S. 291 (1923).

Fed. Baseball Club v. Nat'l League, 259 U.S. 200 (1922).

Fed. Trade Comm'n. v. Motion Picture Advert. Serv. Co., Inc., 344 U.S. 392 (1953).

Hart v. B.F. Keith Vaudeville Exch., 12 F.2d 341 (2d Cir. 1926).

Hart v. B.F. Keith Vaudeville Exch., 262 U.S. 271 (1924).

Interstate Cir., Inc. v. United States, 306 U.S. 208 (1939).

Ring v. Spina, 148 F.2d 647 (2d Cir. 1945).

United States v. Shubert, 120 F. Supp. 15 (S.D.N.Y. 1953).

United States v. Shubert, 348 U.S. 222 (1955).

United States v. Loew's Inc., 371 U.S. 38 (1962).

People v. Klaw, 106 N.Y.S. 341 (Gen. Sess. 1907).

United States v. Paramount Pictures, Inc., 344 U.S. 131 (1948).

Unpublished Sources

Lippman, Monroe. "The History of the Theatrical Syndicate: Its Effect Upon the Theatre in America." PhD diss., University Michigan, 1937.

Rukgaber, Celcile A. "The Theatrical Syndicate and its Effects Upon the American Theatre.", MA thesis, University of Wyoming, 1955.

Shubert, Lee. "Mr. Lee As Told to Ed Sullivan." Unpublished Memoir, *Circa* 1950. Typescript.

Messano-Ciesla, Mary Ann Angela. "Minnie Maddern Fiske: Her Battle with the Theatrical Syndicate." PhD diss., School of Education, Health, Nursing, and Arts Professions, New York University, 1982.

Baker, Dorothy Gillam. "Monopoly in the American Theater: A Study of the Cultural Conflicts Culminating in the Syndicate and its Successors, the Shuberts." PhD diss., School of Education, New York University, 1962.

Acknowledgments

The Shubert Archives are located in the attic high above the stage of the Lyceum Theatre on 45th Street just East of Broadway. They are part of the Shubert Foundation formed under the terms of Lee Shubert's will.

In 1976, the Shubert Foundation established the Archives. A small, dedicated staff, plus volunteers and interns, have indexed thousands of linear feet of Shubert documents dating back to the beginning of operations in the early 20th century. The Archives also publish a newsletter and assist scholars researching the artistic and business aspects of the Shuberts' long association with Broadway.

These offices were once owned by Charles and Daniel Frohman in the days of the Syndicate. Visitors can sit behind the desk in the chair where Charles Frohman and his brother read scripts and made decisions that shaped the theatrical empire of the Syndicate.

I made sure that I sat in this chair in this attic, an almost sacred relic of theater history and what Daniel Frohman called his "sanctuary," as I read the records of the rise and fall of the theater monopolies and cartels of the 19th and 20th centuries. Many of those records had been stored unread under the stage of the theater where new productions are still being staged. On more than one occasion, I crouched low so I could look through the small panel near the floor to view the stage many floors below, as did the impresarios that shaped live entertainment on Broadway. Special thanks to Mark, Sylvia, and Arielle at the Archives for their gracious hosting and generous assistance for the past three years.

I also benefited greatly from the other great archives that tell the story of competition and collusion in live entertainment. These include the Billy Rose Theatre Division of the New York Public Library; the vaudeville holdings of the Harry Ransom Center at The University of Texas at Austin; the Federal Trade Commission library; the Chicago Public Library; the Keith-Albee Archives at the University of Iowa; the Newberry Library; The American Vaudeville Museum Archive at the University of Arizona; and the Madison Historical Society. These archives document the epic battles between the Shuberts and the Syndicate, their brief alliance to do battle with the vaudeville Combine, and the Shuberts' dominance of the industry until the forced break up on antitrust grounds.

I want to thank my wife Laura Matalon, who brought the Syndicate to my attention, inspired me to tackle this project, read my drafts, and supported me all the way on this journey. Thanks to my daughter Jordan Waller for her careful comments of the final draft of the manuscript.

I also want to give a special shout out to my Loyola colleague James Hagy, who shared with me his vast knowledge, and personal collection, of materials relating to the history of magicians in United States theater and vaudeville, and for his invaluable comments on the entire manuscript in draft form. Thanks also to my friends and colleagues Sam Brunson, Barry Sullivan, Anthony Miller, and Peter Kuntz for their comments on the draft manuscript.

Thanks also to Katie Ashcraft, Manny Azenberg, Doug Baker, Meredith Blair, Carl Bogus, John Breglio, Elliot Brown, Arielle Dorlester, Josh Douglas, Bert Fink, Andrea Gabor, Stephen Gabriel, Chris Jones, John Kenrick, Mark Larson, Paul Libin, Mark Lococo, Jeremy McCarter, Suzanne Lipkin, Kevin McCollum, Al Nocciolino, Barack Orbach, Billy Rosenfeld, Rina Saltzman, Roche Schulfer, Jeffrey Seller, Stephen Siegel, Tim Samuelson, Mark Swartz, Studio 659, Jordan Waller, Sylvia Wang, and participants at events at Loyola University Chicago School of Law, the North Shore Writers' Workshop, the University of California-Irvine School of Law, and Yale Law School who provided me invaluable information, assistance, and ideas throughout the research and writing of this book.

Ameer Al-Khudari, Liz Baughman, Eunsoo Choi, Erin Foster, Grace Franklin, Iris Gomez, Stephanie Haines, Meghan Havern, Sam Hunt, Zahrah Khan, Evan Morsch, and Brady Sweet all provided excellent research assistance. Loyola University Chicago School of Law reference librarian Joe Mitzenmacher provided exceptional assistance to me and my research assistants throughout this project. This book was supported by summer research grants and travel support from Loyola University Chicago School of Law and received no external financial support.

Author's Note on Spelling

I must have written or cited the words "theater" or "theatre" hundreds of times while writing this book. The most common spelling of this word has varied over time and between the United States, the United Kingdom, and continental Europe. For the sake of consistency, I have used the most common current U.S. spelling of "theater" in all places, except when referring to names of specific buildings named "theatre" or where I am citing or quoting material using that spelling.

There is substantial variation in calling the top level of vaudeville either "big-time vaudeville" or "big time vaudeville." I have opted to use "big time vaudeville" except when referring to an entity using the hyphen in its name or when quoting from a source that uses the hyphen.

I also use U.S. spelling and grammar conventions more generally except when referring to names of entities or in quoting material from outside the United States.

About the Author

Spencer Weber Waller is a law professor at Loyola University Chicago and an expert in antitrust and consumer protection law. Over the course of his career, Professor Waller has lectured and taught at law schools across the United States and around the world. In addition to teaching, he has been an antitrust and organized crime prosecutor with the United States Department of Justice, a Senior Adviser to the United States Federal Trade Commission, and practiced at several law firms. He is a volunteer attorney with Lawyers for the Creative Arts where he provides pro bono legal advice to authors and clients in the theater industry.

Professor Waller is the author of *Thurman Arnold: A Biography* and many scholarly books and articles. He has invested in several Broadway and touring productions and is a co-producer of 2024 revival of *The Who's Tommy* on Broadway.

Index

Academy of Music 16
actors 46, 115–18, 124 *see also* performers; talent
Actors' Equity Association (Equity) 116, 117–18, 119, 122
adaptations 205–7
Advanced Vaudeville 56, 100–4, 105–6, 169
advertising. *See* publicity
Aladdin (Ashman; Beguelin; Menken; Rice) 202
Alan Wasser Associates 203
Albee, Edward Franklin 26, 121, 122, 130, 132, 133 *see also* Keith-Albee Circuit
  movie industry 152–3
  retirement 153–4
Aldrich, Thomas Bailey 64
"All My Homies Hate Ticketmaster" (Bryan) 222
Alladin 38
Ambassador Theater Group (ATG) 192, 193, 202
American Museum, NYC 25
American Theater Company 9–10
America's Got Talent (Cowell) 21
Annie Get Your Gun (Berlin) 15, 166
antitrust cases/law 3, 7–8, 51–8, 226
  Arnold, Thurman 174
  Clayton Act 53
  DGA 120
  Federal Trade Commission Act 53
  FTC 55
  Interstate Circuit decision 174
  interstate commerce/trade 51, 53–7, 185–6
  Morris, William 106
  movie industry 173–6
  Paramount consent decrees 175–6
  Paramount litigation 174–6, 188
  Paramount Pictures 158, 159
  Pearl Jam 215–17
  presenters 210–11
  Sherman Act 7, 14, 52, 53, 56, 57
  Shubert Organization 55, 56, 58, 120, 173, 177–9, 180–6, 187–8, 189–97, 233–6
  Shubert, J.J. 177, 188, 189–90
  Shubert, Lee 133, 181, 184
  Theatrical Syndicate 51, 53–4, 55–6, 58
  Ticketmaster 215–17, 218
  Ticketmaster/Live Nation 219–24
  triple damages 190
  unions 113–14
Arnold, Thurman 173–5
  Folklore of Capitalism, The 173
Artists and Models (Shubert) 131
Associated Actresses of America 55, 122
Association of Theatrical Press Agents and Managers (ATPAM) 118–19
Association of Vaudeville Managers of the United States (AVM) 238 n. 3
ATG (Ambassador Theater Group) 192, 193, 202
ATPAM (Association of Theatrical Press Agents and Managers) 118–19
Auctioneer, The (Arthur) 62
Auditorium Theatre, Chicago 103
August Osage County (Letts) 211
AVM (Association of Vaudeville Managers of the United States) 238 n. 3

BAA (Broadway Across America) 210–11
Babes in Toyland (Herbert and MacDonough) 79
Bankhead, Tallulah 151
Barnum, P.T. 25, 26
Barras, Charles 5
baseball 56–7, 186, 188
Baum, L. Frank
  Wonderful Wizard of Oz, The 205–6
Beauty and the Beast (Ashman; Menken; Rica) 204
Beck, Martin 29, 105, 107, 148, 153
Belasco, David 40, 42, 59, 61–3
  May Blossom 70
  Shubert Organization 62, 76, 83, 84, 85
  Theatrical Syndicate 47–8, 54, 61–3, 82, 83, 84
Belle of New York, The (Kerker and Morton) 71
Ben-Hur (Niblo) 49, 136, 143, 154
Ben Hur (Wallace and Young) 49, 136
Ben-Hur (Wyler) 49
Bernhardt, Sarah 75–6
Bernheim, Alfred 237 n. 1
big time vaudeville 19
Black Crook, The (Baker et al.) 5, 12, 39, 42, 49, 70
Blackstone Theatre, Chicago 194, 195
block booking 158–9
Blossom Time (Romberg) 139, 163
Blumenthal, Richard 222
Book of Mormon, The (Lopez; Parker; Stone) 204
bookings 13, 27, 28, 147, 191–2, 203 *see also* UBO
  block booking 158–9
  booking agents 30–2, 33, 65, 202–4
  efficiencies 59
  IBA 65
  IBO 203
  League 203
  LITNA 203
Brixton Burglary, The (Sidney) 72
Broadway 7, 20, 193 *see also* tours
  adaptations 205–7
  budgets 205
  COVID pandemic 204–5
  "Direct from Broadway" touring shows 49–50
  Disney 201, 202
  enhancement money 211
  FTP 151–2
  Great Depression 145
  investment/investors 87, 88, 201, 205, 207
  licensed local productions 209
  New Amsterdam Theatre 202
  non-commercial theaters 211–13
  opera 16
  producers 88, 201, 207, 208
  profit 210
  risks 207
  Shubert Organization 75, 87, 139, 145
  theaters 202
  Theatrical Syndicate 47, 49
  tryouts 30, 47, 212–13
  working conditions 46
Broadway Across America (BAA) 210–11
Broadway League 118, 193
Broadway to Paris (Atteridge; Bronson-Howard; Hoffman) 92
Bryan, Zach
  "All My Homies Hate Ticketmaster" 222
Buffalo Bill's Wild West Show (Cody) 15
Burgomaster, The (Luders and Pixley) 77
burlesque 14, 18, 19–22, 27

cartels 3, 14, 25–125, 226 *see also* antitrust cases/laws; circuits; Shubert Organization; Theatrical Syndicate; vaudeville
  antitrust laws 51–8
  booking agents 30–2, 33
  Independents, the 59–67
  labor 113–23
  NIRA 123
  theater 14, 30–2
  UBO 27
  unions 113–19, 121–2, 124, 125
  vaudeville 26–30, 97–108

Cass Theater, Detroit 195
Cather, Willa 6
Cats (Eliot; Lloyd Webber; Nunn; Stilgoe) 203
Celler, Emmanuel 166, 178–9
Charley's Aunt (Thomas) 49
Chautauqua circuit 17, 144
Chicago 76–82, 103, 194, 195–6
Chinese Honeymoon, A (Dance) 73
Cincinnati 195, 196
circuits 13, 25, 32–3, 56–7, 147 *see also* Combine, the; Keith-Albee Circuit; UBO
  Advanced Vaudeville 56, 100–4, 105–6, 169
  Chautauqua 17, 144
  competition 144
  Lyceum 17, 144
  Morris 106
  Orpheum Circuit 19, 28–30, 97, 98–9, 153
  vaudeville 19, 26–8, 29, 56–7, 97
circuses 15
class 63
Clayton Act 53
Clear Channel Communications 210
CNN 215
  Inside Business 215, 217
Code of Fair Competition for the Legitimate Full Length Dramatic and Musical Theatrical Industry 123–5
Cohan, George M. 30, 117
  Give My Regards to Broadway 82, 117
  Yankee Doodle Dandy 117
  You're a Grand Old Flag 82
Colonial Theatre, Chicago 82
"combination system" 12
Combine, the 4, 7, 106, 148
  legitimate theater 101
  power 225
  Shubert-Syndicate agreement 103
competition 4–5, 201, 202, 213, 226–7
  Code of Fair Competition for the Legitimate Full Length Dramatic and Musical Theatrical Industry 123–5
  labor 113
  movie industry 152–4
  presenters 210
  Shubert Organization/Theatrical Syndicate 71, 72, 73, 74–6, 82–3, 85, 88–91, 93, 95, 108–11, 118, 130–1, 137–8, 146, 225
  UBO 100, 101, 102, 103
concert business 8, 215–19
copyright 41, 119
Count of Monte Cristo (Dumas ad. Fechter) 61
COVID pandemic 204–5, 211
Cox Theatre, Cincinnati 195, 196
Cravath, Swaine & Moore 180, 184, 217
critics 94–5
Crucible, The (Miller) 150

Daredevil comic books 37
Dark Victory (Goulding) 206
Davis, Will J. 81
Death of a Salesman (Miller) 150
Debs Eugene 53
Deslys, Gaby 92–3
DGA (Dramatists Guild of America) 119–20
dime museum shows 25–6, 27
"Direct from Broadway" touring shows 49–50
Disappointment, The (Barton) 9
Disney 201, 202, 204
Drama Guild 137–8
Dramatic League 138
Dramatists Guild of America (DGA) 119–20

economy, the 13–14
Ed Sullivan Show, The (Sullivan) 21, 167
England 89–90, 105
Englishman's Home, An (du Maurier) 129
enhancement money 211
entertainment barons 25–33

Equity (Actors' Equity Association) 116, 117–18, 119, 122
Erlanger, Abraham Lincoln 35, 37–8, 110, 137 *see also* Klaw & Erlanger
Auctioneer lawsuit 62
Ben-Hur, producing 154
blacklisting 48
death 146, 147
Fiske, Harrison 61
global syndicate 105
Iroquois Theater 80
movie industry 136, 143
Shubert Organization 74–5, 76, 80, 84, 131, 132, 137–8
Shubert Organization/Theatrical Syndicate merger 110
Shubert, Lee 130, 135, 169
Shubert, Sam, death of 84
Theatrical Syndicate 35, 37, 38, 40, 48, 61
ticket scalping 164
USAC 100
vaudeville 99, 103, 104
Worm, A Toxen 93–4
Ziegfeld, Florenz 130
Erlanger, Mitchell 146, 147
Europe 104, 105

Famous Players Film Company 157
Famous Players-Lasky Corporation 157, 159
Fantana (Shubert) 82
Federal Baseball Club v. National League 56–7
Federal Theatre Project (FTP) 149–52
Federal Trade Commission (FTC) 55
Federal Trade Commission Act 53
Fields, W.C. 30
films. *See* movie industry
fire safety 79–82
First National Pictures 157
Fisk, Harrison Grey 44, 60–1, 65, 85
Fisk, Minnie Harrison 44
Fisk, Minnie Maddern 59–60, 63, 65, 73, 85
Folies Bergère (Marchand) 49, 130
Folklore of Capitalism, The (Arnold, Thurman) 173
Follies of 1909 (Ziegfeld) 93
Forty-Five Minutes from Broadway (Cohan) 82
Fountain 28
four-wall arrangements 208
Foy, Eddie 78
fraud 165–6
Frohman, Charles 11, 35, 38–43, 100 *see also* Hayman & Frohman
criticism 93
death 110, 129–30
ticket scalping 164
Zukor, Adolph 157
Frohman, Daniel 11, 42–3, 59, 75, 152
ticket scalping 164
Zukor, Adolph 157
Frohman, Gustave 38, 39, 40, 42
Frozen (Anderson-Lopez; Lopez) 204
FTC (Federal Trade Commission) 55
FTP (Federal Theatre Project) 149–52

Gilbert and Sullivan 16, 163
Pirates of Penzance, The 16
Give My Regards to Broadway (Cohan) 82, 117
Goldwyn Pictures 154, 158
Gone With the Wind (Fleming) 206
Goodbye, Mr. Chips (Wood) 206
Goodwin, Nat 63
government funding 149–51, 212–13
Grateful Dead 218
Great Depression 123, 125, 145–6, 225
Great Northern Theatre, Chicago 195–6
Great White Hope, The (Sackler) 212
Guys and Dolls (Loesser) 163
Gypsy (Ardolino) 21
Gypsy (LeRoy) 21
Gypsy (Sondheim and Styne) 20–1

Hamilton: The Musical (Miranda) 16, 41, 204, 205, 211
Harry Potter and the Cursed Child (Thorne) 204

Hart, Max 57
Harvey (Chase) 166
Haverly Mastodons Minstrel show 40
Havoc, June 21
Hayman, Al 35, 36, 40, 42, 43, 46 *see also* Hayman & Frohman
  retirement 110
  USAC 100
Hayman & Frohman 35
Hazel Kirk (MacKaye) 41, 209
Heiman, Marcus 147
Hellzapoppin' (Olsen and Johnson) 162
Hollywood 158, 174–6, 206
Holmes, Oliver Wendell 56, 57
Houdini, Hardeen 17
Houdini, Harry 17, 30
house seats 165–6
Hovick, Ellen (June Havoc) 21
Hovick, Rosalie (Gypsy Rose Lee) 21
Hovick, Rose 21
Howells, William Dean 63
Hoyt, Charles 71
  Midnight Bell, A 59
  Texas Steer, A 71

IAE (International Amusement Exchange) 38
IATSE (International Alliance of Theatrical Stage Employees) 114, 115, 118, 119
IBA (Independent Booking Agency) 65
IBO (Independent Booking Office) 203
ice (Incidental Company Expenses) 165, 166
Incidental Company Expenses (ice) 165, 166
Independent Booking Agency (IBA) 65
Independent Booking Office (IBO) 203
Independent Presenters Network (IPN) 210
Independents, the 59–67
industry 12–13, 14, 186 *see also* labor; movie industry
  antitrust cases/laws 52–3
  cartels 14
  enterprises 50
  gentleman's agreements 50
  monopolies 113
  NIRA 123
  rock music 8, 215–19
  theater as 12–13
  trusts 14
  unions 113–14
Inside Business (CNN) 215, 217
International Alliance of Theatrical Stage Employees (IATSE) 114, 115, 118, 119
International Amusement Exchange (IAE) 38
interstate commerce/trade 51, 53–7, 185–6
investors 201, 205, 207
IPN (Independent Presenters Network) 210
Iroquois Theater, Chicago 77, 78–82
It Can't Happen Here (Lewis and Moffat) 149–50

Jane (Lestocq and Nicholls) 42
Jazz Singer, The (Crosland) 159
Jefferson, Joseph 63
Jesse L. Lasky Feature Play Company 157
John Gore Organization 210, 211
Jolson, Al 18, 89, 133
Jujamcyn Theaters 192
Julius Caesar (Shakespeare) 73
justice system 182, 190 *see also* antitrust cases/laws

Keaton, Buster 30
Keep 'Em Laughing (Fischer; Shubert; Shubert) 162
Keith, Benjamin Franklin 26, 27, 73 *see also* Keith-Albee Circuit
  movie industry 152–3
  UBO 97
  unions 121
Keith, Paul 133–4

Keith-Albee Circuit 19, 26–8, 29, 73–4, 97, 153
  mega-Syndicate 98–9
  Shubert, Lee 134–5
Kennedy, Joseph 153
Kern, Jerome 129–30, 136
Kerr, John 70
Key Brand Entertainment 210
Klaw, Marc 35, 36, 37, 38, 47, 130 *see also* Klaw & Erlanger
  Auctioneer lawsuit 62
  Belasco, David, 62, 63
  Iroquois Theater 81
  play piracy 41
  retirement and death 146
  Shubert Organization 131
  Shubert Organization/Theatrical Syndicate merger 110
  Theatrical Syndicate 35, 36, 37, 38, 41, 47
  ticket scalping 164
  USAC 100
Klaw & Erlanger 35, 38, 62, 63
  decline 131
  mega-Syndicate 98–9
  movie industry 154
  Shubert Organization 131
  USAC 100
Klein, William 83, 176, 179–80
Klein & Weir 179
Klobuchar, Amy 222

labor 113–23 *see also* unions
  conditions 46, 114–16, 117, 120–1, 123–5
  FTP 150–1
  independent contractors 119
  strikes 116–17, 118, 119, 121, 122
Lady Teazle (Bangs; Rhodes; Sloane) 82
League (League of New York Theatres and Producers) 203
League of Broadway Theaters. *See* Broadway League
League of New York Theatres and Producers (League) 203
Lee, Gypsy Rose (Rosalie Hovick) 21
Lee and J.J. Shubert Enterprises 85 *see also* Shubert Organization
Legitimate Independent Theatres of North America (LITNA) 203
"Let Me Entertain You" (Styne; Sondheim: Laurents) 20
"Let's Forget Russia and Fight the Shuberts" (Nathan) 182
Lewis Sinclair 150
  It Can't Happen Here 149
Life with Father (Crouse and Lindsay) 177
Life with Father (Curtiz) 177
Lion King, The (John and Rice) 202, 204, 205
LITNA (Legitimate Independent Theatres of North America) 203
live entertainment 9–22 *see also* Broadway; theatre; vaudeville
  adaptations 205–7
  burlesque 14, 18, 19–22, 27
  circuses 15
  as commerce 54, 55
  fair competition 123
  lowest common denominator of 140
  magic shows 17
  minstrel shows 18, 40
  music 10
  music industry 8, 215–19
  operas 15–16
  operettas 16–17
  reputation 10
  sketch shows 162–3
  survival 225–6
  unions 114–16
  variety shows 17, 18, 21, 162–3
  Wild West shows 15
Live Nation 8, 210, 219–24
Lowe, Marcus 154–8, 159
Lusitania, RMS 129–30
Lyceum circuit 17, 144

Macbeth (Shakespeare) 150
McKnight, William 192
magic shows 17

Mansfield, Richard 64, 72–3
Marx Brothers 30
May Blossom (Belasco) 70
Mayer, Levy 81, 100, 104–5
MBA (Minimum Basic Agreement) 120
Meet the Press (Melick) 179
Merry Widow, The (Lehár; Léon; Stein) 108, 163
Metro-Goldwyn-Mayer (MGM) Studios 158
Metro Pictures 157–8
Meyerfeld, Morris 29
MGM (Metro-Goldwyn-Mayer) Studios 158, 159
Midnight Bell, A (Hoyt) 59
Miller, Arthur 150
  Crucible, The 150
  Death of a Salesman 150
Minimum Basic Agreement (MBA) 120
Minnesota Mining and Manufacturing Company (3M) 192
minstrel shows 18, 40
Misérables, Les (Krettzmer and Schönberg) 203, 205
monopolies 14, 113, 120, 139, 178, 226
Morning Telegraph 60, 90
Morris, William 55–6, 100–1, 106–7, 130, 155, 203
movie industry 132, 136, 142, 143
  antitrust laws 173–6
  Code of Fair Competition for the Legitimate Full Length Dramatic and Musical Theatrical Industry 123
  as competition 152–4
  expansion 144, 154
  Famous Players Film Company 157
  Famous Players-Lasky Corporation 157, 159
  First National Pictures 157
  Goldwyn Pictures 154, 158
  IATSE 115
  as interstate commerce 55, 174, 186
  Jesse L. Lasky Feature Play Company 157
  Loew, Marcus 155–6, 157–8, 159
  Metro Pictures 157–8
  MGM 158, 159
  Paramount Pictures 157, 158, 159
  Shubert, Lee 152, 154, 158, 159
  studio system 158, 174–6
  talkies 159
  tent shows 143–4
  ticket prices 144
  Zukor, Adolph 157
Mr. Bluebeard (Cheever Goodwin; McNally; Solomon) 78–9, 81
Mr. Broadway (Sullivan) 167
Mr. Lee (Shubert and Sullivan) 168–70
Mr. Smith Goes to Washington (Capra) 206
Muppet Show, The (Henson) 21
music industry 8, 215–19
Music Man, The (Wilson) 205
My American Cousin (Taylor) 12
My Fair Lady (Lerner and Loewe) 163

Nathan, George Jean
  "Let's Forget Russia and Fight the Shuberts" 182
National Association of Theatrical Producing Managers (NATPM) 107–8
National Industrial Recovery Act (NIRA) 123
National Theatre, Washington, DC 191, 197
National Vaudeville Artists, Inc. (NVA) 55
NATPM (National Association of Theatrical Producing Managers) 107–8
Nederlander Organization 192–3, 194, 202
Nederlander Theatre, Chicago 82
New Amsterdam Theatre, NYC 202
New York City 30, 31–2, 72–3, 85, 136, 192
  see also Broadway
New York Dramatic Mirror 60, 61, 65, 90
New York Review 90–1, 93
New York World 60
newspapers 60–1, 65, 90–1, 93, 111

Ninotchka (Lubitsch) 206
NIRA (National Industrial Recovery Act) 123
Nixon, Sam 35, 43, 60, 110 *see also* Nixon & Zimmerman
Nixon & Zimmerman 35
Notebook, The (Michaelson) 212
NVA (National Vaudeville Artists, Inc.) 55

Oasis 222
Oberdorfer, Jesse 71
Of Mice and Men (Milestone) 206
Oklahoma! (Rodgers and Hammerstein II) 163
Omar (Romberg) 139
O'Neill, James 61
operas 15–16
operettas 16–17
Oriental Theatre, Chicago 82
Orpheum Circuit 19, 28–30, 97, 98–9, 153
Orpheum Opera House, San Francisco 28–9
Outsiders, The (Chance; Clay; Levine) 211

Palace Theatre, NYC 29, 98, 148, 192
Paramount Pictures 157, 158, 159, 175
Passing Show, The (Engländer and Rosenfeld) 18, 89, 131, 140
Passing Show of 1914 (Engländer and Rosenfeld) 139
Pastor, Tony 18–19
Pearl Jam 215, 216–18
performers 114, 121, 124 *see also* actors; talent
Perilman, Nathan 186
Peter Pan (Barrie) 42, 49, 129
Phantom of the Opera, The (Hart; Lloyd Webber; Stilgoe) 203, 205
Pirates of Penzance, The (Gilbert and Sullivan) 16
plagiarism 41
play piracy 41
playwrights 119–20, 124, 150
PMA (Producing Managers' Association) 116, 118
politics 149–151
Pollock, Channing 94–5
Powers, Harry 81
presenters 12, 29, 208, 210
presidential elections 53
Prince of Partha, The (Godfrey) 10
Priorities of 1942 (Fischer; Shubert; Shubert) 162
producers 88, 201, 207, 208
  enhancement money 211
Producers, The (Brooks) 88
Producing Managers' Association (PMA) 116, 118
publicity 40, 90–4

Queen Elizabeth (Desfontaines and Mercanton) 152

race 18, 150
radio 152
Radio-Keith-Orpheum (RKO) 153
Rent (Larson) 16, 41, 211
RKO (Radio-Keith-Orpheum) 153
RKO Studios 135
Robinson, Ethan 134
rock music industry 8, 215–19
Rogers, Will 133
Romberg, Sigmund 139–40
  Blossom Time 139, 163
  Omar 139
  Student Prince, The 140, 163
Roosevelt, Theodore 53, 123, 149
Rosalsky, Otto 54, 55
Rose, Billy 182

Sam S. and Lee Shubert Inc. 82 *see also* Shubert Organization
Saturday Night Live (Michaels) 21
Schiller Theater, Chicago 77–8
Serlin, Oscar 177
Shaw, George Bernard 90
Sherman, John 7, 52
Sherman Act 7, 14, 52, 53, 56, 57

Shoenfeld, Gerry 177, 179, 180, 184, 185
Show Boat (Kern and Hammerstein) 129, 136, 140
Show Boat (Pollard) 136
Show Boat (Sidney) 136
Show Boat (White) 136
Shubert, David 69
Shubert, J.J. (Jacob) 69, 71, 72, 82, 83–4, 187 *see also* Shubert Organization
 antitrust laws 177, 188, 189–90
 brothers, relationship with 73, 86, 88–9, 137, 148, 162, 186, 187, 189
 character 86, 89, 161
 competition, thoughts on 109
 death 196
 ice 166, 167
 Klaw & Erlanger 109
 Loew, Marcus 156
 production preferences 87, 136
 responsibilities 86
 revues 131
 Shubert Organization/Theatrical Syndicate merger 110
 Shubert Theater Corporation 135–6
 USAC 100
 Worm, A Toxen 93–4
Shubert, John 49, 162, 167, 193, 194
Shubert, Lee (Levi) 69–71, 72, 73–5, 83–4, 161 *see also* Shubert Organization
 antitrust laws 133, 181, 184
 brothers, relationship with 73, 86, 88–9, 137, 148, 187
 Cass Theater 195
 character 86, 89, 186–7
 charitable work 161, 167, 170, 187
 competition, thoughts on 109
 death/funeral/estate 186–7, 197
 Drama Guild 138
 Erlanger, Abraham Lincoln 135, 169
 fair competition 123
 house seats 166
 ice 166, 167
 innovation 132–3
 Keith-Albee Circuit 134–5
 Loew, Marcus 154–5, 156, 158, 159
 memoirs 167–70
 movie industry 152, 154, 158, 159
 Mr. Lee 168–70
 production preferences 87, 136
 as receiver 146
 responsibilities 86
 Sam S. and Lee Shubert Inc. 82
 Shubert Organization/Theatrical Syndicate merger 110
 Shubert Select Theatres 146
 Shubert Theater Corporation 135–6
 Sullivan, Ed 167–70
 tours 184–5
 unions 117
 USAC 100
 vaudeville 103–4, 132–4
 Woollcott, Alexander 95
 World Film Corporation 154
 Ziegfeld Follies, producing 148, 163
Shubert, Milton 162, 166
Shubert, Sam 69, 70, 71, 72, 73–5, 78 *see also* Shubert Organization
 death 82–3, 179–80
 Erlanger, Abraham Lincoln 80
 Sam S. and Lee Shubert Inc. 82
Shubert Advanced Vaudeville 132–3
Shubert family 69, 162 *see also under individual names*
Shubert Foundation 197, 202
Shubert Organization 3, 7, 62, 69–84, 85–95, 160–1, 183
 antitrust laws 55, 56, 58, 120, 173, 177–9, 180–6, 187–8, 189–97, 233–6
 bankruptcy 146
 Belasco, David 62, 76, 83, 84, 85
 Bernhardt, Sarah 75–6
 business organization 87–8
 capital 87–8
 Chicago 76–8, 80
 cost cutting 161–2
 criticism of 140
 critics, banning 94–5
 DGA 120
 Dramatic League 138
 entities, control of 88

Erlanger, Abraham Lincoln 74–5, 76, 80, 84, 131, 132, 137–8
exclusivity 86
expansion 76, 85, 108
FTP, competition from 149, 151–2
Great Depression 145–6
house seats 165, 166
investment 87–8
Klaw & Erlanger 131
Klaw, Marc 131
labor conditions 116
Loew, Marcus 156, 157
movies, competition from 152–3, 160
musicals 163
NATPM 107–8
New Opera Theater, competition from 163
New York City 72–3, 85, 136
newspapers 90–2, 93
open door policy 76, 86, 108, 131
opposition 109
playwrights 120
power 139, 225
price fixing 109
productions, quality of 163
profits 88, 137
public ownership 87
publicity 90–5
radio, competition from 152
revues 130–1
Romberg, Sigmund 139–40
Shubert Advanced Vaudeville 132–3
Shubert Foundation 197, 202
Shubert Select Theatres 146
Shubert Theater Corporation 135–7
Shubert way, the 88
support for 182, 183
theatre building 89
theatres, disposing of 184, 191–6
Theatrical Syndicate, alliances with 74, 80, 95, 99–101, 107–8, 109–10, 130–2, 225
Theatrical Syndicate, competition with 71, 72, 73, 74–6, 82–3, 85, 88–91, 93, 95, 108–11, 118, 130–1, 137–8, 146, 225
Theatrical Syndicate, differences from 87
Theatrical Syndicate, mergers with 110, 146–8
ticket agencies/brokerages 164, 166–7, 192, 197
ticket fraud 166, 179
ticket scalping 164, 179
UBO 139, 191, 193
unions 117, 118, 120
USAC 100
vaudeville 99, 100, 101–6, 107–8, 156, 162–3, 225
Worm, A Toxen 92–4
Ziegfeld, Florenz 130
Shubert Select Theatres 146
Shubert Theater Corporation 135–7
Shubert Theatre, Cincinnati 195, 196
Shubert way, the 88
Six (Marlow and Moss) 211, 212
sketch shows 162–3
small time vaudeville 19
South Pacific (Rodgers and Hammerstein II) 166
Spiderman: Turn off the Dark (Bono and Edge, The) 205
sport 56–7
St. James Theatre, NYC 191
stagehands 114–15
Stagg, Jerry 140–1
Stair, E.D. 195
star system 11–12
stock companies 11, 12
Strange Interlude (O'Neill) 138
strikes 116–17, 118, 119, 121, 122
Student Prince, The (Romberg) 140, 163
studio system 158, 174–6
Sullivan, Ed 167–70
Ed Sullivan Show, The 21, 167
Mr. Broadway 167
Mr. Lee 168–70
Toast of the Town 167
Sullivan & Considine theater chain 156
Sullivan and Cromwell 216, 217

Sweet Nell (Crossman) 48
Sweet Nell of Old Drury (Kester) 48
Swift, Taylor 221–2
Syndicate, the. *See* Theatrical Syndicate
Syracuse 70–2

Taft, William Howard 53
talent 89, 102 *see also* actors; performers
  conditions/pay 103, 109, 124, 133
  movie industry 143
technology 4–5
Temple, Anson 77
Ten Little Indians (Christie) 163
tent shows 143–4
Texas Steer, A (Hoyt) 71
theater/s 9–14, 226 *see also* Broadway; tours; vaudeville
  adaptations 205–7
  booking offices 13
  cartels 14, 30–2
  "combination system" 12
  as commerce 54–5
  commercial 226–7
  decline 146–7, 211–12
  differing productions 41
  Drama Guild 137–8
  economics 13–14, 226
  excess capacity 107
  FTP 149–52
  as interstate commerce 53–4, 105, 185–6, 188
  licensed local productions 209
  managers 12, 31–2
  national 151
  as national industry 12–13
  non-commercial 211–13
  over supply 144
  presenters 12, 29, 208, 210
  profits from 140–1
  risks 13–14
  star system 11–12
  stock companies 11, 12
  subscription model 138
  touring 10–12, 13
theater managers 12
Theatrical Syndicate 3, 4, 7, 35–50 *see also* Klaw & Erlanger
  American Theatrical Syndicate Agreement 229–32
  antitrust laws 51, 53–4, 55–6, 58
  Belasco, David 47–8, 54, 61–3, 82, 83, 84
  blacklisting 46–7, 48, 51, 60, 65, 71, 75, 76
  business organization 87
  capital 87
  coercion 46–7
  decline 129–30, 138–9
  efficiencies 59
  Erlanger, Abraham Lincoln 35, 37, 38, 40, 48, 61
  exclusivity 46, 50
  expansion 98, 108
  fees 47
  Frohman, Charles 35, 38–43
  global 104–5
  Hayman, Al 35, 36, 40, 42, 43, 46
  Hayman & Frohman 35
  Iroquois Theater 77, 78–82
  Klaw, Marc 35, 36, 37, 38, 41, 47
  labor conditions 116
  mega-Syndicate 98–9
  movie industry 154
  NATPM 107–8
  newspapers 90, 92, 93
  Nixon, Sam 35, 43, 60
  Nixon & Zimmerman 35
  opposition 44, 45, 47–8, 59–65, 80–1
  power 44–5, 47–9, 65, 108, 225
  price fixing 109
  producer alliances 108
  profits 45
  publicity 90
  revues 130
  Shuman Organization, alliances with 74, 80, 95, 99–101, 107–8, 109–10, 130–2, 225
  Shuman Organization, competition with 71, 72, 73, 74–6, 82–3, 85, 88–91, 93, 95, 108–11, 118, 130–1, 137–8, 146, 225

Shuman Organization, differences from 87
Shuman Organization, mergers with 110, 146–8
theatre building 89
USAC 100
vaudeville 98–9, 100, 101–6, 107–8, 225
Ziegfeld, Florenz 130
Zimmerman, J. Frederick 35, 43, 60
There's No Business Like Show Business (Berlin) 15
3M (Minnesota Mining and Manufacturing Company) 192
Ticketmaster 215–24
Ticketron 219
tickets
Broadway League 118, 193
house seats 165–6
ice 165, 166
Pearl Jam 215, 216
ticket agencies/brokerages 164–5, 166–7, 192, 197
ticket scalping 164–5, 179
Ticketmaster 215–24
Ticketron 219
Toast of the Town (Sullivan) 167
Todd, Michael 195
tours 7, 10–12, 13, 30–2, 137, 147, 207–10 *see also* circuits
BAA 211
competition 144
decline 141–4, 184–5
"Direct from Broadway" touring shows 49–50
dishonesty 144
Drama Guild 137–8
four-wall arrangements 208
FTP 149–50
as interstate commerce 53–4, 105, 185–6, 188
Life with Father 177
multiple 41, 209
non-Broadway 209
Pearl Jam 216, 217–18
presenters 12, 29, 208, 210
profits 207–10
risks 207–8
subscription models 208
tent shows 143–4
Theatrical Syndicate 48–9
ticket prices 144
vaudeville 19, 26–8, 29, 56–7, 97
trade associations 119–20
transport 13
trusts 14, 113 *see also* cartels
Twain, Mark 41

UBO (United Booking Office) 27, 28, 73–4, 97–8, 99, 106
competition 100, 101, 102, 103
labor conditions 121–2
Morris, William 100, 101
new version 147, 148
Shubert Organisation 139, 191, 193
unions 121–2
vaudeville 121–2
unions 113–19, 121–2, 124, 125
Equity 116, 117–18, 119, 122
IATSE 114, 115, 118, 119
United Booking Office (UBO). *See* UBO
United States Amusement Company (USAC) 100, 103
USAC (United States Amusement Company) 100, 103

variety shows 17, 18, 21, 162–3
vaudeville 9, 14, 17, 18–22, 27–30, 97–108, 132–5
Advanced Vaudeville 56, 100–4, 105–6, 169
antitrust laws 55–7
AVM 238 n. 3
Beck, Martin 29, 105, 107, 148
cartels 26–30, 97–108
decline 122–3, 133, 135, 153
dime museum shows 25–6, 27
economics 121
excess capacity 107
international 105
as interstate commerce 55, 57, 186

Keith-Albee Circuit 19, 26–8, 29, 97
labor conditions 120
Loew, Marcus 155–6
mega-Syndicate 98–9
Morris, William 100–1, 106–7, 130, 155
movie industry 152–3
Orpheum Circuit 19, 28–30, 97
profits 98
Shubert Organization 99, 100, 101–6, 107–8, 156, 162–3, 225
Theatrical Syndicate 98–9, 100, 101–6, 107–8, 225
touring circuits 19, 26–8, 29, 56–7, 97
UBO 27, 28, 97–8
unions 121–2
USAC 100
wars 97–108, 132, 169
Zukor, Adolph 155
Vaudeville Managers Protective Association (VMPA) 122
Vedder, Eddie 218
Vienna Gardens, San Francisco 28
VMPA (Vaudeville Managers Protective Association) 122

Waitress (Bareilles) 211
Waller, Spencer Weber 3, 215, 216–17, 220
Walter, Gustav 28–9
Warfield, David 62
Weir, Milton 176, 179, 180, 181–2
Welles, Orson 150
White Rats Actors Union 55
White Rats of America 121–2
Who's Tommy, The (Townshend) 212, 217
Wicked (Chu) 207
Wicked (Schwartz) 16, 204, 206–7
Wicked For Good (Chu) 207
Wicked: The Life and Times of the Wicked Witch of the West (McGuire) 206
Wild West shows 15
William Morris Endeavor agency 203
Williams, Bert 18
Wilson, Francis 63, 64–5, 109
Wilson, Woodrow 53
Wine, Women, and Song (Herk; Liebman; Shubert) 162–3
Wiz, The (Lumet) 206
Wiz, The (Smalls et al.) 206
Wizard of Oz, The (Fleming) 206
Wizard of Oz, The (Tietjens et al.) 206
Wonderful Wizard of Oz, The (Baum) 205–6
Woollcott, Alexander 95
Works Progress Administration (WPA) 149, 151
World, The 64
World Film Corporation 154
Worm, A Toxen (Conrad Henrik Aage Toxen) 92–3
WPA (Works Progress Administration) 149, 151
Writers Guild of America 119
Wuthering Heights (Wyler) 206

Yankee Doodle Dandy (Cohan) 117
Ye Bare and Ye Cubb (Darby) 9
You're a Grand Old Flag (Cohan) 82

Ziegfeld, Florenz 93, 130, 148
Follies of 1909 93
Ziegfeld Follies. See *Ziegfeld Follies*
Ziegfeld Follies (Ziegfeld) 49, 89, 108, 130, 140
black face 18
New Amsterdam Theatre 202
pay 133
Shubert, Lee, versions 148, 163
Zimmerman, J. Frederick 35, 43, 60, 110
see also Nixon & Zimmerman
Zukor, Adolph 155, 156, 157